Forgotten Agenda

Forgotten Agenda

God's Payroll

Whose work is it anyway?

God's Wealth

Whose money is it anyway?

Neil Hood

Authentic

Copyright © 2006 Neil Hood

This volume first published 2006 by Authentic Media
9 Holdom Avenue, Bletchley, Milton Keynes, Bucks., MK1 1QR, UK
and 129 Mobilization Drive, Waynesboro, GA 30830-4575, USA
www.authenticmedia.co.uk

God's Payroll
First published 2003 by Authentic Lifestyle

God's Wealth
First published 2004 by Authentic Lifestyle

The right of Neil Hood to be identified as the Author of this Work has been asserted by him in accordance with the Copyright, Designs and Patents Act 1988.

British Library Cataloguing in Publication Data
A catalogue record for this book is available from the British Library

ISBN 1-85078-681-X

Cover design by fourninezero design.
Typeset by Temple Design
Print Management by Adare Carwin
Printed in Great Britain by J.H. Haynes & Co., Sparkford

Neil Hood, CBE, DBA, FRSE, has juggled a busy life as an international business strategist, university professor, company director, Christian conference speaker, prolific author on international business and economic development, family man and church elder. He was Emeritus Professor of Business Policy at the University of Strathclyde, Glasgow, UK, and a director of, or advisor to, a number of major companies. He had been a non-executive director of eight public companies, including Reg Vardy plc and British Polythene Industries plc. He has advised many governments and international agencies on economic matters. He was Chairman of Scottish Equity Partners Ltd and former Deputy Chairman of Scottish Enterprise. In 2000 he was honoured by Queen Elizabeth for services to business and economic development. His life plan to dedicate his time and skills to Christian ministries was reflected in his being appointed President of Send the Light Limited in 2005, in his involvement with Christian ministries such as Blythswood Care and International Christian College, and in his busy preaching and teaching schedule. Neil was the husband of Anna, the father of two children, Annette (married to Alan) and Cameron (married to Ann), and grandfather to three grandchildren, Emily, Isla and Sarah. Neil's hope and prayer was that *Forgotten Agenda* would prove to be influential in your search for a lasting relationship with Jesus Christ.

Contents

Introduction

The passion with which I wrote the two books included in this single volume in 2003 and 2004 has not diminished. In the lives of many successful Christian people, I remain convinced that busyness, self-generated priorities, poor resource allocation, and gifts that are not on the altar continue to restrict the effectiveness of Christian witness in some of the environments that need it most. The moving feedback and personal confession from many of my readers confirm that. I mainly write for business, professional and academic audiences of all ages since I know them best. They are among the most articulate, influential, and powerful people in the community – a potential Christian elite within our society. What are the consequences of them having continuing bouts of amnesia about discipleship, work and money? They are serious – very serious indeed! Or think of the implications of some of our professional colleagues working "to their own agenda"? I was tempted to call one of the books in the trilogy of which *Whose Work?* and *Whose Money?* are part *Whose agenda is it anyway?* So I will pose that question to you as I introduce you to this combined volume. Might it be true that in the long list of life's priorities, our three related topics are in "any other business"? This is an interesting category in any agenda. It can mean that it's something that nobody wants to address; or it's too big to handle right now and time is short; or that it's a topic that the chairman "wants to kick into the long grass" never to reappear. Have you asked the Lord recently what his view is on your agenda?

Never one to miss the mark in his writings, Dietrich Bonhoeffer pointedly observed, "Christianity without discipleship is always Christianity without Christ." This strips away the external wrapping into which we can readily fit our version of faith, and behind which we can run our own agenda. Honesty requires us to acknowledge that there are many pale imitations of true discipleship which are neither allowed to reach our possessions nor our workplace. As Martin Luther expressed it, "There are three conversions necessary; the conversion of the heart, mind and the purse." How many people have you ever heard giving testimony as to how the Lord had transformed their attitudes to either money or work? Have you ever done it? George McDonald was thoroughly biblical in his remark that, "No man has the mind of Christ, except him who makes it his business to obey him."

When we drill down into the biblical treatment of subjects like money and work and look at the consequences for disciples, there is a general sense of shock about how much we have neglected them. So both these books are in the form of rather loud "wake-up calls". They have been variously described to me as challenging, demanding, impossible to comply with and radical. To which my ready response is, "Does not most of this teaching come directly from the Lord himself?" The fact that it does means that compliance is no less difficult – but for example, are you trying to apply the teaching on money and possessions?; or has it slipped from the agenda yet again? Somehow we feel that because we can manage *our* money in a satisfactory way and meet the various costs incurred in our lives, that *God's* money is being looked after. I start with the assumption in the book that all we have by way of money and possessions belongs to God. Our challenge is how to deploy and allocate these resources to his glory. One of the greatest challenges associated with money is that it needs real mental focus to make sure that it does not possess you – such is the way it is used to monitor success in our society. C. S. Lewis captured this truth very accurately when he said, "Prosperity knits a man to the world. He feels that he is 'finding his place in it', while really it is finding its place in him."

Maintaining a sense of all of our work being designed to be for God's glory, is no less necessary and no less challenging. Each of us need to capture, or recapture, the precise way in which we do our job and realise that it is special to God. In the fervour of the appeals after conferences on discipleship and work, the scale and potential of our work as a mission field overwhelms us – but then Monday comes along, and the mundane and routine takes over our attitudes. This is nothing short of disastrous for the church and the kingdom if the place in which we spend most time and the peer group with which we have most interaction are largely excluded from our witness. Our attitudes to our work are vital and need to be high on our agenda at all times. A. W. Tozer was right to place the emphasis in this way: "It is not what a man does that determines whether his witness is sacred or secular, it is why he does it."

I hope that you find these two books biblical, honest and thought provoking. They reflect my own struggles. They cannot be anything but challenging because that is the way they were presented to us. Think hard again about how much time and effort you devote to reviewing your agenda. Satan is really expert at creating ideal conditions for the "spiritual amnesia" bug to prosper. The effects that flow from this can be devastating. We end up living in the fringes, or the borderlands of true discipleship. As Earnest Worker puts it, "There is no peace in the borderlands. The halfway Christian is a torment to himself and of no benefit to others." Let's ask the Lord to deliver us all from that!

Neil Hood
December 2005

God's Payroll
Whose work is it anyway?

Neil Hood

For our grandchildren, Emily and Isla,
with our prayers that they will grow up
to know Jesus Christ as Lord

Contents

Preface

This is a book written by a fellow traveler through the world of work – not by an expert or a saint. Like you, I share in the trials and triumphs of work. Many of us spend a lot of time talking about our work, but we don't talk much about being a Christian at work. Indeed, for many Christians work almost seems to be a "no go" area – at least as it relates to our minds and our prayers. While we spend a great proportion of our lives at work, and although work dominates much of the rest of our lives, it is rarely the subject of church teaching. When the church does address the subject of work, many claim that its guidance is of little relevance in the "real" world of work in the twenty-first century. Thus the duality of being a Christian and being at work is born, fostered and fossilized. This is not the message of the Bible. Jesus never intended for us to have the inherent skepticism about the application of our faith to our work that some Christians display. Neither did he ask his followers to make a false distinction between secular and spiritual work.

However, I can personally relate to those who have concerns and confusions regarding work. I know many Christians who feel both anxious and guilty about their relationship with the world of work. Moreover, I share some of these feelings. Work is a topic that generates a whole spectrum of emotions. Satisfaction and frustration; fulfillment and boredom; preoccupation and indifference; liberation and exhaustion; clarity and confusion are among the many pairs of adjectives that describe my own experience. You probably share some of them and could add others as well. For some Christians, work is a constant source of anxiety, worry, stress and tension. For others, the dominant issue is that of work-life balance, or the lack thereof. Some Christians find their work constantly fulfilling and readily take its pressures in their stride. Others struggle with uncertainty over either the lack of employment or its terms and conditions. So, paradoxically, Christians with too much work experience some of the same emotions as those with too little work to meet their needs for self-satisfaction or income.

All of the above would be challenging enough, but there are other vital and often unanswered questions for the Christian. What does God expect from me in my work situation? How can I be a good witness in a job I hate? Am I in my job to please my employer or to please God? What kind of behavior distinguishes a faithful follower of Christ when he is heavily outnumbered at work? What do people I work with learn from me about Christ? And how do they learn? How do I handle conflict at work?

This book tackles these and many other related questions. Both the questions and the emotions that accompany them are part of my own daily work experience. This book reflects many years of wrestling with these issues, and I'm still traveling.

Why this book? This book is about Christian behavior both in and out of the world of work. I hope that you find it a "lived in" book that deals with real and pressing issues that you confront in your life – because I confront them in mine. This book begins on the sound biblical footing that although we may have disconnected our Christian practice from our work practice, God has not. We try to face work-related challenges daily, and even hourly, "without God", as it were – because the weekly sermon, the house group, the monthly seminar or the annual event planned to encourage us in our Christian lives all seem to be on an entirely different frequency. Yet the Lord has placed us in this real world of work, the principal context in which the majority of Christians are called to be salt and light, and he has not left us there on our own.

This book is the second in a series of books on Christian living, following *Whose Life Is It Anyway? A Lifeline in a Stress-Soaked World* (Carlisle: Authentic Lifestyle, 2002). *Whose Life Is It Anyway?* challenges Christians to respond to God's call for service. While God has a vast array of resources embedded in each of his disciples, he only uses a few of them because many are not "on offer". *Whose Life Is It Anyway?* examines many of the consequences of discipleship, touching briefly on the issue of work as one of the important realities of the Christian's life. The present volume specifically addresses the many different issues facing the Christian at work. While the two volumes can be read independently, in this book you will find occasional cross-references to matters discussed in *Whose Life Is It Anyway?* that are intended to be thought-provoking. As such, the two volumes complement each other.

While there are helpful books on the Christian at work, there are not many of them. Not surprisingly, it seems to have proved almost as difficult to write about work as it has been to deliver sermons about it. But this is a subject to which the church community – in every economic, cultural and political environment – needs to devote much more attention. We have to debunk the myths that secular work is divorced from, or less important than, church-based activity; that the ultimate aspiration of the Christian should be some form of "full-time" ministry; that the Bible has little of relevance to say to us on this subject, and so on. Having done that, the locus of our daily missionary activity becomes much clearer. I have little doubt that, for all of us, knowing the biblical answer to "Whose work is it anyway?" will provide uncomfortable challenges to the way we as Christians behave in our work environment.

Who is it for? This book is designed to be both practical and inclusive. The word "work" in the title refers principally (but not exclusively) to paid employment. Even that definition embraces many different relationships within the job market. So the issues covered here are of importance to the college student who works part-time in a coffee bar, to the senior citizen transporting disabled people to hospital on a part-time basis, to the senior executive in an international corporation and to the landscape gardener working outside his office window. This book is for Christians in every level of every profession. But it is also for those engaged in a range of other activities that may be entirely voluntary, as well as for those working in environments that are not considered "secular", such as Christian ministries and other charities. It also touches our homes. Most Christian homemakers would agree that domestic activities and work share some common characteristics – although not the salaries! This work environment can certainly generate similar stresses and strains.

You probably find yourself somewhere in that wide-ranging list. I hope so, because I'm convinced that the question in the title is one that we all need to answer on a very regular basis. Indeed, I find it difficult to imagine either a time or a context in which it is not applicable.

What is it designed to achieve? Above all, this book is intended to stimulate thought, prayerful reflection and action. The ideal outcome would be that more Christians bring their faith back into their work. After all, Christianity is a set of beliefs that should affect our behavior. It's just possible that you have not thought about work in the way it is considered here, and therefore you may never have felt the full force of biblical teaching on your own behavior. My prayer is, therefore, that this book will lead us all as Christian readers to have a more integrated approach to our whole lives – including our work. The Bible knows no other approach! After all, God calls us to serve and glorify him in every part of our being and in every area of our lives.

Style and sources The book is based on the Bible and focuses on applying its principles. In the pages that follow we are more concerned about the fundamentals of Christian living in the work environment than about techniques for witnessing. There are some excellent complementary books on that subject to which I on occasion refer the reader. Throughout, the book addresses difficult situations in work life and examines their consequences for Christians. The approach is an honest one – not merely offering a theology of work that does not relate to where Christians have to live every day. This is not a technical book, nor is it presented in theological language. It's written in an accessible style, with regular breaks for personal reflection and challenge. Illustrations, case studies, life examples and personal incidents are extensively used – many of them from my own experience, suitably disguised where necessary.

For almost all of my Christian life, since my days as a student, I have been an avid reader of Christian literature. Many Christian writers have made a profound contribution to my life, and it is inevitable that I have reflected some of their thinking here. Where possible, these writers are acknowledged – either in the text or in the short list of further reading at the end of each chapter. In other instances, I have illustrated various points using relevant quotations from some standard sources.[1]

Structure The various issues we will explore in order to answer our core question are divided into four related parts. In Part One, Guiding Principles for Our Work, Chapter 1 introduces the overarching question of the book, looks at the artificial separation of faith and work, and sets out the relationships with work that God presumes for his people. Chapter 2 then explains what it is that is special to God about our individual work and asks whether God is in our attitudes to it. Part Two, Keeping a Perspective on Our Work, deals with that important topic in Chapter 3, exploring the paradoxes surrounding work and outlining the Christian way of making sense of the world of work. Part Three, Learning through the Practice of Our Work, includes Chapters 4 to 8. These five chapters cover issues ranging from being aware of dangers at work; recognizing that work generates conflict with our colleagues and our owner; meeting the challenges of discipleship at work; dealing with the moral dilemmas posed in many work environments; and meeting crises in our personal experiences of work. Part Four, Progressing in Our Work with God, comprises Chapters 9 and 10. Chapter 9 considers how we need to work in line with God's plan, while Chapter 10 draws out our response to the core question as we weigh our work in the correct set of balances.

Acknowledgments So many people have wittingly or unwittingly provided the raw material for this book throughout my working life. I am grateful to them all – although I did not always feel that way when I worked with some of them! My gratitude extends to many others who read and helpfully commented on *Whose Life Is It Anyway?* and encouraged me to write further on such practical topics. These people, along with other business colleagues, were among those who were kind enough to endorse that book. I am once more much indebted to my personal assistant, Irene Hood, for help with this and many similar projects over the past decade and more. Mark Finnie and his whole team at Authentic have been very professional and encouraging throughout the whole process of tuning my mind, spirit and laptop to the realm of Christian writing. They deserve my sincere and unreserved thanks for that. Peter Little deserves special mention for his outstanding work on the design and production of these books. Finally I am, once again, most grateful for the sterling and insightful contribution of my truly gifted editor, Tara Smith.

Neil Hood
October 2002

[1] These quotations have come from a wide range of reference works, including: *Gathered Gold*, compiled by John Blanchard (Darlington: Evangelical Press, 1984); *Sifted Silver,* compiled by John Blanchard (Darlington: Evangelical Press, 1984); Edythe Draper, *Quotations for the Christian World* (Wheaton, IL: Tyndale, 1992); F.B. Proctor, *Treasury of Quotations on Religious Subjects* (Grand Rapids MI: Kregel Publications, 1977); *5000 Quotations for Teachers and Preachers*, compiled by Robert Backhouse (Eastbourne: Kingsway Publications, 1994).

PART ONE
GUIDING PRINCIPLES FOR OUR WORK

1
Work, the Bible and You

"Do not work for food that spoils, but for food that endures to eternal life, which the Son of Man will give you. On him God the Father has placed his seal of approval." (Jn. 6:27)

Outline This chapter introduces the book and our core question. It also explores some of the challenges that face Christians in the work environment and outlines principles that are foundational for understanding the biblical view of work. The chapter asks three questions and sounds a note of warning.

Whose work is it anyway?: An introduction
This, the central question, is set in the context of our lives. Then we consider a series of very different Christian responses to the relationship between work and faith.

How do I relate to the secular view of work?
A comparison between the world's view of work and the Christian's view reveals fundamental differences. This section confronts the Christian's temptation to keep work and faith separate.

What kind of relationship with work does the Bible presume?
This section sets out six of the foundational biblical principles concerning work.

A warning and a challenge
The warning concerns how receptive our world is likely to be to our practicing the Christian way at work. The chapter concludes by posing some searching personal questions about the application of these principles.

Whose work is it anyway?: For many of us, this is an awkward,
An introduction difficult and demanding question.
Perhaps it's one you would prefer not to
answer. When I first thought about this book, I wasn't sure I wanted to
answer this question either. I suppose I've known the Christian answer to this
question for years, but I have feared the implications of living it out. Being a
follower of Jesus Christ is one thing, but taking him into each and every work
situation is quite another. And, even then, introducing him there would not in
itself be enough. God's call is to behave as Jesus would have behaved. I
know that I am not alone in being profoundly troubled by this challenge.

*Our co-workers may
or may not have
strong belief systems
or faith of any kind*

To some degree, the nature of the challenge lies in
the complexity and diversity of our work
environments. The people we work with are
invariably very different and have a variety of
personalities and needs. They range from the
consistently friendly and open to the permanently
restless and negative. Their lives mirror both
triumph and tragedy. Our co-workers may or may
not have strong belief systems or faith of any kind.

Their interests and aspirations are all different, as are their attitudes to
work, interpersonal skills, their ability to communicate and listen and so
on. All of these differences emerge before we even consider what they think
of our faith and what behavior they expect from us when we testify to being
Christians. But the differences do not even stop there. When working with
people we face many stresses and strains in relationships, personality
clashes and different reactions to work pressures. Handling change at work,
especially when it has a negative effect on us personally, is another difficult
issue. And what about having to make tough decisions about people in
areas such as promotion, discipline, sickness and lay offs? Daily work brings
us a constant stream of moral choices, both large and small. The way we
make these choices adds up to our Christian behavior.

But diversity is only one of the many dimensions of the challenge. We also
have to consider our attitude to work and the different motivations that drive
us. Money, fulfillment, self-esteem, status, striving for a better society and
necessity are but a few of the motivating factors that appear in surveys on
this subject. Meanwhile, for an increasing number of people, happiness and

work are apparently not closely related – while stress and work evidently are. Equally, long working hours appear to be less connected to more productive work than they are to sickness and fatigue. Christians are not exempt from these pressures – and they affect our behavior in the workplace.

This is only a small sample of the myriad of issues that we typically face on a daily basis. Already we are tempted to say that it is too difficult to link being a Christian with the secular world of work – it would be better to keep these two worlds apart. For many of us, giving in to that temptation is a real danger. But we cannot be truly Christian if we try to keep living and working apart, by whatever means. Difficult though it is, it is to this that God has called us.

But we cannot be truly Christian if we try to keep living and working apart, by whatever means

So that you can understand my perspective and know that I relate closely to, and feel passionately about, this subject, let me share how work affects my life. But first, I acknowledge my own lifelong struggle to keep a balance between home, family, church and work. I have never found this easy and I encourage you to remember this as you read on. Because of the diversity of my interests in business, academic and public life, no two work days are the same for me. I have constantly to adjust to different places, people and environments. Few of them are in any way receptive to Christian faith. Some are openly hostile and marked by their cynicism. The work I do is invariably with strong-willed, successful and highly focused people. Sometimes I am managing them directly; in other contexts I advise them. I travel a lot and work long and irregular hours. Problems and challenges abound. And a lot of my life is lived in the public eye. My work is very diverse. For example, I might be simultaneously helping to grow a business and hire senior people, while working with a large program of lay offs in another company and feeling the real pain of such decisions. Meanwhile I might be mentoring someone through a business or personal crisis, or both. On other days I will be working on a radical change program in an organization, knowing that this will have a profound impact on the lives of many people. As part of my responsibility for the governance of companies, I might be trying to resolve complex ethical problems in different cultures or make commercially risky decisions in an informed way. I work a lot, and I constantly face the

TABLE 1.1

Responses to "Whose work is it anyway?"

"I have no idea! But the last person I would want to associate with this job I hate is God – if that's what you are implying. Do you know anything about the real world?"

"This is not a valid question. I only work for my employer, and that's that. If I want to know for whom I work, I just look at my monthly bank statement. Of course I'm a Christian – but that's another dimension of my life."

"I know the answer to this question. The Bible shows me that my work belongs to God, but I don't have any idea how that might make a difference in what I actually do every day. The whole issue is a mystery to me."

"Good question – but I can't see how biblical principles on work derived from a totally different environment can have anything to say about my work. The Bible is just not good on this kind of stuff."

"I've been a Christian for years and have genuinely opened up all of my life to God – but I've never been asked this question before. I'm not sure that I can handle the answer, especially if it means changing my behavior."

"The thought of really bringing God into my work situation scares me. My attempts at Christian witness there have been rebuffed for years and I'm struggling as it is. I just can't take this any further."

"I have a seriously important and senior job, you know. Yes, I'm a Christian – but I'm also my own man. The pastor has touched on some of these issues, but I filed them all in my in-basket. After all, what does he know about business and professional life? And anyway, I didn't get where I am by being Christ-like."

"Depends what you mean. There are times when I'm very Christian at work – I'm great with illness and family problems. But this is a rough industry; hard decisions need hard hearts, you know. I was never a fan of soft management skills. Tough, but fair, that's me."

"I did know that God had a plan for my life and my career, but I didn't know that it extended into my behavior at work. It's something that I'm not always proud of. This blows my mind. Where do I go from here?"

reality that God can be crowded out of my life. He sometimes is. Yet I am clear that he wants me where I am and that he has a specific expectation of me to live for him in all circumstances. Is it always comfortable? No. Do I always represent God well? No. Do I sometimes hanker for a simpler, less pressure-filled life? Yes – even if only momentarily. Those who know me best smile at this prospect. But there are real tensions for all of us in our relationships with work, and I readily acknowledge them in my life. That is why I have written this book.

One of the latent and universal, yet unresolved, areas of tension between the old creature and the new creature in Christ lies right here. Is it my employer's work? Or is it God's? In what sense can it be both? Not only is the question unresolved – it's often not even discussed or confronted in Christian teaching. Why? It's probably because it falls into that "very difficult" area. Few Christians are confident that the Bible has much to say about work-life problems in the twenty-first century. Over the years I have had many conversations with Christians on this and related subjects. Table 1.1, on p.18, sets out some of the views I have heard expressed. You might relate to some of them. Indeed, I might be describing you. Others you might think are not very "Christian" – and therein lies part of the tension.

☑ ACTION: Do any of these comments describe your attitude to work, now or at some time in the past? Try to write down a short description of how your faith relates to your work as you begin to read this book. We will revisit these views later.

Do any of the responses in Table 1.1 sound familiar? At least some of them probably do. These responses suggest confusion, anxiety, a wide variety of interpretations of appropriate Christian behavior, a perceived gap between faith and work and so on. They should not surprise us; nor should we judge. These views do, however, highlight some of the potential danger areas in the Christian's relationship with work. These dangers include partitioning our lives, losing our sense of calling and being shaped by the world's behavior. The reality is that, for some Christians, the duty to self is the greatest of the commandments. It's not just busy people under pressure who face these hazards. We all do. Sherman and Hendricks say that "faith and work is a raw, open nerve for many Christians".[1] While the goal of the material that follows is to heal this wound, cleaning and dressing a wound can be painful – and some aspects of this topic are difficult to confront. In all of this, however, we have the power and strength of the great physician himself.

How do I relate to the secular view of work?

Because a person's attitudes to work and experiences of work are very personal, generalization is difficult. But the prevailing "spirit of the age" surrounding work has created a worldview with common features in most developed countries. Whether we like it or not, this is the air we breathe. This view might even be implicit in the contract you hold with your employer. He hired you because he thought that everybody has this kind of philosophy of life. This worldview includes the beliefs that success means attaining both wealth and status, and that this success is derived from achievements at work. How many times have you heard, "I've made it!" after a promotion? Driven by these imperatives, there is much evidence of the spirit of expediency. "To succeed is tough, therefore I will do whatever it takes to achieve it." This type of statement is often made palatable by the vague qualification of "within limits" – to suggest a moderated and tolerable type of behavior. Those who hold to this view believe that the purpose of work is seen as self-fulfillment – one by-product of which can be that a career becomes an idol. Furthermore, I compare my idol with yours. So we have a futures market in false gods. We are all worshiping them and eagerly anticipating their promises. As has been said, "Too many Christians worship their work, work at their play and play at their worship". Sadly, this is all too often true. Others try to disguise this idolatry and their motivations with statements such as, "This is all for the family"; "I work to live, not live to work"; "I will know when I have enough money/ success/status, and then take life easy" and so on. God is nowhere to be seen in any of these features of the secular view of work – not least because each person designs his own god. We will pause here as we approach a serious hazard.

☑ **ACTION:** Lots of Christians are tempted to try to weave God into such secular perspectives on work by attempting to spiritualize their own behavior. Ask yourself whether you are doing this; and think hard about the consequences. How would you describe in a few words how work fits into your life?

You probably recognize at least some of the above features as representing the world of work. Is the world of Christian faith to be regarded as a separate and very different world? It is tempting, and sometimes convenient, to think this way. Three sets of behavior can flow from this type of compartmentalized thinking, as illustrated by the following simple picture of a house with two rooms.

1. The rooms of faith and of work are never simultaneously occupied. There is a connecting door and we simply walk from one to the other as required. The two rooms are in the same house, but the activities that take place in each are largely separate. This is the way we like it. It keeps life simple.

2. We demonize the work room as somewhere we go under a set of compulsions such as earning a living, supporting our lifestyle, complying with social norms and so on. We are there reluctantly, and somehow it is less important than what happens in the faith room. There is more threat there than there is opportunity. Indeed, we might even feel rather guilty about being at work too often or even being there at all. Being in the faith room is a much higher calling.

3. We see the faith room as a good place to be. Life there, on the whole, is comfortable. But our tendency is to discount the value of faith – either because it appears too demanding or because it seems not entirely applicable to the work room. This attitude is often a long-term consequence of being polluted by the atmosphere that surrounds us at work. Faith ultimately suffers. Indeed, we end up only needing the work room to live in, and we leave the faith room for others to occupy. The end product of this is spiritual emptiness.

Without overanalyzing the metaphor, think about where you stand in this picture. Lots of us are most comfortable with a lifestyle of daily commuting between the faith and work rooms. You might tend towards behaving in one of these ways rather than another. An honest appraisal of our experience might suggest, however, that we often display all three types of behavior. In so doing we reveal how we really relate to the secular world of work.

What kind of relationship with work does the Bible presume?

The theme text for this chapter from John 6 implicitly raises this question. Do Jesus' words here infer that our daily work is always to be regarded as inferior? Or does he mean that we should stop working for a living? Or is it that our daily work contributes nothing to what God is doing in the world? By looking at what Jesus says in the context of the Bible as a whole, we can see that he implies none of these things. Rather, he is addressing here the specific problem of attitudes to work. His audience seemed to be solely interested in material and physical satisfaction. Apparently they could not lift their minds above this. Jesus' words were cautionary to his audience then, and they are even more so now. Jesus Christ directed this teaching to bring a fresh focus to their living by pointing them towards himself. And Jesus clearly explains this guidance, "on him the Father has set his seal of approval". This sign of authenticity is vital to us. Only Christ can satisfy eternal hunger; only he can put our lives into perspective and guide us to know the answer to "Whose work is it anyway?".

Only Christ can satisfy eternal hunger

The question before us, "What kind of relationship with work does the Bible presume?", will recur throughout the book in many different contexts. At this stage we need to establish and understand some of the basic biblical principles concerning work. I have selected six of these principles, all of which are interrelated. We will then build on these in subsequent chapters. As you think about these principles and begin to relate them to your work, recall the words of James Moffat. "Great as is the power of God, he cannot work in a vacuum or with empty minds or with hearts filled with prejudice." This subject will engage our minds and our hearts in a very practical way.

God as a worker

From the first pages in the Bible, the subject of work confronts us. For example, the creation record refers several times to God engaging in work and to his satisfaction with what he had made. "God saw all that he had made, and it was very good."[2] This activity was evidently something that, having been completed, led to his being refreshed and rested. We see this in Exodus, "On the seventh day he rested, and was refreshed".[3] Thus, even in these early references, we see traces of both God's attitudes to work and his behavior in it. But it does not stop there. God starts with creation and moves on to the work of providence, judgment and redemption. God's work is creative, orderly and constructive. In all of this, God enjoys perfect job satisfaction (something we rarely have). Although unique, the work of God remains a model for human work – in spite of the fact that the connection between the work we do and its contribution to God's work is not always obvious.

God and human beings as co-workers

The principle of being co-workers with God is also established early in the Bible and consistently reinforced throughout. God planted a garden and charged humankind to cultivate and protect it.[4] Human and divine co-operation abounds as people become partners with God. "Unless the LORD builds the house, its builders labor in vain".[5] In this context, the attitude of the worker towards God is one of dependence, service and worship. The result of that attitude is evident in passages such as "May the favor of the Lord our God rest upon us; establish the work of our hands for us – yes, establish the work of our hands".[6] There is little doubt that the Bible sees our work, provided it is work in which God can be honored, as being done in co-operation with him. But this collaboration has other consequences as well. It implies that we seek to apply as much of God's model of work as possible. In this relationship we are the junior partners, and we are learning from our Master. What

God planted a garden and charged humankind to cultivate and protect it

implications, for example, does this have for seeking to maintain harmonious relationships at work? For our work being characterized by order and creativity? For us being satisfied within it? It is possible to conclude (and sometimes we do so too readily) that, because of sin, none of our work completely fulfills God's intentions. In later chapters we will look in more depth at just how practical and possible all this is.

Work as a calling

The biblical sense of Christian "calling" is first and foremost that we are called to belong to Jesus Christ. It's a calling to belong to and imitate Christ in all dimensions of life – including where we work. "That's just fine", you might say, "I've no problem with this in principle." But it doesn't just stop there – there's much more detail to come. As John White observes, "It is one thing to know how God thinks, it is quite another to want what he wants". Paul, in his letter to the Corinthians, says that "Each one should remain in the situation which he was in when God called him".[7] You might well ask what this can possibly mean in today's geographically and socially mobile society. Paul was illustrating the point that the particular calling of God reaches into every part of our lives. In this context the focus was on the domestic, cultural, social and occupational aspects of their lives. There was no hiding place for them, any more than there is for us in this matter. It's possible that you and I do not always like what God has called us to do. We would prefer a different job, in another place or in a distant culture. Such a spirit of discontent can blind us from ever seeing our current work as a calling. It is worth noting that Jesus took time out to answer questions from tax collectors and soldiers who were asking how they should display his moral and spiritual values in their occupations now that they had come to follow him.[8] He told the former to be honest in their tax collection, and he told the latter not to extort money or falsely accuse people and to be content with their pay. Pretty detailed stuff!

Work as stewardship It is tempting, when considering the important biblical principle that work is intended for self-fulfillment, to forget that it is also part of our stewardship of God's resources vested in us. In terms of self-fulfillment, the instruction "Be fruitful and increase in number; fill the earth and subdue it"[9] does point to part of God's purpose for our lives. Yet, for many people, the concept of self-fulfillment through the particular work they do is very difficult. Monotony, risk, persecution and the pressing necessity to earn money might be among the many reasons for this. Viewing work as stewardship can be no less challenging for similar reasons. Christians hold three things in stewardship, and they each have a work dimension. First, we have natural talents from birth – the parts of our personalities, skills and aptitudes that mark the similarities and differences between us. These natural talents usually shape our choice of work. Second, we have the truth of the gospel, the indwelling Spirit and the gifts received from God. We did not know about these when we were born, but we were told about them and

We have the truth of the gospel, the indwelling Spirit and the gifts received from God

they have affected our lives. The Bible assumes that these are indelibly engraved in our hearts. Finally, we hold in stewardship the possessions acquired during our lifetimes – these we have generally accumulated by applying our skills and experience to work. The foundational biblical principle is that all three categories of resources belong to the Lord. The first two we take to work every day, whether we use them there or not, although there is no doubt that Jesus expects us to apply these to our daily work. See, for example, the parable of the talents in Matthew's gospel.[10] The worker is a steward who serves his master, and the master in turn gives the opportunity to work and sets the time frame. The worker has a choice as to how to deploy the resources given to him and must exercise moral responsibility in their use. The master judges on the basis of service and the reward is his approval. It's interesting to note that there are no financial rewards here. Approval in and of itself is enough for these workers – very unlike the expectations of reward in our world. Rather troubling, isn't it?

Work as service

Closely linked to both calling and stewardship is the principle that work is not only for self-fulfillment but also for the benefit of the community. In the great Philippian passage on imitating Christ's humility, Paul writes, "Each of you should look not only to your own interests, but also to the interests of others".[11]

In effect, where we might place an either/or between service to God and the community, the Bible assumes that we think of our work as both. John Stott takes this further. "Certainly the Bible regards work as a community project, undertaken by the community for the community. All work needs to be seen as being, at least to some degree, public service."[12] This idea is probably not foremost in our minds. The ethic of service is more evident, perhaps, in caring professions, although I regularly

> All work needs to be seen as being, at least to some degree, public service

hear Christians who work in these jobs disagree because of the pressures under which they function. Many types of work that we engage in, and many of the attitudes that we take to work, seem to be quite distant from this ideal. Moreover, some of the work decisions that we have to make bring out the tensions between public and private interests. For example, sometimes people lose their jobs for the good of the whole organization, it can be difficult to balance safety at work with practical operations, and so on. But there is a wider social aspect of this service, namely that of viewing our work as enabling us to help others in need. For example, in his teaching on living as children of light, Paul observes, "He who has been stealing must steal no longer, but must work, doing something useful with his own hands, that he may have something to share with those in need".[13] We need to be forcefully reminded of this in a society in which many Christian people see their incomes as being primarily (or solely) to sustain a lifestyle to which they aspire. The needs of others rarely come into their reckoning.

Work as bringing glory to God

This is perhaps the most challenging principle of all, because it is all-embracing. I can see some of my work doing this, but not all of it, and not all of the time. It can be good work by earthly standards, my way of doing it can be laudable and my behavior exemplary – but it still may not bring glory to God. The "gap" may be in my motives, in my attitudes, or even in my testimony when no one around me knows who my real Master is. "Bringing glory" implies that God's purposes are revealed and fulfilled. "So whether you eat or drink or whatever you do, do it all for the glory of God."[14]

> "So whether you eat or drink or whatever you do, do it all for the glory of God."

This principle by its very nature infers an act of worship in our work. And, for many of us, work does not often feel like something that can be considered worshipful. I'm convinced, however, that God does not want to keep us in the dark about how we can bring him glory in our work. Faithfully applying the six principles set out here will bring God glory. Our work can be our witness, but we usually need to use both actions and words. Augustine was right when he said, "What I live by, I impart".

A warning and a challenge

The German theologian Christoph Ernst Luthhardt was correct in observing that "the view we entertain of God will determine our view of the world". As we have reflected on these principles regarding work, we are all aware that the world around us is not neutral as to how we try to apply them. Let me suggest that God is not neutral either. These principles are part of his instruction to us that we ignore at our peril. Know your God, know your world is a sound principle. In general, the world around us is hostile to faith. John expresses it in these terms, "For everything in the world – the cravings of sinful man, the lust of his eyes and the boasting of what he has and does – comes not from the Father but from the world. The world and its desires pass away, but the man who does the will of God lives forever".[15] Jim Packer translates the essence of this verse by describing "everything" as encompassing the pleasure, profit, power and promotion motives. Christians share some of these motives; it would be dishonest to deny that. But verse 17 confronts us with the simple truth that the world and its value systems have a limited life. We will not find the true answer to our question by pursuing them. We will develop this important issue further in Chapter 5.

I'll let C.S. Lewis have the last word: "There is no neutral ground in the universe: every square inch, every split second is claimed by God and counter claimed by Satan". That's the battle we should expect to wage as we ask God to give us a fresh perspective on our personal world of work.

Challenge No1

Take the opportunity here to pause, think and pray. Take each of these six principles and test them against your present practice at work. This might lead you to ask the following types of questions:

1 Is God's model of work in any way reflected in my behavior at work and in my attitude to work?

2 Am I conscious of God as a co-worker?

3 To what extent do I regard my present work as God's calling for me?

4 Do I take all of God's resources that I have in stewardship to my work? How can I make preparations to do this each day?

5 What sense do I have of serving God and the community in my work? And where does it show?

6 In what way does my behavior at work bring glory to God?

Further reading

Field, David, *The Bible and Christian Living* (London: Scripture Union, 1987).

Stott, John, *The Contemporary Christian* (Leicester: IVP, 1992).

Triton, A.N., *Whose World?* (London: IVP, 1970).

Yancey, Philip, *Reaching for the Invisible God* (Grand Rapids: Zondervan, 2000).

Endnotes

1 Doug Sherman and William Hendricks, *Your Work Matters to God* (Colorado Springs: NavPress, 1987).

2 Gen. 1:31.

3 Ex. 31:17 (RSV).

4 Gen. 2:15.

5 Ps. 127:1.

6 Ps. 90:17.

7 1 Cor. 7:20.

8 Lk. 3:12-14.

9 Gen. 1:28.

10 Mt. 25:14-30.

11 Phil. 2:4.

12 John Stott, *Issues Facing Christians Today* (London: Marshall Pickering, rev. edn, 1999).

13 Eph. 4:28.

14 1 Cor. 10:31.

15 1 Jn. 2:16-17.

2
The Importance of Your Work in God's Eyes

"The Word became flesh and lived for a while among us. We have seen his glory, the glory of the one and only, who came from the Father, full of grace and truth." (Jn. 1:14)

Outline   Before we look further at how to make sense of the world of work from a biblical perspective, we need to consider how God sees the work in which we are engaged. Unless we each know how our work matters to God and how it can make a difference for his kingdom, we run the risk of seeing faith at work as an optional extra. This chapter poses two central questions and then takes a brief look at some biblical pictures highlighting the attitudes God desires at work.

What's so special about my work?
We examine the following four elements of Christian character in order to better understand our personal work responsibilities for God: to be a witness; to be shaped by God; to show God's love in action; and to bring him glory.

Is God in my attitudes to work?
This section stresses the vital importance of this question by thinking about some aggressive contemporary attitudes to work that daily surround us.

The attitudes at work that God wants
This final section looks at three of the words that the New Testament uses to describe a Christian: God's temple, God's partner, God's disciple. Some challenging lessons emerge from the attitudes at work that are implicit in these pictures.

What's so special about my work?

We concluded the first chapter with six biblical principles concerning work, but I often find myself one step removed from these principles. In this second foundational chapter we will flesh out these principles personally and practically as we seek to answer our core question, "Whose work is it anyway?". It is very easy to be so caught up in the daily routine – the preoccupation with tasks and deadlines, the need to respond to the pressures and changing demands of work – that we lose any real sense that our work actually matters to God. Christians are wisely advised to start the day with God and reaffirm their sense of purpose and mission. But it is all too easy to overlook that discipline in the hustle and bustle of the day. It is necessary but not sufficient to make us aware that the work that each of us does, as well as how we behave while at work, are of real importance to God. If I can discern God's purposes in my work at all, to what extent can I do this? Work, with all its minutiae, can so dominate each hour of our working day (as well as our time outside of work) that we forget the strategic reason why God has placed us where we are. In fact, many Christians seem quite unaware that there is any strategy at all behind why we do what we do.

"What's special to God about my work?"

There are plenty of people (Christians among them) who will readily bore you for hours with the details of what's special about their work. In doing so, they are really responding to the question, "What is special to me about my work?". On the negative side, this type of conversation betrays traces of self-importance, power, professional status, earning power and so on. More positively, all people need to feel that their work is worthwhile and contributes to both their needs and those of society. Few people dislike talking about their work. We are seeking the answer to a rather different question, however: namely, "What's special to God about my work?". As we shall see, to find the answer to that question we need to understand God's intentions for his disciples. It's highly improbable that the God who called us to follow him does not have a purpose for us in the place where many of us spend two-thirds of our time and up to half of our lives. To deny this purpose would be to presume a very partial calling and a rather spurious form of discipleship. In addition to understanding the nature of discipleship, we need to consider the spirit and attitudes that we bring to our work. John Oxenham's prayer is very challenging in this regard, "Lord, turn the routines of work into celebrations of love". I know that I will never be able to do this until I can answer our core question. So I'm bound to ask what exactly is so special to God about my particular work? What kind of a person does God call me to be in my work situation? The following four dimensions of godly behavior lead us towards an answer.

To be a witness   We can only implement Jesus' great commission if we assume that our whole lives are open to his instruction. "Therefore go and make disciples of all nations, baptizing them in the name of the Father and of the Son and of the Holy Spirit, and teaching them to obey everything I have commanded you. And surely I will be with you always."[1] While this passage does not explicitly mention secular work, it is difficult to see how potential disciples could be either reached or taught without engaging with them in work situations. Jesus not only worked as a carpenter himself, but he also went to visit people at their places of work (on their fishing boats, at tax collection offices and so on) and challenged and taught them in terms of living out their faith in these situations.

The great commission includes the instruction to teach the nations "everything" Jesus commanded – and he taught plenty about behavior at work! Jesus' attitude towards our work is a key to its special importance and should destroy any notion we may have of keeping faith and work apart. Our workplace may well be the only place where our colleagues will ever be exposed to Christians. But does that mean that evangelism at work should be our only priority? If this were the case, the actual work that we do would be secondary and of much less significance. We might then regard our work as "only a job" and a means to an end. With such an attitude, we would be unlikely to bring glory to God by our performance and behavior at work. Our work would then fall far short of the standard set in several biblical passages. Ephesians, for example, encourages disciples to "Serve wholeheartedly, as if you were serving the Lord, not men, because you know that the Lord will reward everyone for whatever good he does, whether he is slave or free".[2] Such passages make it very clear that God is looking for excellence in our work, part of which is effective witnessing. It's that combination that's important to him. We are to be living examples that Christianity actually works.

To be shaped by God   It has taken me some time to see how God has used my different work experiences – good and bad – to shape me for his service. It can be difficult to see the bigger picture of how God is shaping us when we have a boss who always takes all the credit or who seems to survive by conflict in all his work relationships, or when we have colleagues who are cynical about our beliefs. These experiences do not always feel like a positive shaping. Yet, for many of us, the places where we have worked and spent so much of our lives have been important for the development of our faith in God. And each of us has been shaped in a different way. On occasion, the more negative the situation is, the more we cling to our faith. God doesn't always change the work, but he does change the worker. Paul attributes much to this divine process in the phrase "we are God's workmanship"[3] – literally, we are his living works of art, with all of the craftsmanship and uniqueness that this picture implies. By a process of "keeping in step with the Spirit",[4] we have come through it. Sadly, not all Christians have persevered through this testing. I know too many young professional Christians who have been shaped more by ambition, money and power than they have by faith. Their relationship with the Lord, once so right, has gone seriously wrong. In contrast, consider how Joseph's ability to provide leadership in Egypt was honed through his experiences of abandonment and slavery. This painful journey finally led to the palace and a unique position of leadership. Similarly, Daniel moved all the way from being a prisoner of war to ruling one third of the kingdom of Babylon. From the outset, his witness at work was awesome. In terms of performance excellence, he and his colleagues were better than their godless peers by a factor of ten.[5] Most of us would be happy with a factor of two. If we allowed God to shape us just as he wants, he would have his special servants in the places where we work. At the moment there might be a void there – a void created by our resistance to his purposes.

God doesn't always change the work, but he does change the worker

This principle of seeing our work in the context of a right relationship with God extends across the widest possible activity spectrum. This book is for all kinds of workers, and so is the Bible. All of us need to know the answer to the question "whose work is it anyway?". In Colossians, for example, slaves (the lowest members of society) were told, "obey your earthly masters in everything; and do it, not only when their eye is on you and to win their favor, but with sincerity of heart and reverence for the Lord. Whatever you do, work at it with all your heart, as working for the Lord, not for men, since you know that you will receive an inheritance from the Lord as a reward".[6] We can scarcely imagine the menial, demeaning and wretched tasks that such slaves did in these times. Yet God himself regarded such work as being done for him. Conversely, the most powerful members of society who had become Christians were called to a very different kind of behavior than they had exhibited in the past. In a world where their slaves had no rights of any kind, in Christ God charged them to "provide your slaves with what is right and fair, because you know that you also have a Master in heaven".[7] What a powerful reflection of the impact of the Spirit on their lives! Christ introduced both parties to a higher dimension to their work, to an overriding set of obligations. Jesus Christ reminded them that he was Lord of their specific work environment. It may be surprising to see the assumption in these passages that God dominates our work. We may try to marginalize him, but that's obviously not his plan. How far short of this plan we all fall!

To show God's love in action

Showing God's love is linked to our special role as witnesses but applies more specifically to behavior at work. Now we are in really tough territory. The work behavior of many Christians would not stand up to the scrutiny of their peers, never mind that of the Lord. Some Christians are characterized more by their awkwardness, arrogance, pettiness and bullying tactics than they are by Christ-likeness. The church's greatest handicap is the ungodly lives of those who profess to follow Christ. C.H. Spurgeon once remarked, "If your theology doesn't change your behaviour, it will never change your destiny". When asked what the greatest commandment was, Jesus said, "'Love the Lord your God with all your heart and with all your soul and with all your mind.' ... And the second is like it: 'Love your neighbor as yourself'".[8] This is a challenging mandate – to love God, love others and love ourselves. The practical implications of these words are immense. Loving God involves obedience. How often do we prayerfully analyze our job and work behavior? How often do we ask whether and where the love of God is evident in this behavior? Should our love for God

> *The work behavior of many Christians would not stand up to the scrutiny of their peers, never mind that of the Lord*

not show in the way we treat people, our work methods, our performance, our motives and so on? For example, how is it evident in dealing with a difficult customer in a retail store? In a manager's relationship with an awkward employee? In the life of an exhausted nurse taking care of an ungrateful patient? We might be tempted to ask, "What does love have to do with my work?". The biblical answer is – everything.

But there is a mystery and a reality here. It was within God's power to clone us when he called us. To make us all alike would have somehow been simpler. Yet he has taken us, with all our faults, and through the power of the Spirit God is able to transform us so that we can express his love in our actions – and in our work. That's how a woodworker, a banker, a truck driver, a doctor, a plumber or a teacher does God's work. Part of this love is expressed through relationships at work. But this love is also evident through our other forms of service such as in helping others and caring for our families and for others who are in need. Although William Tyndale wrote these words several centuries ago, they are wholly biblical and contemporary in their application. "There is no work better than another to please God; to pour water, to wash dishes, to be a cobbler, or an apostle, all is one; to wash dishes and to preach is all one, as touching as the deed, to please God."

There is no work better than another to please God

To bring God glory

In this vital matter we face a massive challenge. In our work we are called to lead the people with whom we interact to thank and praise God. For what, you may ask? For what they see of Christ in us; for the Spirit-induced differences in our lives; for our demonstration of the love of Christ; for our practice of faith; for our integrity; for our concern for others and so on. The words "in order that we, who were the first to hope in Christ, might be for the praise of his glory"[9] imply all of that and more. It would be very easy to give up and say that this calling is quite impossible on several counts. "The people I work with neither know nor worship God"; "nobody here thinks like that – if I'm a decent person, they would not know who to thank (if they even thought of thanking anybody)"; "people do notice differences, but only in the usual ways – good or bad, kind or rude and so on – why do they want a reason?"; "this is a dreadful work atmosphere, there's no way that God is getting glory out of this". All of these responses lead to a single reasonable, if challenging, answer. I will have to both live as a follower of Christ and talk about the person I am following. How else can people make the connection? Christians are called to be more than "good people". This poses problems for some Christians. They rightly contend that it is better to walk than talk. It is necessary, in fact, to both walk and talk. Many of us in the developed world, and especially in Europe, live in post-Christian societies. Large sections of the population have little memory or concept of what it means to follow Christ. Being a Christian is not, in their eyes, materially different from being anything else. People need signposts as to why we behave as we do, and we have to provide them.

The New Testament writers consistently tell us that the glory of God's nature, character, power and purpose are now to be seen in Jesus. As the writer to the Hebrews says, for example, "The Son is the radiance of God's glory and the exact representation of his being, sustaining all things by his powerful word".[10] Our theme text for this chapter is another example. John writes of the voice of God that still speaks through the Bible by the power of the Spirit. Jesus is in us through the Spirit – and, for the moment, warts and all, we are part of that continuing voice. In every sense, the work of "bringing glory" continues, in part, through us. But how will we know if we are bringing glory to God? We may in fact never know in this life. While you can know your cholesterol count, blood pressure or resting heart rate, none of us has a "glory indicator". We are assured, however, that God is pleased with obedience to our calling, and a natural outcome of that obedience is to bring glory to his name. While our task is to manage the inputs to our work, God measures the output.

There is, however, another crucial aspect of bringing God glory. Throughout the Bible, work and worship are closely linked. Indeed, one of the Hebrew words for "work" is on occasion translated as "worship". Mark Greene makes this connection by observing that "work is a seven lettered word".[11] When a Christian works, he is also worshiping. Do you have any sense of that day by day? Wrong attitudes at work and about work are bound to lead to poor quality worship – or to no worship at all. God is thereby "doubly" robbed of

Throughout the Bible, work and worship are closely linked

glory – because we are not leading others to give him glory and because we are not worshiping him ourselves.

The prayer of David, when he was preparing for the temple that his son Solomon was one day to build, set the pattern for all ascriptions of praise in the Bible: "Yours O LORD, is the greatness and the power and the glory and the majesty and the splendor, for everything in heaven and earth is yours. Yours, O LORD, is the kingdom; you are exalted as head over all."[12]

Jesus picked up the essence of this response in the prayer that he taught to his disciples.[13] As William Barclay reminds us, "I cannot say amen [to these words] unless I honestly say, 'Cost what it may, this is my prayer'". Such indeed is the magnitude of the challenge to bring God glory in our life and work.[14]

> ☑ **ACTION:** We have explored four ways in which we are to contribute to God through our work. Review and assess your own recent job experience in each of these four areas. Pray that you will be able to see this honestly and in a balanced way. We all have a lot to learn about this subject and a long way to go to apply these principles more perfectly. How would you answer the question "What's so special to God about my work?".

Is God in my attitudes to work? The attitudes we bring to our work play a major role in determining what our unique contributions will be. As you went through the exercise above, you probably felt some pain about your current behavior. I know that I have. We explore this further by looking at the "spirit of our age" regarding work. How and where does this spirit affect our work that matters so much to God? What follows is in very sharp contrast to our discussion above. I found the following attitudes as I scanned a number of business magazines that I normally read. I searched the individual and company profiles for some current evidence on prevailing attitudes to work. I did not have to look for long – these role models were brimming over with opinions that seep into the media and training courses all over the world. These people are opinion formers who help to set the context in which many

Christians have to work. Here are ten of their views about themselves or others they admire.

1. "He has always been mindlessly competitive."
2. "This man needs to be a control freak at all times."
3. "He is consumed by ambition."
4. "To succeed, you have to regard everybody else as the enemy."
5. "I regard work as a promotion machine."
6. "He's a person who is amoral in all things – the end always justifies the means."
7. "The secret of my success is, find the money formula first and fast."
8. "The 24-7 work culture suits me; I don't want a family life."
9. "He's adrenalin-fuelled, committed to the max."
10. "A team builder, noted for his delegation and trust – but not too much of either."

You'll notice how assertive and aggressive these statements are. There are some extreme remarks here, and many of them sound very negative. Some levels of ambition and competitiveness might be necessary ingredients of good personal work performance – the kind that brings glory to God. Others, such as the reference to an absence of morals or zero respect for family life, could not be considered Christian. Whether you know many people like these or whether you are a person with similar characteristics may depend on the type of work that you do. You may be at the early stages of a career and such views have so far bypassed you, or you may be in mid-career and all of this sounds like "business as usual". It is not only "the captains of industry", however, who use this language. I have met such driven people in very different walks of life. Many of them would regard being described in some of these ways as a "badge of honor". While they often disdain such pointed language, they show much evidence of these traits. And some of them are Christians.

We saw above that our work is special to God – at least that is what he intended it to be. But whether it is in fact special will depend on our attitudes and behavior. Look again at the ten attitudes above, thinking of it as looking in a mirror where you see both yourself and some parts of your immediate work environment.

☑ **ACTION:** Do you display any of these extreme characteristics in your attitudes to work? If you do, think carefully about how that might affect the distinctive contribution from work that God is looking for from you. If you are brave enough, test the opinions of those you work with to see how they perceive you. What will you do to change any ungodly attitudes? If these types of attitudes are evident around you, pray that they will not pollute you.

The attitudes at work that God wants

The One who made us knows our weaknesses – and our potential – and he gave us the Bible as our manual for living. Noting that Christian ethics were not developed either in the cloister or for the cloister, John Stott observed, "... the New Testament context of the Christian life is the noisy, busy, challenging arena of the workplace and the marketplace".[15] What we are doing here, then, is reconnecting something that has too often become disconnected. We can confidently say that it was not the Master's intention to disconnect work and life from faith. To that end, the Bible contains many helpful perspectives on the type of attitudes we need in order to speak for God through our work. In this final section we explore three of them.

God's temple

Paul poses the question, "Don't you know that you yourselves are God's temple and that God's Spirit lives in you?".[16] He goes on to say just how sacred that temple is and that "you are that temple". This is a powerful metaphor. And it is founded on a very high view of men and women. Perhaps, for some of us, this is just too high a view. The expectations built into it might seem beyond our abilities – especially in the work environment. However, the value that Christians have in this world lies in the unique relationship they have with God. That's the working assumption of the Bible. That's what Christ died for. Pressing this picture further, we have to ask ourselves about the activity that goes on in this temple, the extent to which it actually belongs to the living God. Who else lives there? Is this temple of ours a historic monument or a center for worship and witness? Moving into even deeper water, that means that you took the Spirit to that meeting when you behaved mercilessly in berating a junior colleague for a minor offense. The Spirit was there when you lied to the customer about the product problems he has been having. The Spirit witnessed you fudging the expenses claim. The Spirit was there, waiting, when you had an opportunity to witness but remembered that you never mix faith and work as a matter of principle. If this makes you weep, weep on. Sometimes this is the sad fact of Christian life at work. The issue is not whether I can live like Christ, but whether I can let Christ live in me. My body is the container – is the Spirit evidently in it?

The issue is not whether I can live like Christ, but whether I can let Christ live in me

God's partners The idea of partnership and sharing is integral to Christian life. The very idea of a partnership is rooted in the purely business and commercial sense of the term. As such, it is very relevant to our study of work. No partnership works unless there is sufficient common purpose between the parties; they have to have good reason for being in that relationship; and the reason has to be durable through good and bad times. Partnerships rarely survive for long if one of them is "sleeping", or taking no active part in the relationship. Is "partner with Christ" listed on your physical or mental biodata? Do you have a sense of doing (or not doing) your share of God's work? Without exception, all Christians are named as partners in the grace of God. Paul built on this idea when he thanked God for "partnership in the gospel from the first day until now, being confident of this, that he who began a good work in you will carry it on to completion until the day of Christ Jesus".[17] It is indeed encouraging to find that the Bible recognizes our need for ongoing help to deliver on this role. While a partnership needs strength, it also requires the right spirit. It simply cannot be made to function if I have to be reluctantly dragged into taking the Lord into my working life. You can assume that God has work that he wants you to do together where you work; but in you he may not always have a willing partner.

God's disciples The Christian is characteristically a learner. This must be his lifelong aim – based on an attitude of humility that wants to know more about the person he has pledged to follow. For most of us, work can be a difficult environment – and one in which we all make mistakes. The first rule for every learner is to admit that others may be right and he may be wrong. Unplanned words, unforeseen situations, unhelpful colleagues are only some of the things that can induce behavior in us that is far from Christ-like. We need to remember that what we are learning about is the greatness and all-sufficiency of God in all of life's challenges. Other people need (and some want) to learn that from us. Many people simply don't read the Bible. In our working lives, we do not always hear it in the words expressed to Philip, "Sir, we would like to see Jesus".[18] These truth-seeking Greek travelers exhibited a hunger for God that our peers do not always have. The "request" is often silent; the office mood indifferent; the questioning cynical and sneering; the words taunting. But people do look for the evidence of both our following and our learning. What do they see? If they were taking notes, how would their "diary of a Christian" actually read?

Challenge No2

This chapter covers some rather personal material about God's expectations of, and our attitudes to, our work. Take time now to spend a few minutes in prayerful reflection about the following:

1 Determine what you think is special to God about your present role at work. It is essential to consider this now, so that the material in the following chapters will be challenging and life-changing.

2 Over recent years, has your work had more impact on you than God has? Or have you felt that God has worked with you to make it possible for you to handle the different attitudes in your work environment?

3 How do you relate to the idea of your current work as "worship"? Think of comparisons with how you prepare for and engage in worship, its impact upon you, your attitude while worshiping, how focused you are and so on.

4 How could you bring more glory to God through your work? Or what has to change in order for you to start to bring him any glory?

5 As you reflect on the pictures of a temple, of partners and of disciples that we looked at in the last section, decide which has the most relevance for how you relate to your work.

6 One conclusion that a Christian could draw from this chapter is, "I work for God". Are you able to say that?

Further reading

Dunn, Jim, *Lifewise Guide to Work* (Eastbourne: Kingsway Publications, 2000).

Green, Michael, and McGrath, Alister, *How Shall We Reach Them?* (Milton Keynes: Nelson Word, 1994).

Tippett, Sammy, *The Prayer Factor* (Amersham: Scripture Press Foundation, 1989).

Westcott, David, *Work Well: Live Well: Rediscovering a Biblical View of Work* (London: Marshall Pickering, 1996).

Endnotes

1 Mt. 28:18-20.

2 Eph. 6:7-8.

3 Eph. 2:10.

4 Gal. 5:25.

5 Dan. 1:20.

6 Col. 3:22-24.

7 Col. 4:1.

8 Mt. 22:37, 39.

9 Eph. 1:12.

10 Heb. 1:3.

11 Mark Greene, *Thank God It's Monday: Ministry in the Workplace* (London: Scripture Union, 1994), p. 36.

12 1 Chr. 29:11.

13 Mt. 6:9-13.

14 You might like to pursue this further by reading William Barclay, *The Plain Man Looks at the Lord's Prayer* (London: Collins, 1964).

15 John Stott, *The Incomparable Christ* (Leicester: IVP, 2001), pp. 96-97.

16 1 Cor. 3:16.

17 Phil. 1:5-6.

18 Jn. 12:21.

PART TWO

KEEPING A PERSPECTIVE ON OUR WORK

3
Making Sense of the World of Work

"But in your hearts set apart Christ as Lord."
(1 Pet. 3:15)

Outline   We now move from foundational principles about work to some of the pressing issues that confront us as we try to orient ourselves in our work environment. Chief among these concerns is confusion about the world of work – where work is heading and how we fit into it. All of the following issues can and do disturb Christians. It is essential to understand work from a Christian perspective. In this chapter we address three questions and end with a series of biblical lessons about "making sense while standing still".

What paradoxes do we find in work?
This section examines five areas of inconsistency, including work itself, time, age, stress and identity.

What's happening to work?
This section briefly reviews some of the major trends affecting work and current issues that often make work "feel different" for Christians. Included in this list are risk and uncertainty, change, individualism, performance, morality and pollution.

Is there a Christian way of making sense of work?
Convinced that the answer to this question is "yes", we explore here the need for a fresh perspective, clear vision and a renewed spirit – each of which can only come from the Lord.

Making sense while being still
Based on three different cases in which people were asked to be still to be delivered, instructed and restored, we explore the relevance of all three to our relationship with work.

What paradoxes do we find in work? This chapter builds upon the first two, which set out some of the great biblical principles concerning work and rooted these in how we contribute to God's kingdom through our work. This chapter focuses not so much on a comprehensive review of the many ways work is changing as it does on asking how Christians might interpret and respond to such changes. Whatever the context (and each one varies considerably), can we make (Christian) sense of work? We would probably all agree that at times this is really difficult. Yet without such an understanding it is unlikely that we will be effective Christians at work through the various twists and turns of career, circumstances, employment opportunities, family responsibilities, health and so on. Christians take comfort from the fact that "Jesus Christ is the same yesterday and today and forever"[1] and cling to such biblical constants in times of change. But we can too easily forget these assurances in the midst of difficult situations. It is tempting to respond to the many complexities of the work environment by saying that we simply cannot make any sense of them. But that's scarcely good enough. God's purpose is not best served by our wandering in the dark. Part of the confusion surrounding the world of work lies in the many paradoxes associated with it. As we consider five of these paradoxes below, we will see that each one has Christian consequences.

Work The first issue about which it is easy to make self-contradictory statements is work itself. Work is something we all need to do, yet most of us seem to have either too much or too little of it; work is either too exhausting or not challenging enough; work can generate excessive rewards or none at all. For some, work is characterized by chronic busyness, while for others its most striking feature is crushing boredom. Some people seem incapable of anything other than total commitment to their work, while others have a casual relationship with it and seem to perpetually live at the edge of the job market. Some members of our society are almost too qualified for the jobs that are available, while others do not have enough skills. There are Christians in all of these different categories, and some face such paradoxes on a daily basis. The type of work available to us also varies, and not always in the ways we want. In countries such as the United Kingdom, the United States and France, only between 50 and 60 per cent of

Work is something we all need to do, yet most of us seem to have either too much or too little of it

workers are in full-time employment; with many others of working age employed part-time, in contract employment or self-employed. Work is associated with status and standing, and its absence with the opposite. Charles Handy expresses this well. "We seem to have made work a god and then made it difficult for many to worship".[2]

Time We think that we should have more time, yet we appear to have less. In spite of the fact that people now generally live longer and have higher levels of efficiency and more leisure, we never seem to have enough time. In order to accommodate other societal changes, organizations tend to offer more time flexibility in work contracts. Meanwhile, many people feel overworked – in part because they need more money and in part because the organizations that employ them want to operate with fewer people. Lots of people simply choose to have little time in order to maximize the money they earn or (more unusually), vice versa. This battle with time has several consequences for the Christian. In some jobs, it's clear that both success and survival are on a collision course with marriage and parenthood as God designed them. Neither do many of us have the time to form relationships with people as "salt and light". The societies in which many of us live operate seven days a week to support the high service levels that we expect, to accommodate demands for leisure and so on. Christian service suffers and the church is the poorer because some of its best resources are lost to this lack of time. In such situations (and many of us are in them), something has to change. We will return to this issue later in the book.

> The societies in which many of us live operate seven days a week to support the high service levels that we expect

Age There are also many paradoxes with regard to age and work, and particularly concerning skill and experience. While many organizations trumpet that their real asset is people, they seem content to lose the skills and experience of relatively young people through early retirement. Increased life expectancy, together with the growing costs of financing retirement and low population growth, are beginning to contribute to a reversal of that trend in some countries, which will produce an older cadre of workers. Some of these workers will have a portfolio of different activities, part paid and part voluntary. Churches that have long benefited from healthy early retirees may no longer do so. Another age paradox for older Christians is much (apparent) leisure, but no spare time. I meet many highly skilled Christians who cannot think what they could possibly do with their skills for God in their retirement. So they just travel a lot. There are many others who have much to offer and have a different answer to "Whose work is it anyway?". They may not all agree with Jonathan Swift's remark "that no wise man ever wished to be younger". But their work continues in this spirit, "And whatever you do, whether in word or deed, do it all in the name of the Lord Jesus, giving thanks to God the Father through him".[3] This is good advice for all ages, all times and all cultures.

Stress The issue of stress can also be full of paradox for Christians. "I am convinced that I am in the job God wants me to do. But why is it so very stressful? And why is it getting worse?" There are usually several factors underlying such comments. There is pressure from the demands imposed on us by our environment, peers, colleagues and family. The irony is that most of us need some of these pressures to function at our best. Other underlying factors include the consequences, physical and mental, that flow from these demands. These can include tiredness, illness, disorientation and breakdown. Such symptoms can be both recurring and very serious. Sometimes changes in our work situation cause stress – notably retirement, job change and taking on new responsibilities. All of us can also relate to stress that comes from relationships at work; from ambiguities about our role; from specific conflict situations; from our own temperaments and so on. Christians live with stresses from many different sources. Not all of church life is joyous. Personality clashes and disputes over practice and theology only serve to exacerbate the life stresses that some Christians face. Many Christians say that the greatest stresses in their lives are church related, and not from their secular work. Sometimes the high standards of behavior set out in the Bible cause Christians to feel under pressure. Even reading Christian books, like this one, that draw these matters to their attention can cause stress! This is a difficult area, and the solution is not to offer trite and neatly packaged solutions. Usually we need to tackle both the source and the symptoms. And, to go back to where we started, we regularly need God's confirmation that we are in the right job. While joy and peace can be scarce commodities, finding them again is essential.[4] As the psalmist

I am convinced that I am in the job God wants me to do. But why is it so very stressful?

says, "When I was in distress, I sought the Lord; at night I stretched out untiring hands and my soul refused to be comforted".[5]

Identity Finally, I want to touch briefly on the issue of identity and self-esteem. Work can also generate extremes in this area. Too much ego can breed pride and independence; too little can be both negative and destructive. This lack of identity can leave people stranded, without an evident place in society. Many of us use the role we do (or did, or aspire to) at work as a way of introducing ourselves to others. Remarks such as, "I am a plumber"; "I was a teacher"; "I plan to be a doctor" all testify to the importance we attach to our roles. People without employment often struggle with a sense of identity and have a sense of failure, a simmering anger and a lack of confidence. Christians are not exempt from such emotions. On the other hand, an excess of ego is often expressed in arrogance, pride and a cynical disregard for others. Both extremes show unhealthy relations with the concept of work. We may well not understand what has happened to us professionally, or why. But we cannot glorify God in our work, whatever that may be, if our sense of self is distorted. If we are full of ourselves and our own importance, or if we have no confidence, the result is the same. We are not acknowledging that our sense of self needs to come from God – from our creation in his image and from our redemption by Christ on the cross. Jesus pointed out the damaging effects of both these extremes. The Pharisees were at one extreme, the woman at the well at the other. Our self-esteem rests solely on God's grace – not on where our pay comes from, the size of our office or the length of our entry in *Who's Who*. The psalmist encourages all of us with these words, "You made him (humankind) a little lower than the heavenly beings and crowned him with glory and honor".[6] We should not, of course, confuse the need to know ourselves and be confident as to who we are with biblical teaching on self-denial. Jesus was very clear in his call to the disciples, "If anyone would come after me, he must deny himself and take up his cross daily and follow me".[7]

✔ ACTION: Are some of these paradoxes, or perhaps others, currently affecting your own work life or your perspective on work? Which do you find most difficult and why? It has been said that the Lord didn't burden us with work: he blessed us with it. In your current work situation, can you honestly say that you agree with that?

While we can comment on these paradoxes in general, we can't solve them here. All of us need to resolve them at a personal level by revisiting some of what was said in the first two chapters. For example, if you struggle with work and time, consider honestly whether your approach to both of these brings God glory. This follows the route of obedience, rather than asking someone for a formula or an algorithm to make your work life better. If we look for the biblical answer, we will find that God wants honor in our personal, family, church, work and community lives.[8] Many Christians have shelves full of books on work-life balance that have made no difference whatsoever to their lives – not because they can't read, but because they don't obey. The only person who can really fix these problems is God, through the power of his Spirit.

The Bible is the only book that teaches us what a healthy Christian life is like

But we have to be willing to do what he says. When God called us, he did not ask us to join a cafeteria line and pick up the parts of the Christian menu that pleased us. If we are to bring God glory, we may need to resolve some paradoxes associated with our personal work – and fast. The Bible is the only book that teaches us what a healthy Christian life is like. We ignore it at our peril.

What's happening to work?

The aim of this section is not to gaze into a crystal ball, however fascinating that might be. We will, rather, reflect on how Christians are to respond to the ever-shifting world of work with their timeless values. For years, experts have been heralding a workplace revolution. In essence, they describe the following scenario: jobs for life are dead; many more jobs are flexible; the pace of work is accelerated; white collar jobs become a thing of the past; and everything of significance for volume employment moves to countries where costs are much lower. As a consequence of some of these trends, people are said to be tiring of long hours of commuting; work-life relationships are in serious imbalance; and more people are either opting out of work altogether or seeking self-employment in the hope that it will bring a lifestyle of choice. Taken together, these trends are often referred to as "the transformation of work", and they have been keeping publishers and pundits alike busy for years. Many of these trends will strike a chord with us. They will confirm what we feel and see. But, in fact, a number of them have actually been happening much more slowly that we have been led to believe. Others changes, such as self-employment, working from home and more frequent job changes, are growing more in perception than in reality.

All of this is not to deny that we live in times of unprecedented change in terms of many of the variables that determine the nature of work. The heightened pace of scientific discovery and technological change, for example, is likely to demand higher levels of education and training, generate much new employment and further transform the way we work. As innovation accelerates and becomes more geographically widespread, competitive conditions will intensify for many industries. Meanwhile, medical knowledge is doubling approximately every five years, and unprecedented ethical issues therefore abound. The Internet is growing both exponentially and globally, with all kinds of positive and negative implications. Both management and employees will have to come to terms with lifelong learning in such an environment – at a social and economic cost. New graduates today might expect to have up to five or six different careers, depending on life expectancy and retirement age. Two-income families are already the norm in many developed economies, and work practices are likely to have to adjust even more to this reality. For these and other reasons, birthrates have already declined in many of these countries. On the business side, companies will have to reshape themselves even more frequently, as they come to terms with globalization. No business is now too large to be a takeover target – and so the uncertainty multiplies. In all of this, time is becoming the world's most precious commodity.

We are often told that the workplace of the twenty-first century requires a different set of skills and a different kind of leader from those needed in the "industrial age". This line of argument usually goes on to say that in economies where knowledge, creativity and innovation are prized, people are the "bottom line" and their potential must be harnessed, rather than instructed. Although I live in a world where these attributes are prized, I don't see much evidence of these attitudes. You probably don't see it either. In a similar vein, the new employment era is supposed to be one of flexible, non-bureaucratic organizations in which people have more power to choose employment opportunities and to negotiate terms and conditions. In this world, employability replaces employment security as the basis for employment contracts. But there are significant gaps between this rhetoric and the reality of employment for many people. Meanwhile, many surveys show that work

Many surveys show that work dominates people's lives to the detriment of other interests, including family

dominates people's lives to the detriment of other interests, including family; that they want to alter this pattern; that they are searching for work-life balance and so on.[9] But I don't meet large numbers of people, including Christians, with the will to actually change their life priorities or patterns to achieve any of these longed-for goals.

No one knows for certain what the future of work will be. But some of the present trends clearly do concern Christians. Over recent years, I have discussed work issues with lots of different people who follow Christ. They communicate much confusion and many different emotions about their world of work. Some of their uncertainty concerns the future, but much of it is about the present. For many, and for various personal reasons, work feels different. Perhaps we can make better sense of work by asking "why?". Here are some of the reasons Christians give.

Risk and uncertainty These come in various guises. Work is less secure than it once was for many people. Employment tenure is one reason, others include not being perceived to be ambitious enough, having preoccupying interests "external" to work and skills becoming obsolete.

Change The chosen careers of many people have changed in ways that make them question why they are there. Many people feel uncomfortable in an increasingly competitive and aggressive work environment. Some of these changes call for greater time commitments or for them to be rather different kinds of people.

Individualism The spirit of the age promotes teamwork but lauds individualism. This is difficult for some Christians because it is self-seeking. Others feel that it smacks of "new age" and have difficulties when it is built into some of the personal development programs they are required to undergo. Finding yourself becomes more important than finding God.

Performance Christians aspire, or should aspire, to excellence in their work. In many contexts, excellence is being redefined. For example, it often includes high time demands outside working hours; infinite flexibility in work patterns; implicitly measuring performance by hours at work beyond the stated norm; being of necessity a "corporate" person who gives all to the organization and so on.

Morality The dramatic change in attitudes to sex has affected the workplace and has many implications for working relationships. Christians need to exercise care and show greater wisdom than ever in these areas. Even when values are discussed, they are set out in morally neutral terms. They sound persuasive, but often they are not put into practice. For some, the workplace is a morality-free zone.

Pollution There is a danger that, as values are discounted and faith as a basis for life is further discarded, Christians can become more and more like the people they work with – by a process of drift. Part of this is the struggle for many to be salt and light when the people to whom they witness have no framework into which to fit Christianity. Another dimension of this insidious pollution is the worship of the god of materialism.

☑ **ACTION:** Consider the concerns you have about making sense of your work – in the present or as you think about the direction in which it seems to be going. In doing so, you may add to the list of six areas cited above – or completely change them. Which of these issues are the most pressing for you at the present time? And how are you trying to resolve them?

Is there a Christian way of making sense of work?

While the modern workplace can be both demanding and confusing for Christians, it is where God has placed us. Some of its many anomalies involve us; others are evident around us. Both can be equally perplexing. We are puzzled about the highly trained person who has skills in abundance but no steady employment, and the multi-skilled individual who is repeatedly made redundant. What about that Christian friend who does not know where to turn, and for whom every work-related door closes? What about the completely immoral neighbor who always prospers at work? How can we accept the dishonest, deceitful and incompetent colleague who has cheated her way to the top? And what of the migrant worker, driven by economic imperatives, whose lifestyle is beyond your comprehension because he faces long-term, often indefinite, separation from family and friends? Or the two parents who work on opposite shifts for forty weeks a year and rarely see their family together? Or the person in the next estate who works by satellite only and never sees a colleague other than by video conference? How about the executive who goes to New York and Tokyo alternate weeks for meetings and often does 80,000 air miles per month – and who claims to be fulfilled by all of this? These are just a few examples of the world of work in which Christians live.

Interesting though all such cases may be, what is essential is that we make Christian sense of our own personal work. How do we do that in the midst of all of life's demands? How do I know that what I do "fits in" with God's purpose for me? To address these and other related questions, let me encourage you to think in the following way. As my career has progressed, I have found that making sense of my daily work depends on ...

Perspective The place from which I am viewing it. Viewed from the hustle and bustle of everyday life, it is very difficult to see work clearly. We live in the world of the "perpetual now". The immediate crushes in; the deadlines and priorities are dominant; the stresses and strains of relationships are only too real; and there is always risk and uncertainty. We need to consider God's perspective. Why did he lead me here? Why he is keeping me here? What is it that he wants done while I am here? What does my work look like, viewed from heaven? Does God get enough (or any) space to give me his perspective on my work? Seeing ourselves from God's perspective often requires that we are still – one of the hardest things to achieve in modern life.

Vision The eyes through which we see ourselves and our work are crucial. It's easy for all of us to see our work in the classic terms as earning a living, providing for our families and so on. But when God looks at your work, what does he see? Does he see faith? Witness? Love? Or does he see total commitment to every possible priority other than his own? Inconsistency of practice? A reluctance to identify with his kingdom? Knowing how God sees us would surely challenge our behavior.

Spirit What is the condition of your heart as you look at your life and work? What are your attitudes to God? Are you willing to hear and obey? Are you open to redirection? Often this boils down to what we are trying to achieve in our work. What's in your heart about your work? Are you planning to maximize money, status, promotion, reputation and so on? And how does that compare to what God wants you to achieve? Have you made a point of asking him? And, frankly, does God have any place in your attitude to work?

These three categories for making sense of work have several common features. They are all spiritual exercises; they are independent of the present and future shape of work; they apply to all work situations; and they are all about the lordship of Christ in our work. As the theme text for this chapter points out, making sense of work is only possible if we set apart Christ as Lord – giving to him the reverence and respect that is his due. The following section reinforces the importance of these points with some biblical lessons on how God speaks in the stillness – provided we are willing to be there to hear him.

Making sense while being still

There is much evidence that the pressures that come from work affect a Christian's stillness. The effects may not be evident on the surface. Many of us are experts at masking inner turmoil with external calm; while others claim to rejoice in the inner peace of God while visibly living with a high degree of anxiety. For others, life in general, and work in particular are associated with neither external nor internal stillness. The Bible makes it clear that God would have it otherwise. So the Lord said to Israel, "In repentance and rest is your salvation, in quietness and trust is your strength, but you would have none of it".[10] That's the problem for many of us. It's not that God hasn't provided. It's rather that we don't want to know. How does a passage like "the peace of God, which transcends all understanding, will guard your hearts and your minds in Christ Jesus"[11] relate to your attitude to your daily work? Perhaps not at all. For most of us, peace and work don't fit into the same sentence. God, however, promised to bless his people as he led them to stillness in some very unlikely circumstances.

Many of us are experts at masking inner turmoil with external calm

Be still – to be delivered The Israelites were under intense pressure. Having just left Egypt, they were terrified as an army marched towards them to take them back. The Egyptians had quickly decided that to allow this ready supply of slaves to leave was an economic disaster. Ahead of them lay the Red Sea. They were in turmoil, critical of their leaders, fabricating rosy memories of how good life really had been in Egypt, acting as if they were on their own. Sound familiar? In that unlikely context, the word from Moses was, "The LORD will fight for you; you need only to be still".[12] Humanly speaking, being still at precisely that moment in their lives was improbable. It was the last thing on their minds. Many of us would have been building rafts or testing out our long-distance swimming abilities. Yet it was in that situation, and through their subsequent rescue by the parting of the waters, that God assured them that he would "gain glory".[13] The moral of this incident? No stillness, no glory. As M. Eckhart observed several centuries ago, "Nothing in all creation is so like God as stillness."

Be still – to be instructed We all need to have a refreshed perspective. To a group of people who seemed to have forgotten how God had blessed them in the past and preserved them through natural and political disasters, David brought God's message. "Be still, and know that I am God."[14] They were encouraged to have supreme confidence in the promise of God's ultimate sovereignty. And so are we. But first their memories had to be stirred. And so do ours. It's usually best done in stillness. In this setting, being still enabled God's people to recall his track record in their lives, to remember who he really was and to re-establish their faith in his future purpose.

Be still, and know that I am God

Be still – to be restored G.K. Chesterton once said, "The one spiritual disease is thinking that one is quite well". So it was with Elijah, in that his greatest trial came shortly after his one of his greatest triumphs. He had just defeated the prophets of Baal before King Ahab with an impressive display of God's power. Now he was on the run from Jezebel, in fear for his life. He assumed that he was the only prophet left, and consequently he bore all kinds of burdens that were not his to bear. God's challenge to him was, "What are you doing here, Elijah?".[15] Told to stand on the mountain to witness God's presence, he found that it was not in the wind, earthquake or the fire, but in "a gentle whisper".[16] It was a voice that could only be heard in the stillness. The experience on the mountain was calculated to allow him to experience God's presence again, to recalibrate his life to God's power again, and to give answers to God's questions as to what he was doing with his life. We need to be able to do all three of these as well if we are to understand the answer to the question, "Whose work is it anyway?". We will consider this incident in Elijah's life in greater depth in Chapter 8.

The examples above illustrate how foundational stillness is to our lives in general, and to our working lives in particular. But more than that, as we see in the examples above, we also need deliverance, instruction and restoration in order to keep making sense of our work. We need deliverance from its pervasive demands, from the priorities of the world and from the temptation to think that it is ours, not God's. We need instruction on God's perspective to prevent us from making complex what is simple in his eyes. And we need restoration from the tendency to think that we are alone when trying to find the right relationship with both our work and our God. Edna Becker's poem helps to direct us to the imperative that is stillness.

If, like the lake that has the boon
Of cradling the little moon
Above the hill
I want the Infinite to be
Reflected undisturbed in me,
I must be still.

Challenge No3

Try to find a way of being still as you reflect on this chapter. That might be a tall order if you are on a commuter train, on your coffee break in a machine shop, with the children at home or in any number of situations that seem far from stillness. But try to find a still time soon and reflect on the following:

1 What aspects of your work do you find difficult to make sense of? And why?

2 Is Jesus Christ the Lord of your work? In what ways does that show, in your own heart and in the work environment?

3 Many readers will be confused and have fears and uncertainties about their roles in the world of work. Spend some time prayerfully applying the concepts of perspective, vision and spirit.

4 How can you build more stillness into your pattern of life?

Further reading

Anderson, Jock, *In the Stillness* (Carlisle: Alpha, 1999).

Lucado, Max, *Let the Journey Begin: God's Roadmap for New Beginnings* (Nashville: Word, 1998).

Packer, J.I., *Rediscovering Holiness* (Ann Arbor, MI: Servant, 1992).

Stott, John, *The Incomparable Christ* (Leicester: IVP, 2001).

Endnotes

1 Heb. 13:8.

2 Charles Handy, *The Empty Raincoat* (London: Arrow, 1995), p. 26.

3 Col. 3:17.

4 A very helpful discussion on this topic is to be found in Westcott, *Work Well: Live Well* (London: Marshall Pickering, 1994), Chapter 6.

5 Ps. 77:2.

6 Ps. 8:5.

7 Lk. 9:23.

8 See passages such as Col. 3 and Eph. 6 on these topics.

9 The scope of this chapter precludes a deeper examination of these trends in the world of work. You might wish to look further into them in books such as the following: P. Rayman, *Beyond the Bottom Line: The Search for Dignity at Work* (New York: St. Martin's Press, 2001); J. Ciulla, *The Working Life: The Promise and Betrayal of Modern Work* (New York: Times, 2000); L. Worrall and C. Cooper, *The Quality of Working Life* (London: Institute of Management, 1999).

10 Isa. 30:15.

11 Phil. 4:7.

12 Ex. 14:14.

13 Ex. 14:17.

14 Ps. 46:10.

15 1 Kgs. 19:9.

16 1 Kgs. 19:12.

PART THREE

LEARNING THROUGH THE PRACTICE OF OUR WORK

4
Danger – Christians at Work

"The LORD does not look at the things man looks at. Man looks at the outward appearance, but the LORD looks at the heart." (1 Sam. 16:7)

Outline   Throughout Part 3, we will consider Christian practice at work. Chapters 4 and 5 begin with a series of health warnings about dangers and conflicts. As we have seen, God designed work to be positive, but it does have built-in hazards. The three dangers discussed below are only a few of the many that are possible to identify. They reflect my own experience both as a participant in, and an observer of, the world of work.

What dangers?
This introductory section establishes that the Christian really does face dangers associated with work.

Applying New Age thinking to our work
In a brief review of this phenomenon, we evaluate the way in which it has influenced much of this generation's perspective on work and how it can subtly seep into Christian thought.

Failing to be a witness at work
The four cases in this section illustrate some of the many challenges that Christians face when witnessing in the workplace. This section also addresses the widespread and highly damaging issue of hypocrisy.

Making a god out of a career

We see here that each of us is capable of gradually sliding from displaying good Christian discipleship in work to making our work a god. This section also sets out the characteristics of idol worship.

A matter of relationships

We conclude the chapter by acknowledging that the only known Christian antidote to these hazards is to revisit our relationship with the Lord. Is it rich or poor? We learn from the experience of Psalm 63.

What dangers? Having laid the foundations and stressed the need to make Christian sense of our work, we now need to face up to some of the hazards associated with the competitive work environment in which many of us operate. While all of us recognize an element of futility in our work, this is especially painful for the person who is not a follower of Christ. Work-related glamor and successes are short-lived. Above all else, sin has a major impact on our co-workers (both Christian and non-Christian), and therefore affects our relationships. And we ourselves are far from exempt from its wiles. John Blanchard was right when he said, "we are born in sin and spend our lives coping with the consequences". As a result, there are many sin-induced dangers at work. Dangers and opportunities, however, are often quite closely linked. The Chinese characters for both are identical – literally, crisis is "an opportunity riding the dangerous wind". So Christians can find that circumstances which carry a serious threat at work may also generate enormous opportunities. The environmental effects of sin on work are all around us. Sin has made work harder and brought many frustrations and conflicting emotions. But, at the same time, the broken and dysfunctional lives of colleagues often open their eyes to the need for faith. Similarly, we can try to turn situations of conflict into positive outcomes or bring some form of assistance to our peers in the midst of crises. While the three hazards discussed below are quite far-reaching in their implications, they may not be particular sources of danger for you. But think twice (or three times) if you don't consider that there are any dangers associated with your work. We will deal more fully with the opportunities that these dangers present later in the book, in Chapters 6, 9 and 10.

✔ **ACTION:** As you read the following section, think about the particular dangers that you face at work. Make a list of them. And then try to fit them into the three categories below. To what conclusions does this exercise lead you?

The Bible gives us good grounds for being on guard in our work. Jesus assumed the implicit dangers when he sent out the 12 disciples. "I am sending you out like sheep among wolves. Therefore be as shrewd as snakes and as innocent as doves".[1] Paul reflected this attitude with the advice, "Do everything without complaining or arguing, so that you may become blameless and pure, children of God without fault in a crooked and depraved generation, in which you shine like stars in the universe as you hold out the word of life".[2] This is quite an assessment of our context, and a challenging job specification! Do you think that you are fulfilling its terms? Think about just how much expectation of danger is built into that advice. It is also important to remember that Jesus said, "If the world hates you, keep in mind that it hated me first".[3] These verses add to our understanding of God's perspective on our work – an issue that we noted as vital in Chapter 3.

Looking more closely at some of the dangers associated with work is like switching on the lights in the lighthouse. We are familiar with the waters, but not with all the hazards. There is a chart, but we don't always consult it. Life on the ship is busy, and everyone is preoccupied. The Master is on the ship somewhere, but not always at the helm – because we like to share the steering. And there are rocks in abundance.

Applying New Age thinking to our work

Pause to reflect before you protest that this is not one of your personal dangers. You might contend, "I have no idea what this is, and no interest in knowing". Or perhaps, "I've never knowingly met someone with such ideas – don't they dress up in strange clothes, have dreadlocks and hug trees?". Some do, but most don't. And there are a lot of people with such ideas in business suits, thinly disguised as your colleagues. That's part of the problem. Few of us have enough time to study every passing fad in world thinking. But we all breathe the same air, and it's full of strange ideas that erode the Christian view of life and work. We are all probably unknowing victims of it. We started to meet New Age ideas in

Chapter 1 when we were looking at the prevailing worldview of work. It is an intrinsic part of the "spirit of our age".

New Age is an umbrella term, connecting a whole series of disparate movements that attempt to underpin a vast array of different lifestyles.[4] The name "New Age" comes from the astrological theory that presumes that each star lasts for 2000 years. The Age of Pisces (the fish symbol of Christianity) has passed, we are told, and we are now in the Age of Aquarius. New Age is a powerful mixture of mysticism, nature religions and the occult – often packaged as a very soft sell. Many bookstores are full of its literature, and the pervasive presence of its ideas in the media has made a huge impact in many walks of life – from schools to airport executive lounges. The best summary of the disparate beliefs of New Age that I have read is that by John Stott when he describes it as: "All is God", "All is one", and "All is well". In this way of thinking, for example, God is not a person but a creative force; the way to find him is to look within ourselves, not in the Bible; the priority in life is to find our own self at whatever cost. The only salvation in New Age is self-salvation. The route to success is self-realization. There are no moral absolutes, and guidance in all things comes from within. The net effect is to underpin a set of lifestyles in which "anything goes". By its tolerance of all views, it implicitly erodes the mandate to follow Jesus Christ as Lord. In fact, New Age constitutes a root and branch challenge to all aspects of our Trinitarian faith. Christian belief is seen as ill-founded, too narrow, not sufficiently open to new ideas and ultimately a delusion. New Age thinking can seriously damage Christian health.

The only salvation in New Age is self-salvation

I recently had a fascinating experience in the London Underground. The train compartment was relatively quiet, and two ladies near me were in earnest conversation about their eclectic New Age reading. Having covered recent horoscopes, lifestyle choices in their personal affairs and some aspects of the occult, one of them reached into her bag and produced a copy of *Mere Christianity* by C.S. Lewis. "There's great new age thinking in this", she said, "all about liberating the person." The other readily agreed, and asked her if she had read any of Max Lucado's work. "There's some really good material in these Christian bookstores, you know" was her conclusion. There is bad news and good news here in this story. On the one hand, people view

Christianity as just part of a cocktail of ideas and as having nothing unique to say. On the other hand, God can use people's openness to Christian ideas and to reading Christian literature to bring them to Christ.

For the Christian church, such a "pick and mix" approach to beliefs is not a new problem. A verse such as "See to it that no-one takes you captive through hollow and deceptive philosophy"[5] could have been written last week about life in the twenty-first century. The Greco-Roman world of the first century shared many common characteristics with ours. Surrounded with such a clutch of philosophies, Timothy was advised to "keep your head in all situations".[6] The following is a summary of some of the more obvious current New Age dangers to our Christian way of thinking about work.

My work is mine. I do it my way, for my ends. It has nothing to do with a calling from anyone else, because nobody else matters.

Whatever your relationship with work is, it is just fine. It should not be subject to challenge from higher authority – because you are the only authority that counts.

Your work doesn't matter to God. You are a witness to your own journey; love is a detached and vague concept; and you are working for your glory.

If work makes sense to you, that's all that matters. Forget God's perspective – he has much less right to one than you have. After all, it's your life!

✔ ACTION: Honestly appraise how you think about work in a Christian way. Consider whether some of the above attitudes have not on occasion infiltrated into your own thinking. There are moments in all of our more tense working days when some of this might sound quite appealing. You may find that such ideas have crept in at particular moments, although perhaps you did not know where they came from. In Paul's farewell to the Ephesian elders, he warns them, "I know that after I leave, savage wolves will come in among you and will not spare the flock".[7] Pray that God will preserve you from wolves of all types, including those that come in sheep's clothing.

Failing to be a witness at work We saw in both Chapters 1 and 2 that God calls Christians to be witnesses at work. James S. Stewart expressed this in forceful terms. "The real problem of Christianity is not atheism or scepticism, but the non-witnessing Christian trying to smuggle his own soul into heaven." Ouch, that hurts! We should first acknowledge what is involved in witnessing. Much of witnessing involves love in action – being Christ-like in character, showing forth the fruits of the Spirit and, of course, looking for the opportunity to tell others about the good news of Jesus Christ. Jesus summarized this lifestyle when he said, "In the same way, let your light shine before men, that they may see your good deeds and praise your Father in heaven."[8] All of us live and work in very different situations. But let's begin with the assumption that there are few better places than the workplace for a non-Christian to see the difference that Christ does (or does not) make in the lives of his followers. One of the best ways to explore this whole area is to look at the following representative cases and ask what they say to us and what dangers they highlight. And we will look at how closely witnessing is linked to Christian character in Chapter 6, where we consider discipleship at work.

All of us live and work in very different situations

Four case studies: Christian witness at work

● *Michael – the separatist.* Michael was a youth leader and a Christian. At age forty he was also the highly successful manager of a local electronics company. In his role as youth leader he had recently written letters to parents whose children attended his club, seeking written permission for their teenagers' attendance at summer camp. Joe, one of his line supervisors at work, had children in Michael's club and had received a copy of this letter. Joe wanted clarification about health and safety at the camp, the qualifications and experience of the leaders and so on before he agreed to let his two sons go. He was really delighted that Michael's church was taking an interest in his boys, and he was amazed that someone of Michael's caliber was giving time to this. Joe didn't have any personal interest in God, but he was determined to let his family choose their own way in life. In fact, the summer camp was only one of the reasons why he asked for an appointment to talk with Michael. Joe had some problems with his marriage and, knowing that his boss was a Christian, he wanted some advice. He had never spoken to anyone about these problems before. Joe had a lot of respect for Michael, who was rather remote from the workforce but respected for his open style of management and his fairness. An appointment was made. Michael was very pleasant, and he satisfactorily explained the details of the camp over a cup of coffee. However, when the real reason for the meeting emerged, he reacted rather differently. "I'm sorry, Joe, I don't talk about personal matters with the staff – have you spoken to the human resources team? Or what about coming to our church on Sunday? Our pastor is great on marriage. This is a matter of principle for me." Joe thought that the Bible said something about love and care for others; he left both embarrassed and disillusioned. He vowed that he would never look for help in that direction again.

● *Bill – the hypocrite*. Bill was a bully at school and had been one ever since. He was a rather volatile person, very competitive, and he always dominated conversations at work and leisure. He was not popular – as the annual office party games revealed. Everybody in the office had views about Bill, and they were not all bad. He could be very kind, but when he was he made sure that everybody knew about it. He was rumored to be a churchgoer, but people were all a bit vague about where and when. Overall, he was not a bad colleague, unless you were a woman. Basically, he thought women were less able at work than men – and he thought that political correctness was a way of keeping accurate election scores. Worst of all, he sometimes made sexually inappropriate comments and Mary, who had joined the company six weeks ago, was the latest victim. She was a quiet, bright and attractive girl, and this was her first job after leaving college. She found Bill disgusting. On Sunday past, Mary passed a downtown church and was sure that she saw Bill go into it. He saw her too, and before she could disappear around a corner, Bill eagerly rushed out of the church to ask her if she would like to come in. "Hi Mary, this is a special week of events geared for your age group – great band, lots of smart young men." Her response to Bill is unprintable.

● *Jenny – the secret disciple*. A very competent young corporate lawyer, Jenny was just five years out of graduate school with a bright future. Her work was demanding, and long hours were just part of her job. She managed to be minimally involved in her local church, but it was tough. She regularly had to work weekends. "No way to the twelve-hour day" was the practice slogan – meaning that nothing less than fourteen would do. Jenny was a follower of Jesus Christ – a commitment that dated from a campus mission. But, as far as she could tell, there were no other Christians in the practice. She might have found that there were – if she ever had time to talk about something other than the latest takeover defense or that prospective management buyout at the other end of town. Jenny always wore a fish badge, but it was neatly tucked behind the collar of her gray suits. The opportunity to witness never seemed to arise. Then, three years later, Mark joined the practice. Jenny and he had attended the same college, where he was a real "Jesus freak". Everybody knew about his faith; he was fearless. He was so fearless, in fact, that the senior partners pondered a little at his interviews. But he was a class act, and "a bit of variety would do us all no harm" was their conclusion. They hired him. Mark was introduced to Jenny at his welcome cocktail party, "Hey Jenny, still praising the Lord, I hope!" he called from a distance. Jenny managed a positive, but scarcely audible, response. "Now there's a surprise", said the senior partner. "I'm not sure that we have room for two of you lot." Neither Mark nor Jenny quite knew what to say. And it occurred to Jenny that she now faced some real challenges in order to make her witness credible in this law firm. She saw that she was very open to a charge of hypocrisy.

The opportunity to witness never seemed to arise

● *Rachel – the quiet planter.* From the time her brothers played with toy trucks on the lawn, Rachel wanted to be in the construction industry. Her parents hoped that this crazy idea would go away; her teachers saw that it wouldn't. When she was in high school she made the decision that she was going into construction, and the marginal compromise was that she would train first as a civil engineer. Rachel kept saying that this (improbably, some thought) was God's will for her life. From the time she started site visits, she was barraged by wolf whistles and cat calls. Rachel could handle this. She was excellent at her job, and soon the leading agents were asking for her to handle their sites. She had the distinctive gift of listening to people, whether they were working cranes or digging drains. Unlikely though it might seem, men old enough to be her father would at times take a small Bible from her. She always carried them in her rucksack. She had some hard taskmasters who had little time for women on sites, let alone a Christian one. Some made her life really difficult. But her witness was effective, her seed sowing consistent. She was often asked to pray for family problems. Five years later, she changed jobs to work in a civil engineering consulting company in the same city. She and Robert planned to marry, and her construction job had recently involved too much traveling. A year later she received a letter from Carlos, who had tracked her down. He wanted to tell her that his daughter had become a Christian by reading the Bible she gave him four years previously. Her life had been in ruins and her wayward behavior had caused great distress to her parents. Her family witness had been such that he and his wife had also come to Christ. Rachel (and Robert) thanked God that they both knew the Lord of the harvest.

☑ **ACTION:** Reflect on the following questions.

Was Joe's expectation of Michael a reasonable one? Was Michael right to respond to Joe in the way he did? How else could he have handled this situation?

What is the way back for Bill in terms of his relationships with Mary and his colleagues? If Bill asked you for counseling, what advice would you give him?

How might Jenny and Mark work together to bring glory to the Lord in this company in the months ahead?

What have you learned from Rachel's story or from observing others like Rachel in the work context?

Are there any parallels between these cases and your own practice as a Christian in the workplace?

Read the theme text at the beginning of the chapter. What was going on in the hearts of the Christians involved in these cases? What do you think God's view of them would be?

There can be few greater threats to the cause of Christ than hypocrisy. So the case of Bill deserves special mention. In or out of the work context, there is no sin more roundly condemned in the New Testament. Others are quick to spot and despise hypocrisy. It's one of the easiest sins to commit, and we can all be guilty of it. And when we separate work and faith, hypocrisy is bound to occur. Somehow we think that what happens at work doesn't matter quite as much as what we are among our Christian peer group. Nothing could be further from God's truth. The Bible refers to hypocrisy of several types. Noting some of these types might help us avoid it. Hypocrisy occurs when alleged beliefs are not consistent with behavior. It can involve play-acting goodness – doing or saying things to be seen. When someone breaks God's laws in the name of religion and hides his true motives under a mask of pretense, that is hypocrisy. One of its many manifestations is when a Christian vigorously condemns sin but continues shamelessly to sin himself. Most observers find this hard to take. In the end, hypocrisy develops its own blindness and so attracts the Lord's condemnation. Referring to the returning master assessing his servants, he said, "He will cut him to pieces and assign him a place with the hypocrites, where there will be weeping and gnashing of teeth".[9] Even as you read this, you may think of cases known to you in which hypocritical behavior has been very damaging to Christian witness at work. We all need to examine our own lives and motivations.

> *Hypocrisy occurs when alleged beliefs are not consistent with behavior*

Making a god out of a career

Our theme text for this chapter comes into its own here. In matters relating to careers, improving the "outward appearance" can be very tempting. Promotion, recognition, status and its associated trappings are the substance of success in the workplace for most of us. That's the dimension that people see – and it may be the one that we want to see, too. But such external indicators may, or may not, be part of God's plan for our lives. What is evident in 1 Samuel, and in the rest of the Bible, is that God measures us according to what is going on in the heart. This, then, is where we must focus our attention – otherwise following Christ is a hollow practice. The Lord wants us to do well at our work and to enjoy our achievements. And so doing may well lead to rapid career progression that can be to his glory. That is wholly consistent with what we learned in Chapters 1 and 2. But seeking to "do well" as an end in itself can destroy Christian life and move us from being God-honoring to being self-honoring. If we are solely focused on achieving such measures of success, we are well down the route to making a god of our careers. The problem is that, even in some Christian communities, many people place a premium on material progress, without any more than a nod in the direction of spiritual progress. The externals can look great and may impress others, but the heart may be spiritually bankrupt. We may be gilded outside but destitute inside. May God deliver us all from this.

Think carefully about the following words from the psalmist:

Not to us, O LORD, not to us but to your name be the glory, because of your love and faithfulness.[10]

I have not met many Christians who set out to make a god of their careers, but I have seen plenty of examples of this happening along the way. Few of them like to describe their relationship with work in this way. It implies excess, lack of control and a loss of a sense of perspective, and few Christians are comfortable with that. A.W. Tozer said that "an idol of the mind is as offensive to God as an idol of the hand". Work and careers can become just that – idols of the mind. We have probably all heard versions of the following. "Sure, I'm driving 150 per cent for promotion, but that's what God wants isn't it?" "When I reach the top of my mountain, I'll have a better view of the foothills – and see the rest of my life much more clearly." "People exaggerate how committed I am to my work. I've always had it fully under control – it only looks bad from the outside. The Lord understands." On the face of it, these are neither good nor bad comments. The only person who can test such statements for their "idolatry content" is God, who knows the heart. But, believe me – test them he does!

I have not met many Christians who set out to make a god of their careers

Having established that there are very real dangers here, let's pause to consider the following vital questions that we should all apply to our careers on a regular basis.

Lordship in practice. Is Jesus Christ the Lord of my career ambitions? How much conversation and consultation have I had with him about them? How often have I exposed them to the light of his words in the Bible?

Idol worship. Has my relationship with work moved into the unhealthy zone in which I worship my career more than God? Danger signs here might include an absolute preoccupation with work at all times, a desire to only talk about work and achievements and so on.

Altar call. Have I recently asked the Lord if I am doing my work in such a way that he could bless it? Does my behavior at work have, or deserve, his seal of approval?

When John wrote to the church in Ephesus and told them, "Dear children, keep yourselves from idols",[11] he probably did not have careers specifically in mind. There were few towns with more connections to the ancient gods, and no town more proud of them. So there were plenty of alternative gods around. But his advice was generic and applies to all objects of false devotion, to anything that leads Christians to abandon the real for the illusory. An idol is anything that we worship instead of God and which we allow to take the place of God. Could this be a career? Yes, it could. Could this be your career? Certainly.

As William Cowper wrote in the eighteenth century,

> *The dearest idol I have known*
> *Whate' er that idol be,*
> *Help me to tear it from thy throne,*
> *And worship only thee.*

☑ **ACTION:** Having thought seriously about these three questions, let me encourage you to take this a little further. From our observations of how people around us treat idols of all kinds (money, celebrities, sports heroes, business moguls, artifacts, etc.), let's recall the ways in which idols exert influence in order to honestly question our own relationship to our careers. To do that might not be comfortable, but it is necessary. Note that there is a potential work dimension in each of the seven issues. Jesus cannot be Lord of our lives if (or while) such things are true of us.

Idols are held in reverence.

Idols are the most important thing in the worshiper's life.

Idols determine the character and standards of behavior of the worshiper – and other worshipers have a lot of influence, too.

The hero is the role model – whatever his values; and the worshiper wants to copy him.

The worshiper wants to spend more and more time with his idol – it's his prime source of satisfaction.

Worshipers are blind to everything else, and so their judgment is thereby often impaired.

Idols are a point of reference at all times. For the true worshiper, it's all he wants to talk about; how he measures others; all that he sees as having value.

A matter of relationships The intention of this book is not solely to highlight problems. We all need solutions and some guidance as to how to avoid such hazards in our own lives. The temptation, however, is to address such issues with Band-Aids and look for short-term fixes. Taking our three topics in turn, we can easily illustrate this. Regarding the problem of New Age thinking, we might say, "I'll remove every book with such ideas from my library". Although this is a good idea, these ideas are also embedded in our culture, media and in many other secular practices. To stop reading about them is not enough – whereas to refocus on Christ as Lord is the perfect antidote. On the question of witnessing, you might think, "You make a forceful point, I'll leave some Christian literature around in the office, school or play group – this will ensure that my position is understood". This is commendable – but what about making some real changes in the way you live by taking (or making) opportunities to talk to people about Jesus, by watching your tongue, by showing love to that colleague who is unkind to you? On the question of making idols out of our careers, we might concede, "Yes, I do need to cool it a little – the job can take possession of my life at times – it always helps me when I go more regularly to the sports club". Exercise probably does help, but will that change the roots of the idolatry? I know no other solution to this but to reconsider the fundamental question of your relationship with God. This really is the heart of the matter.

One of the best illustrations that Jesus gave of a man with a work problem was in the parable of the rich farmer. Work was foremost in his mind – new barns, extended planting, better husbandry, productive gains and enhanced returns. His fertile business mind was clearly working overtime, and he was perhaps the kind of man in whom you would want to invest. But how did he relate to God? The passage concludes, "Yes, a person is a fool to store up earthly wealth but not have a rich relationship with God".[12] That's where we end this chapter, acknowledging that only a "rich relationship" can deliver us from these dangers. In this we are greatly helped by Psalm 63. David wrote this psalm in the desert, at a low point in his life. All relationships are two-way. If both parties don't participate, it just won't work. David gives us four couplets to illustrate what God provides on his side, which in turn calls for something from each of us. For clarity, the following is expressed in an "I do", "you do" format.

● *I looked; you loved.* God's person and power were there for David to see. "I have seen you in the sanctuary and beheld your power and your glory."[13] The effect of these work hazards that we have been examining is that they cloud our vision such that God becomes less visible, and ultimately invisible, to us. David looked again and saw God's love with freshness. God asked him, in return, to fully respond to this love. "Because your love is better than life, my lips will glorify you."[14] God is there. Where are we?

Our work is fundamentally part of God's provision

● *I praise; you provide.* David pledges to praise God in all dimensions of his life. How often, in the intensity of the workplace, does the praising of God disappear? A lot. We may casually note that the fun has gone from our work; with it often goes the Christian joy. For

God's part, David acknowledges that "My soul will be satisfied as with the richest of foods; with singing lips my mouth will praise you".[15] Our work is fundamentally part of God's provision. He did not design it to detract from our worship of him.

● *I remember; you renew.* The pressures of work often crowd out our time to think. What we know about God we too easily forget. Few of our co-workers would reward us for meditating – but God does. David's meditation time was in the "watches of the night". However and wherever we can, we need to make time to remember. That very process brought David its own rewards. His relationship with God was so much better as a result. "Because you are my help, I sing in the shadow of your wings."[16] Such was the benefit of God's renewal.

● *I hold on; you hold up.* There are many times when we feel the force of this couplet, and all we can do is hold on – whether in work or in any other aspect of our Christian experience. "My soul clings to you; your right hand upholds me."[17] God's response is quite amazing – he gives each of us his full attention with his powerful right hand. But how good are we at clinging?

Further reading

Howard, J. Grant, *Balancing Life's Demands* (Portland, OR: Multinomah, 1983).

Ortberg, John, *If You Want to Walk on Water, You've Got to Get Out of the Boat* (Grand Rapids: Zondervan, 2001).

Packer, J.I., *God Has Spoken* (Aylesbury: Hodder & Stoughton, 1979).

Smart, Dominic, *When We Get It Wrong* (Carlisle: Paternoster, 2001).

Endnotes

1 Mt. 10:16.

2 Phil. 2: 14-16.

3 Jn. 15:18.

4 If you would like to read further on this topic, see Caryl Matrisiana, *Gods of the New Age* (London: Marshall Pickering, 1985); Michael Green, *The Dawn of the*

New Age (London: Darton, Longman & Todd, 1993); Douglas R. Groothius, *Revealing the New Age Jesus: Challenges to Orthodox Views of Christ* (Downers Grove, IL: IVP, 1990).

5 Col. 2:8.

6 2 Tim. 4:5.

7 Acts 20:29; see also verses 25 to 38.

8 Mt. 5:16.

9 Mt. 24:51.

10 Ps. 115:1.

11. 1 Jn. 5:21.

12 Lk. 12:21 (NLT).

13 Ps. 63:2.

14 Ps. 63:3.

15 Ps. 63:5.

16 Ps. 63:7.

17 Ps. 63:8.

Challenge No4

This chapter has covered many gritty and difficult matters, some of which are virtually 'no go' territory in much Christian conversation. Take a few moments to reflect on the following:

1 If the quality of our relationship with God is directly linked to our vulnerability to dangers at work, consider what this means for you. Is yours a rich relationship with God? If not, in what ways has your work damaged that relationship? Praise God if your work experiences have enhanced your relationship with him.

2 Try to identify the dangers that you have faced at work over recent months or years. Some of them may be quite different from those mentioned here. If you have not done so already, what steps can you take to enlist God's help to minimize their effects?

3 Pray about the challenge in Dan Greene's words, "Witnessing is not a spare-time occupation or a once-a-week activity. It must be a quality of life. You don't go witnessing, you are a witness". How would your current reputation at work stack up against this challenge?

4 Ask the Holy Spirit to highlight any area of your working life in which you are guilty of hypocritical behavior, ask forgiveness for it and pray for the power to both minimize the effects of past hypocrisy and avoid it in the future.

5
Conflict and the World of Work

"Do not be overcome by evil, but overcome evil with good." (Rom. 12:21)

Outline   How frequently have you heard someone say, "work would be fine, were it not for the people I work with (or for)"? You probably hear a version of this quite often. We are still concerned with Christian practice here in this chapter, which accepts the reality of workplace conflict of different types and levels of severity. This chapter is based on the biblical view of the world. We will look at work conflicts in two very different dimensions – with our colleagues and with our owner – noting that an understanding of both is vital for knowing whose work it is that we engage in.

Christians, work and the world
This introduction reminds us of God's view of our present world. This in turn draws our attention to five important things that we have to remember about it as we think about conflict at work.

Conflict – with our colleagues
We begin this section by looking at some lessons from my personal experience of work-related conflict, followed by four case studies about conflict at work. Finally, we look to Proverbs for some helpful and demanding advice about how wise people should shape their relationships.

Conflict – with our owner
In looking at this dimension of conflict, we trace the ways in which Christians can be in dispute with God and thereby lose any sense of peace in their lives. We point to ways in which this can be restored and by which we can live our working lives to his glory.

Christians, work and the world

In some ways I am reluctant to point to the expectation that there will be some measure of "conflict" for the Christian at work. This is because I enjoy my work – perhaps too much at times. On the whole I find my work stimulating and fulfilling, and so "conflict" is not the first thing I associate with it. I know of many other Christians for whom this is not the case – for a whole variety of reasons, many of which are beyond their control. There are difficult dimensions to this topic for all of us who are on God's payroll, because all of us do face conflicts at work at some time. As Oswald Chambers says, "life without conflict is impossible". For our purposes here, the word "conflict" incorporates a whole range of tensions, disagreements and levels of friction that at times characterize work. They may be neither violent nor continuous, but they all affect our spirits in a negative way and have the capacity to damage our witness.

Life without conflict is impossible

When looking at conflict, we must begin with the biblical perspective on our world. While what we think of our world is interesting, what God thinks is much more important. The word the New Testament uses most frequently to refer to "the world" has a strong connotation of "order". Indeed, the biblical sequence of God's work – order (in creation), disorder (through sin), redemption (in Christ), new order – involves the harmonious integration of various (and at times hostile) elements and energies. The ultimate aim is to unite all things in Christ. We may not immediately think of disorder and rebellion as being the backdrop to our world and work environment, but God does. The following verses personalize and sum up this situation, "the sinful mind is hostile to God. It does not submit to God's law, nor can it do so. Those controlled by the sinful nature cannot please God".[1] This being the case, how are Christians to relate to this world? You might well say, "We can't hope to get anywhere as witnesses in the world if we are in constant conflict with people". That's correct, and Jesus was not in such constant conflict. But he recognized only too clearly the reality of the world he loved, and the character of the people for whom he died. He also experienced a great deal of hostility in his work – from expected and unexpected quarters. What, then, do we need to remember about our world as we look for the answer to the question "Whose work is it anyway?" and, in particular, as we address the topic of this chapter? I would suggest five things.

● *Understand the present reality.* We should not miss the presumption behind Jesus' prayer to his Father for the disciples, "I have given them your word and the world has hated them, for they are not of the world any more than I am of the world".[2] Yet this prayer was not for their removal from the world, but for their protection in it. We must thank God for his understanding and provision here, for we know that we need his protection.

● *Be aware of our own history.* We need to remember what we came from, how recently, and the effects of the hangover from the past. Here's one way of remembering. "As for you, you were dead in your transgressions and sins, in which you used to live when you followed the ways of this world and of the ruler of the kingdom of the air, the spirit who is now at work in those who are disobedient."[3] We should be confident about our salvation while remaining aware of our weakness. Our strength is, like Paul's, made perfect in weakness.

We should be confident about our salvation while remaining aware of our weakness

● *Read the health warnings.* There are many such warnings that apply to our work. They include the caution against entanglement, "No-one serving as a soldier gets involved in civilian affairs – he wants to please his commanding officer"[4] and an acknowledgment that it's easy to fall in love with this world, "Demas, because he loved this world, has deserted me ..."[5] In the context of the shortage of time, we also find wise counsel to avoid being sucked in by the world. Rather, we should be like "those who use the things of the world, as if not engrossed in them".[6] That's exactly where most of us want to be with our work – but we rarely are.

● *Realize that it is not neutral.* Our peers may at times seem indifferent to our Christian faith, but the world is not. I am much struck by Jim Packer's interpretation of the verse, "For everything in the world – the cravings of sinful man, the lust of his eyes and the boasting of what he has and does – comes not from the Father but from the world".[7] As we have seen, he calls these "the pleasure, profit, power and promotion motives". It is very easy to pursue all of these motives to excess – so we must remember their origins and not be deceived. Decorate them as we might, soften them as we may, this is the reality of our world – and God sees it as it really is.

● *Live positively within it.* With all of the above in mind, we should celebrate the great truth that one telling proof that we are Christians is that we can overcome the world – just as Jesus did: "... for everyone born of God has overcome the world. This is the victory that has overcome the world, even our faith".[8] We are both called and empowered to live victorious Christian lives in the full knowledge of the nature of our fallen world. But we always need to be able to see the world through God's eyes – otherwise we will lose our way. Speaking to our hopes and aspirations as Christians, C.S. Lewis was right to advise, "Aim at heaven and you will get earth thrown in; aim at earth and you will get neither".

In concluding this introduction to the context in which we face conflict, I am reminded of the wise words of John Stott about the hazards of "double listening"[9] – namely listening to both the word and the world. Stott notes that we have to hear the one with humble reverence, anxious to understand and obey, and the other with critical alertness. We need to pray that God will help us to distinguish between the quality of advice from these sources.

☑ **ACTION:** Take some time to review your own relationship with the world in the light of these five observations. For example, have you been assuming that the effects of the world on you are neutral and passive? Are these "health warnings" shaping your attitudes in the way in which God intends? Pray about the advice in our theme text from Romans 12 as it applies to your work environment.

Conflict – with our colleagues We all experience conflict with our colleagues from time to time. We have probably all asked the question, "What is the God-honoring way to handle this (present) conflict?". Who has not wrestled with directing the principles of Christian love towards a bitter, aggressive and spiteful colleague? Who has not wondered if the fruit of the Spirit was evident in our lives when we were in intense disagreement at work over a matter of principle? We need to accept, first of all, that we don't get exemption from Christian fundamentals in such situations. The three characteristics of what it is to be a Christian remain unchanged – namely believing, doing and being. We cannot have

Christian "dressing down" days at work when we leave salt and light in the closet at home, when grace is parked in the next county, and when love is coming in next week's mail. As has been wisely said, an account of our faith is an account of our lives. All of the principles set down in Chapters 1 and 2 apply to our work in times of conflict as well as in times of peace.

I have had much personal experience with this difficult subject. It is important to remember that not all disagreements and debates at work lead to conflict – nor should they. It is essential to encourage open communication and discussion to avoid building up negative feelings that place serious stress and strain on relationships. Reason and rational behavior, however, are singularly absent in times of intense conflict. They are absent, that is, except in the Christian heart – where the Spirit lives. But the Spirit's presence may not be evident. At times it can be difficult to remember that he is there, and it is Satan's business to help us forget it. In general, I have not lived my working life "in conflict" with my colleagues – although I have met some Christians who have. Indeed, their autobiographical milestones consist of triumphs in past work conflicts – tales of their victories, in effect! I've never been content with this approach to life, which suggests that personal gain and a form of sustenance come from the pain of others. A better starting point for the Christian is to distinguish between conflict creation and conflict resolution. Surely our focus should be on the latter wherever possible, and we should be known for our ability to assist in such resolution. It is hard to see, for example, how a Christian can be either working in partnership with God or living to bring him glory if he is known at work for being a perpetual source of conflict. This is where the proper meaning of Christian meekness – namely strength under discipline – comes in. For a Christian to be accused of being diplomatic, a peacemaker and willing to resolve workplace conflicts is no bad thing – even though those qualities may be interpreted as weakness. We should recall Jesus' radical teaching on the attitudes to be fostered in his disciples.[10]

I am not naïve about any of this. I face many situations at work that draw me into conflict, and there are many more that would if I did not purposefully try to defuse them. Because I abhor idleness and poor performance, dislike pretentious and arrogant people, have a distaste for lack of truthfulness and

> *Not all disagreements and debates at work lead to conflict — nor should they*

transparency and tend to "suffer fools badly" in all walks of life, these are things that draw me into conflict. Also, I truly detest seeing junior people or individuals low down in a hierarchy being poorly treated by their bosses. On occasion I come across personalities that I could easily clash with – because we are such very different people. I am a rather direct individual, and although I have a slow fuse and do not get angry too quickly, I do express my opinions quite forcefully. When I was younger, some of my real conflicts were with people who tried to manage me, and who (in my youthful opinion) were less than competent, had few leadership qualities and made bad decisions. Looking back on my own past, I can identify some simple principles for managing through conflicts at work. Some of these are listed below.

1. *Let God take control of the conflict*. People have different personalities, but there is much to be said for not flaring up immediately, controlling our tongues and praying about the situation earlier rather than later – this includes praying for the other person or persons. Anger too often takes control of our thoughts, words and actions. The danger is that we sometimes fail to see that the Lord has a vested interest in how a work problem is going to be resolved.

2. *Resolving conflicts*. Christians often lead the way in solving conflicts at work – either because it is their job, or because they have the inner inclination to do so. Either way, the end of a conflict in a work context (in a fallen world) is not always peace – it can be merely the absence (or deferral) of strife. The challenge is to show Christian grace through the process and in the aftermath. That's not easy.

3. *Things to avoid*. Christians are to avoid using abusive language, sending rage-filled e-mails and dictating wrathful memos in the heat of a conflict situation. Neither should we allow situations to develop to the point where conflict is inevitable – the ongoing relationships at work may not matter to others, but they do to Christians. We should not think, either, that we are on our own but know how to ask advice, share with trusted people and seek a mentor. The final thing to avoid is thinking that conflict at work does not matter to God. If we are in partnership with him, it matters a great deal.

The final thing to avoid is thinking that conflict at work does not matter to God

4. Ask God what he is trying to teach you. This is the tough part. In principle, I recognize that God can use a difficult and stressful work experience to shape our character. But, in the thick of it, that is not always easy to accept. But I agree, if somewhat reluctantly, with the point made by Erwin Lutzer, "More is at stake than your personal victory. Conflict is the main ingredient in God's character development programme". I confess that sometimes I rather wish it wasn't.

☑ **ACTION:** Take time out to think about the sources of conflict in your work, your behavior in the midst of such situations and how the four principles above apply to your own experience. Have you been able to bring God glory in any of these conflict situations – in the short term or the longer term?

Cases of conflict at work

Conflicts come in all shapes and sizes. In the four cases below, consider the behavior patterns of the Christians concerned and ask what lessons you could learn from them – both positive and negative. Try to cast yourself in the role of an adviser to Nigel and Mary. The cases of David and William and Alex and Fred introduce the added dimension of Christians working together in secular work. What can you learn from their behavior?

● *Nigel and Frank – testing God's plans.* Nigel was a successful young academic – not quite at the top of the ladder but, in the opinion of some, too young to be promoted further. He was a Christian and had no interest in academic politics. When a new senior post in his department was advertised, his colleagues encouraged him to apply. An influential member of the interview panel briefed him "off the record" that he would not be appointed because the panel considered him to have been too successful for his age. Nigel regarded this remark as very unprofessional, although kindly intended. As a Christian, he did not want to cause waves and decided to leave it to God. Frank, an outsider with an impressive academic record, was duly appointed. Nigel was very disappointed, but he accepted this outcome and vowed to be as helpful as possible. It quickly became evident, however, that Frank had no managerial ability. In fact, his general handling of his colleagues ranged from poor to dreadful. Even more difficult was the fact that he had a very egocentric personality and seemed to thrive on generating new disputes with colleagues on a daily basis. Nigel struggled with this, seeing that he could have done the job so much better and wondering what God was trying to teach him in all of this strife. He struggled hard to avoid conflict, but it was impossible. Frank simply thrived on creating it – he seemed to need to open up a new battlefront with somebody new at least twice a day. Nigel did not want to be seen to be acting out of his own disappointment at not getting the new post. And, to make matters even worse, Frank was a secular humanist who had already made it clear that he had little interest in people of faith. After much thought and prayer, Nigel decided to try to speak to Frank about his many relationship problems with a view to offering some help. Frank was incensed. "Are you trying to suggest that I have a personality problem? Just because people here seem to like you and don't understand my style? Please mind your own business." Nigel was dumbfounded. How could it be part of God's plan to bring this man into his life?

● *David and William – a clash of values*. David was a Christian, but he was also a tough, fair and direct businessman. He had a good track record of taking care of his people. He ran his plastics business very well and was widely recognized as an industry leader, both technologically and commercially. He was always willing to help people, especially with finding employment. This spirit of generosity had sometimes caused him problems. David had hired William, an active lay preacher and church elder – but a man conscious of his rights and rather forthright in his demands for them. In effect, he was not always a user-friendly type of employee. In hindsight, the hire was a marginal call at best. When the company faced severe competition for its European and Far Eastern markets, David had to announce a program of plant closures, restructuring and lay offs. William could not handle this. Although he was not directly affected, he mercilessly criticized David, behind his back, for his unchristian behavior. David found out about this criticism from a friend at a local church and was very angry. He confronted William, "I do not want to have to do this. But if I don't, there will be no company to employ any of us". William took the high moral ground and said, "This action of yours will destroy the Christian witness in this town for the next decade. You should simply resign in protest". David knew that, if he did, the business would fold. The banks would only support him through this difficult time because of his past performance and good stewardship of their money. David was tempted to make sure that William was on the list of those to leave the company – but he considered that would be wrong and likely to be misinterpreted.

● *Alex and Fred – partners in trouble.* Alex and Fred, both Christians, were business partners in an information technology company. They were at college together and during that time pledged that sometime they would start a business together. It would be founded and run on Christian principles, with integrity, honesty, regard for people and so on, yet developed in such a way as to give them a competitive edge in their market place. They kept in touch in the early years of their careers, although one was in Dallas and the other in London. Seven years after graduation they met in New York and, six months later, New Dawn Consulting was formed as a partnership. Their original vision was undiminished. For the first five years, the business prospered and their families grew closer together. Too close, as it happens, because Alex's wife left him to have an affair with Fred's younger brother. The business partners were devastated, but in spite of the raft of mixed emotions this situation caused, they decided to stay in business. This was not easy, and inevitably each took sides in the family problems. But the business relationship did survive – until, that is, Fred discovered that Alex had been producing false invoices in his side of the company in order to inflate the performance of his division. Fred knew that Alex was under great pressure with the children. The divorce had been messy and expensive. Alex had not personally gained from these actions and there was no fraud. But there was deceit, and the basis of trust was broken – perhaps gone forever. Fred wondered how he could raise this topic with Alex without losing a long-standing friend. Conflict seemed inevitable, and at a time when Alex was very vulnerable.

● *Mary – joining a war zone.* Mary was a hospital administrator who had just taken up a post in a busy general hospital. She was forty-five years old, her children had grown up, she had completed a refresher course and was fired up for this job. She was sure that this was what God wanted her to do. After all, there had been stiff competition for the job and she was amazed that she had come through as the favored candidate. The first week was great. Senior and junior colleagues were welcoming and seemed to want to chat about social and work issues. "What a terrific witness opportunity this will be", she thought. But she gradually became aware that there was a serious agenda underlying some of the friendly comments. "Has anyone told you about the complex personal life of the boss?" "My advice is not to trust anyone here – because they will not trust you." "The doctors are the gods here, everyone else is treated like dirt – just watch and you'll see." "You will have to quickly decide whose side you are on here – there are three, by the way!" By the end of the first month, Mary's stress levels were at an all time high. Although she was not in conflict with anyone personally, judging by the whispers in the corridor everyone else seemed to be. "This is a version of the war of the worlds", she told her husband John, "I'm worried about conflict by association". John wasn't a Christian but remembered Mary's conviction that this was the job for her. Rather unhelpfully, he reminded her of that. Mary wondered where to go from here.

Lessons from Proverbs   The Bible is not short on relevant advice concerning conflict. Some of this advice is found in Proverbs, a book that contains many wise words about how people should relate to one another.[11] Although Proverbs is not a business manual, it does contain lots of things that we need to know. What follows here touches on only a few of these pieces of advice. Conflict situations tend to expose attitudes that are normally hidden, and one attitude that is often absent from situations of conflict is a generosity of spirit. Therefore, counsel such as "A generous man will prosper; he who refreshes others will himself be refreshed"[12] is worth listening to. Here, the "refreshing of others" implies behavior that is generous far beyond reason. Such is God's expectation of his followers. We know from experience that conflict and criticism often go together. On occasion, it is our job to bring critical appraisal to different individuals. Before we approach such situations, the Bible encourages us to think carefully and note that "The purposes of a man's heart are deep waters, but a man of understanding draws them out".[13] You may not feel that you are always such a person – and neither do I. The care with which we speak in all situations is the subject of much comment among our peers. "Reckless words pierce like a sword, but the tongue of the wise brings healing."[14] Equally difficult to apply is advice such as, "He who answers before listening – that is his folly and his shame".[15] The challenge for all Christians in situations of conflict is to

A generous man will prosper; he who refreshes others will himself be refreshed

consider "what is wisdom's way here?". In all of these verses, the responsibility rests on the wise person – the follower of Jesus Christ. After all, God does not command either obedience or wisdom from those around us at work, but he does require us to be wise. In the heat of a moment of conflict or in its aftermath, you might wonder whether this is reasonable. "Does God expect something of me that I can't deliver?" No, but he can deliver. If you're inclined to say, "I just can't take this type of unrealistic advice anywhere near my work situation", I would encourage you to think again. When you say that, you are saying something very serious about the lordship of Christ in your life – which we will now consider.

Conflict – with our owner   I know many Christians who have lost the peace of God in their lives because of their work. You might be among their number. This path to "conflict" (an absence of peace and therefore of harmony with God and his purposes) with the Lord can begin at any number of different points. It may have come, for example, from a promotion too far; from adopting a lifestyle that demands a total commitment to earnings; from drifting into a work-related social environment that drags people away from Christian fellowship; from adopting the values and culture of the workplace in order to survive its rigors; or from a total separation of work and faith because it just makes life too complicated and faith is not considered important in the workplace. It may even have come from being in perpetual conflict with work colleagues, and from just giving up the fight. However it may have happened, many have lost this peace and do not know how to get it back.

Peace is a very full and positive word in the Bible. It involves "wholeness", a state of integrity, harmony and completeness of a person in a community. Salvation through faith in Christ restores this wholeness. Jesus said, "My peace I give to you".[16] This peace was his legacy to his disciples. It's not a legacy locked up in a remote bank vault or lost in a galleon at the bottom of the ocean. Nor can one have it only after complex litigation. What kind of peace was it? Firstly, it was inward and not dependent on outward circumstances. "That's easier said than done in my work", you might say (and I agree). Yet this is what Jesus left us. It can be achieved; and he wants us to have it.

Jesus said, "My peace I give to you"

87

Secondly, it was linked to his vocation and the single purpose that integrated his life. This, too, is quite a challenge for us. Many of us live complex lives, juggling numerous priorities. The call of God is to integrate co-working with him towards a very clear end. It's very easy to live lives of separate compartments, inviting the Lord into some of them but consciously excluding him from others. We might choose to live that way – but how can that achieve the goal of bringing glory to his name? That's the plan, and he is the master planner. Thirdly, his peace came from obedience to the Father. Our peace will only come this way as well – don't look for peace without obedience.

In the fourteenth century, Petrarch observed that the five great enemies to peace were "greed, ambition, envy, anger and pride". How many of these five vices have strong links to work and money (the product of work) in our contemporary environment? They all have, in some instances – and so Christians find themselves in conflict with their owner – the one that they have pledged to make the Sovereign Lord of their lives. How can we resolve this conflict? There is little doubt that having and sustaining inner peace with God has everything to do with how my will relates to his will and purpose for my life. There is, as C.H. Spurgeon remarked, the need for another conflict to be reinstated in many of our lives. "If you aim to have peace with God, there must be war with Satan."

The five great enemies to peace were "greed, ambition, envy, anger and pride"

There is a further kind of conflict with our owner which is the enemy of peace. This conflict stems from discontentment – with how the world of work has treated us, with our position in it, with the way in which others have fared better in their careers, with feelings of being underpaid, undervalued, passed over and exploited. Because of such feelings some people despise their jobs – a state of mind not conducive to bringing God glory. These very real problems are getting worse as our societies (and, sadly, our churches) become more success oriented. In some ways this leaves a whole group of Christians "in dispute" with the Lord, with some bearing a grudge against God. I have great sympathy for such people. At the spiritual level, these issues can only be addressed by finding God's answer to a simple question, "Why am I here, Lord?". The biblical answers lie in being reassured about who we really work for and in having confidence in his choice of employment location for us. "Whatever you do, work at it with all your heart, as working for the Lord, not for men".[17] To answer such questions we also need to lift our sights from this life to the next, "I consider that our present sufferings are not worth comparing with the glory that will be revealed in us".[18] But, for some, such comfort is not real enough to deal with present hurts. The Bible is clear that, for better or worse, our faith develops within our place of work. How, for example, can a verse like, "Since we live by the Spirit, let us keep in step with the Spirit"[19] possibly exclude the major part of our lives that is taken up with secular work? As Ian Clark summarizes so well, "the disciple of Christ knows his own personal weaknesses but realises that, so long as he keeps in Christ's company, nothing is impossible".[20]

In order to resolve conflicts with our owner we need to receive and accept his plan for our lives. Although this process can be difficult, we need to take a longer-term perspective on our lives than we will get from our peers. This poem by Alex Muir, one of my early Christian mentors, has spoken volumes to me over many years. To the best of my knowledge it has never before been published.

The Plan

When I stand at the Judgement Seat of Christ
And he shows his plan for me:
The plan of my life as it might have been
Had he had his way; and I see
How I blocked him here and checked him there
And would not yield to his will;
Will there be grief in my Saviour's eyes
Grief though he loves me still?

He would have me rich but I stand there poor,
Stripped of all but his grace:
As memory runs like a haunted thing
Down the years it cannot retrace:
Then my desolate heart will well nigh break.

With the tears that I cannot shed,
I'll cover my face with my empty hands
And bow my uncovered head.

Lord of the years that are left to me
I yield them to thy hand:
Take me, melt me, mould me
To the pattern thou hast planned.

☑ **ACTION:** If you are "in conflict" with the owner, try to trace when and why it started. In diagnosing your situation, you might want to think about the symptoms in areas such as time allocation, determining priorities, following God's advice (see the section on Proverbs, above), your relationship with God, your attitude towards your work and so on. Spend some time seeking and confirming that you and the Lord are working to the same plan in your work. To do this properly you might need to briefly write out your career plan and then ask what signals you believe God has given to either confirm or change it. It is unlikely that you will find peace as long as your plan diverges from that of the Lord!

Challenge No5

There are many difficult challenges in this chapter. Reflect on the different but closely connected sets of relationships in your work and on God's view of the world in which you live your Christian life. (This will also help you to prepare for the next chapter on discipleship at work.)

1 How does the love of God show in your life at work?

2 Christians have a ministry of reconciliation. Is it one that you practice at work?

3 One of the fruits of the Spirit is kindness. How have you displayed kindness (or how might you have done so) in a situation of conflict?

4 You trust in God. But do people who work with you trust you?

Further reading

Anderson, Neil T., and Rich Miller, *Getting Anger under Control* (Eugene, OR: Harvest House, 2002).

Curran, Peter, *All the Hours God Sends?: Practical and Biblical Help in Meeting the Demands of Work* (Leicester: IVP, 2000).

Kendall, R.T., *Total Forgiveness* (London: Hodder & Stoughton, 2001).

Zigarelli, Michael A., *Faith at Work: Overcoming the Obstacles of Being Christ-Like in the Workplace* (Chicago: Moody Press, 2000).

Endnotes

1 Rom. 8:7-8.

2 Jn. 17:14.

3 Eph. 2:1-2.

4 2 Tim. 2:4.

5 2 Tim. 4:10.

6 1 Cor. 7:31.

7 1 Jn. 2:16.

8 1 Jn. 5:4.

9 Stott, *Contemporary Christian*, Ch. 6.

10 See, e.g., Mt. 5-7.

11 Michael A. Zigarelli's *Management by Proverbs: Applying Timeless Wisdom in the Workplace* (Chicago: Moody Press, 1999) is a very helpful book that outlines these principles in the managerial context.

12 Prov. 11:25.

13 Prov. 20:5.

14 Prov. 12:18.

15 Prov. 18:13.

16 Jn. 14:27.

17 Col. 3:23.

18 Rom. 8:18.

19 Gal. 5:25.

20 Ian Clark, *Reservoir of Power* (Glasgow: Pickering & Inglis, 1980), 'Foreword', p. 2.

6
Discipleship at Work

"This is to my Father's glory, that you bear much fruit, showing yourselves to be my disciples."
(Jn. 15:8)

Outline   Jesus asks us to follow him and learn from him. Because the Lord blesses us with his Spirit in our hearts, he accompanies us to work every day. But can those with whom we work see enough – or indeed any – evidence of that? This chapter investigates just how effective our discipleship can be in a work environment, provided that we depend on God every step of the way. After proposing that we do some new thinking about work, this chapter poses three questions and gives lots of biblical answers.

Fresh thinking about my work
First we examine why we need to think in a new way about our work in order to fulfill our calling as disciples, then we recall the objectives set for us and marvel at the way in which Peter introduces the example of Jesus.

What are the people I work with learning about Christ from me?
Our colleagues learn from us as we demonstrate our Christian character. We will look at two specific aspects of this character, namely integrity and the ways in which we demonstrate the fruit of the Spirit in our lives at work.

... and how do they learn?
Jesus chose salt, light and seed sowing to illustrate the behavior that he is looking for in our witness at work. We will flesh these out with some real-life applications.

What difference has Jesus made so far in my work?
In the spirit of performance review, this section sets out some very practical evidences of Christian character for each of us to address in self-assessment.

Fresh thinking about my work

You may regard the heading above as a joke. "I hardly ever stop thinking about my work – that's my problem. I don't want a Christian book telling me that I need to think about it even more." Or you might think, "the only way I can cope with my stressful work is to switch off the moment I walk out of the office door and not think about it until I go back again". While many of us can relate to both of these comments, we will have seen by now that we cannot achieve the Lord's standard of discipleship with these attitudes. Most of us probably do need to think more about our work – but in a different way, to specifically and prayerfully address the questions set out in this chapter. These questions, including "What are people I work with learning about Christ from me?", "And how do they learn it?", "What difference does Jesus make in my behavior at work?", "What do God's people look like at work?", are not popular or easy ones. In the challenging words of Joseph Bayley, "Jesus didn't commit the gospel to an advertising agency; he commissioned disciples".

Most of us probably do need to think more about our work – but in a different way

Having begun our study of practice with some cautionary thoughts on some of the dangers and conflicts associated with work in Chapters 4 and 5, we now consider how Christian discipleship applies to our work. But maybe for some of you that is a step too far – the very idea of taking Christ into your particular work environment is still alien. Or you may think that biblical teaching about discipleship sets out an unattainable model, having more to do with idealism than with reality. Many Christians think that way – and act accordingly. Why? Are we not being taught properly? Are we swayed by social and economic pressures? Do we not really know what work-based ministry looks like? Or is it all too difficult? All of these explanations, and many others besides, are quite possible. Most of us have to work with ill-tempered and short-sighted people at some point and have to be responsible to some very unpleasant and unreasonable bosses. We all struggle in these situations to see past the immediate circumstances and remember that "It is the Lord Christ you are serving".[1] Our point of departure, in light of what we learned in Chapters 1 and 2, is that God wants to go to work with us each and every day. In Chapter 2 we asked, "What's so special to God about my particular work?". We noted that the answers included the following:

- To be a witness
- To be shaped by God
- To show God's love in action
- To bring God glory

If we were able to deliver on these four goals, we would be effective disciples for the Lord in our work situation. We would produce the evidence that lies at the heart of our theme text for this chapter, because we would truly be "showing ourselves to be his disciples". If that is the "what" (and it is), the essence of this chapter is to ask ourselves "how do we achieve this?". That's what we have to think about individually and in greater depth. To be passive or neutral about how we approach work is not an option if it is our intention to truly follow Christ.

To be passive or neutral about how we approach work is not an option if it is our intention to truly follow Christ

A disciple is, as the root of the word indicates, a learner. Any Christian disciple has to want knowledge, to realize that applying it is a lifetime task and to be flexible enough to accept that others may be right and we may be wrong. There is no better place to start than with Peter's explanation of Jesus' example. "To this you were called, because Christ suffered for you, leaving you an example, that you should follow in his steps."[2]

This Greek word for "example" had its origins in primary education. It refers to the lines that teachers drew on wax tablets for children to follow as they wrote. In my case it was a slate in a village school, but I well remember the teacher's lines – largely because I had a problem staying within them. I always found the z's difficult, and I did the s's in reverse. What did the teacher do? First she wrote perfect letters at the top of the slate, so that I could copy the correct thing. And then, when I still couldn't do it well, she put her hand over mine to guide me through the shape of the letter. Christ does both of these things in our lives every day – if we let him. But having a superb example without any help can be very discouraging and demoralizing. As I watch the British Open or US Masters golf tournaments, I only want to throw away my own clubs. The professional standard bears no resemblance to the game that I play. I will simply never be able to attain that standard. But the Lord gives both an example and the Spirit to make discipleship at work possible. And we don't have to be perfect to be effective.

What are the people I work with learning about Christ from me? Martyn Lloyd-Jones hit upon a humbling truth when he remarked, "If you try to imitate Christ, the world will praise you; if you become like Christ, the world will hate you!". While there is a sense in which the world welcomes a measure of goodness, people find too much goodness threatening. What does being Christ-like entail? Following are some different aspects of Christian character and behavior.

a) Integrity Let's start by thinking about integrity at work – while recognizing that it is only one aspect of Christian character. According to the dictionary definition, integrity means "adherence to moral principles". It is a word associated with wholeness, uprightness, honesty and purity – all highly desirable evidences of Christ-like behavior. We know, for example, that it is essential to be honest at work with people, with problems, with success and failure, with the acceptance and exercising of authority and so on. If we are not honest, we have no right to be heard by anyone. And, if we are not honest, we rarely are. As Christians, we might even be tempted to hijack the word "integrity" and say that only Christians display this quality. Charles Colson says that "The three most important ingredients in Christian work are integrity, integrity, integrity". But I regularly see people who are far from Christian, or indeed from any faith, practice with a very high degree of integrity. It is therefore necessary to distinguish between the drivers of good behavior at work and integrated Christian practice. They are two very different things – I could comply with the former (and it is vital that I do) without people learning anything very much about Christ from me (see Table 6.1).

TABLE 6.1

Drivers of Christian practice at work

Focus	Content	Scope	Accountability
Law	Statute	Universal	Courts
Secular morality	Codes of conduct	Compliance	Peer groups
Salt and light	Bible	Ambassadors	God

A Christian has to embrace all three of these focus areas at work. And none of us can operate the "on/off" switch in matters of integrity by choosing which moral principles we prefer to embrace or by deferring them on a bad day. Nor can we arrange our affairs by a dual morality, running our personal lives by one set of principles and our business lives by another.

Some Christians try this, and they fail miserably as ambassadors for Christ. Indeed, they succeed only in bringing the cause of Christ into disrepute. Both "peace with God" and witnessing for Christ depend on an integrated life. Table 6.1 tells us that it is important, for example, to comply with the law. But we have to recognize that the law is a moral floor, setting only minimal standards of behavior. Do you remember Jesus' conversation with a certain rich young man? This man was legally compliant in all regards, yet he walked away from the greater and tougher demands of the Lord – to sell his goods and give to the poor.[3] We are to fully adhere to the law as well as to various codes of conduct that surround our work, but this is not enough. Doing that is part of getting us to first base with our fellow workers, and helping to establish our credentials as Christians. Of course, obeying the law is also part of being good citizens as God instructs us to be. Table 6.1 illustrates only one of the distinctively Christian callings, namely to be true ambassadors for the Lord as "salt and light". To fulfill this calling requires a new Spirit-led set of moral principles that are the foundations of Christian integrity. If we live in this way, people will learn a lot about the beauties of Christ through us.

Both "peace with God" and witnessing for Christ depend on an integrated life

A good integrity test for us all comes from the nineteenth-century pen of Josiah Gilbert Holland. In spite of his language, these words are for both men and women.

> *God give us men! A time like this demands*
> *Strong minds, great hearts, true faith and ready hands;*
> *Men whom the lust of office does not kill;*
> *Men who possess opinions and a will;*
> *Men who have honour; men who will not lie.*

> ☑ **ACTION:** Do you consistently display Christian integrity at work? Think of specific incidents when your behavior either helped or hindered a work colleague from learning about Christ. What lessons has God been teaching you in this area of integrity? How have you been responding to his prompting?

b) Christian character As we move to the central importance of wider aspects of character, we need to acknowledge that the people we work with may see more of the negative side of Christianity than they do the positive. Christians should adhere to the moral imperatives of the Bible – and so shun lying, adultery, stealing and so on. In so doing, they communicate a message to their peers. But can anyone I work with see positive evidence of the graces of the Spirit in my life? Without them, they will see little of Christ – since they are his virtues. A gardener cannot manufacture fruit – it only comes from the life that is in the plants – a life that the gardener does not initiate. The nature of each plant determines the fruit that it bears – apple trees don't produce strawberries. Each fruit also contains the seed for still more fruit. Christians produce fruit only by the Spirit – hence the great Pauline injunction, "Since we live by the Spirit, let us keep in step with the Spirit".[4] The Bible clearly sets out the characteristics that God wants to see in our lives.[5] The difficulty comes in applying these to the work situation. Their presence, or absence, will determine what those I work with learn about Christ. Although Table 6.2 cannot possibly be exhaustive, it illustrates what is expected of us in this area. Reflect on the illustrations below and how they apply to your conduct at work. Although this is unlikely to be an easy exercise for any of us, we need to remember that the Lord is always there to forgive us and to help us to change.

TABLE 6.2

The fruit of the Spirit in work

● *Love*. Divine love is the root of all the other fruits. Love cannot thrive where there is hatred, bitterness over an injustice or hostility over a lost promotion. Love cannot exist when you treat people ruthlessly, in the politics of the office, in the midst of jealousies over career advancement, when employers or employees are not respected. Loving is at least as demanding an obligation in the workplace as in the rest of life – if not much more so at times.

● *Joy*. The Christian's inward peace and sufficiency should not be affected by outward circumstances – but it often is. Joy doesn't sit well with cynicism, with constant complaining about my job, with my reputation for being negative about everything and everybody. Nor is it easy to show joy when work is not creative or fulfilling, or when boredom and uncertainty are its main ingredients.

● *Peace*. Sourced in God alone, this peace is often not visible in the midst of tension and stress at work. It implies a community of people in right relationships with one another and with God. This is not common in a work environment, but it is what the Christian works for and actively seeks to contribute to. The Christian needs a sense of peace that he is working where God wants him to be. The Christian is to show evidence of inner peace in worrying situations and in times of contentment, as well as through mood swings – none of which is easy.

● *Patience*. A courageous endurance that does not quit, we need to show patience towards God, towards people and towards ourselves. We show it towards God when we want something or someone changed and work is full of inconveniences. We show patience with people when anger, bad temper, spiteful behavior and retaliation would be the easy way. We show it to ourselves when we fail in our witness and report slow progress in producing these other graces.

● *Kindness*. The divine kindness out of which God acts towards human beings is often lost at work due to the formality of organizational structures and reporting lines, aloofness and the process of figuring out how to show it and not appear weak. Preoccupation with our own affairs can stop us from displaying kindness. Sometimes we use the excuse that difficult colleagues would not understand it, or that we are rebuffed when we try to be kind. Kindness is often costly and inconvenient to put into practice – yet it is one of the hallmarks of God's people.

● *Goodness*. We are expected to be good and to do good – since goodness is love in action. For this goodness to have a positive impact, our motives must be pure and we must avoid hypocrisy, boasting and dishonesty at all times. Goodness and integrity are closely linked. We should not be afraid of having a reputation for doing good – it can be a vital witness to, and product of, personal faith.

● *Faithfulness*. This includes the qualities of loyalty, reliability and dependability – all of which are highly valued in most work contexts. They are characteristics that often make even timid disciples stand out because of the sheer quality of their performance. This is an area in which the Lord looks for excellence from us – and in displaying faithfulness we bring glory to him. But such faithfulness can also lead to willing workers being overloaded and promoted beyond their own comfort level.

● *Gentleness*. Often translated "meekness", gentleness involves the right use of power and authority, or power under control. This is unlikely to feature in many modern training manuals where self-assertiveness, focus and aggression are at a premium. Gentleness requires us to avoid throwing our weight around, misusing authority and insisting on our own rights unnecessarily.

● *Self-control*. This is the application of discipline whose aim is fitness for service. Years of Christian witness at work can be destroyed in a momentary loss of self-control – whether in a business meeting, in a heated argument or at an office party. Exercising self-control requires self-restraint in all things, including in working relations with the opposite sex, alcohol, addiction to work, ambitions and language.

It's difficult to think of anything more radical and counter to the prevailing work culture than the contents of Table 6.2. You might say, "The behavior implied here is from another world, and it's light years from mine". And you would be right. It is a brief for the citizens of heaven – and you are one of them as a disciple of Christ. Or you might think, "Whoever wrote this has no earthly idea about the world of work in the twenty-first century". Well, actually he does – since he is the sovereign Lord of all things. You might protest, "There's no way I could take on this remit – no way!" But as a Christian you already have. So the real question becomes, "Where do you get the power to deliver on it?". It's the work of the Spirit to make us like Christ in character. Only the Spirit can produce the fruit of the Spirit. And it will only be produced if we keep in step with the Spirit. It's a waste of time trying to counterfeit these features – there can be no glory for God by that route. Nor can we pick and choose which of them we will specialize in. They are a package. But we should remember that, with the Lord, failure is not fatal – as the lives of Peter and David demonstrate. Yet we also need to know what success looks like. So if we are to work with and for the Lord, we need to closely examine the example – hence the focus of Table 6.2. Did

Jesus take these attitudes into the carpenter's business at Nazareth? He certainly did. He saw it all first hand in the working life of a small trader, with all the complexities that brought. We must assume that he worked in a highly moral way, achieved excellence and treated people with great respect. He displayed such graces where he was, doing what was his to do. Oswald Chambers is right: "If our spiritual life does not grow where we are, it will grow nowhere". You and I are co-workers with the Lord where we work right now, no matter how good or bad it feels there.[6] Our central task is to portray something of Jesus in that setting. And our character usually speaks much louder than our words.

In making ourselves aware of the awesome nature of the task of displaying Christian character at work, we must not miss the fact that God requires this fruit for a purpose. We display the fruit of the Spirit not so that others can admire it (or us), but so that they will desire it. People around us are looking for a Christian faith that actually works. As Warren Wiersbe perceptively observes, "People around us are starving for love, joy, peace and all the other graces of the Spirit. When they find them in our lives, they know that we have something that they lack."[7] I recently heard a radio commentator say, "It's the God part that's missing in our lives, so we've turned to poor substitutes". One of our roles is to show how to fill that gap. One of the principal ways that we do this is by living out these graces. We attribute them to Jesus Christ, and we want others to do the same. Glorifying the Lord is indeed the driving force – that is the essence of the opportunity – and this in turn is a central part of the answer to our "whose work is it anyway?" question.

☑ **ACTION:** Your first inclination might be to take a break here – to pause, think and pray. Pause to get a new sense of what God wants from you in your work situation; think about the opportunities that the evidence of these graces in our working lives would, or do, create; and pray that you will keep in step with the Spirit to make this possible. Part of this might involve an honest "character check" and some self-assessment on these nine features. On a scale of one to ten, how would you score yourself in terms of how you display each fruit in your working environment? This appraisal will help you to better understand how people are learning about Christ through you – and what it is that they are learning. In the light of all this, list some things you can do to be a more effective witness for Christ in your daily job. George Duncan once said, "The fruit of the Spirit is not excitement or orthodoxy; it is character".

...and how do they learn? We have seen that our workmates are learning (or failing to learn) about Christ through observing our characters – the kind of people we are in a wide variety of circumstances. These include contexts in which there is little other human support and minimum Christian peer pressure. Without living in constant anxiety, we need to recall that these observations are being made all the time, building up a picture of who we truly are. Would we recognize ourselves if we were able to see that picture? More critically, does the Lord recognize it as an example of discipleship in practice? This section explores three of the many biblical pictures that summarize the behavior that the Lord desires from us at work.

Salt and light "You are the salt of the earth. But if the salt loses its saltiness, how can it be made salty again? It is no longer good for anything, except to be thrown out and trampled by men. You are the light of the world. A city on a hill cannot be hidden."[8] These metaphors are both powerful and pointed. They clearly remind us of the responsibilities that Christians have in all dimensions of their lives. In Jesus' time, salt was an important substance that purified, preserved and gave flavor – by becoming an integral part of whatever it was applied to – yet it also kept its distinctiveness. In the right amount and in the right recipe, salt is a very effective ingredient – even in these health conscious days. But salt can be painful in wounds, and it is bad news for growing most plants. God does not want us to live low-sodium lives at work – sparingly bringing this essential ingredient to our workplace or leaving the salt in our kitchen cupboard back home. On the contrary, our workplaces need Christians who are wholeheartedly involved and who bring a wholesome contribution. Bringing the values and virtues of the kingdom and the qualities of the Christ to work is often profoundly difficult. When do we need to do this? Almost constantly! Our Christian character shows, for example, when we bring a different view to decision making and choices. It shows in the reconciliation of fractured relationships, in countering the evil that surrounds us and in bringing the Christian standard to bear on a multitude of situations. Sometimes we need to speak up when keeping a low profile might seem like a better, or easier, idea. We need to bring Christian values to tough situations when they are not welcomed or when most other colleagues are priding themselves in being "value-free". At it's best, being "salty" means being, and being known to be, Christian in all things at work. It has everything to do with our individual lifestyle and character. The thrust of this verse is that "you and only you" are the salt of the earth. For disciples this is a primary responsibility. If we renounce this responsibility at work, we damage the cause of the kingdom. The pressures to conform and to comply to other norms of corporate culture, styles of working and to kinds of behavior that are really alien to maintaining "saltiness" increase daily. Only the Spirit can help us both to identify these and to resist them.

Sometimes we need to speak up when keeping a low profile might seem like a better, or easier, idea

Jesus came as the "true light that gives light to every man".[9] As his disciples, we inherit that mantle. This light is not just a matter of passive shining, difficult though that is. Being light involves sharing the good news of the gospel. To give illumination once again requires both good deeds and good words. Work should be a very fertile setting for witness because it is a ground upon which so many things are held in common. Many of the barriers between the church and the world are absent, people face the same drudgeries, tensions, excitements, frustrations and triumphs, and so on. It is the real world for most people. Conversation is often more open as a result – and, often, so are lives. This creates opportunities for listening to personal problems, passing on a relevant Christian book, giving a Christian perspective on contemporary issues and so on. This is not always pain-free, however, because this light often brings unwelcome exposure to both people and situations. In the workplace this light challenges dishonesty and malpractice of all kinds. If Christians do not handle the light with care, they can become the subject of sneering allegations about being the conscience of the organization. Shining without judging is difficult – but essential.

Seed sowing Some aspects of the parable of the farmer sowing his seed have always fascinated and encouraged me and readily apply to the work context.[10] The farmer sowed his seed in a very liberal way. In Jesus' time, the sower threw the seed to the wind as he walked through the field with a seed sack by his side. There was neither time nor inclination to take all the stones away first. The sower simply took the view that a certain proportion would land in good soil. It was not a case of planting the odd seed in regimented rows. At the moment of sowing, no particular attention was paid to the quality of the soil – if it had been, farmers would have saved a lot of money buying seed! At that stage, the receptiveness of the soil was a second-order problem, and seed landed in all types of soil. The sower would carefully choose, however, the month and day to launch his season. So there was a plan behind what appeared to be random. It is also important to note that not all the seed that Jesus himself sowed bore evident fruit. Much of the soil was very hostile – but he continued to sow. In this parable, three out of the four soil types were unfruitful. In our work contexts, our daily task is to sow seed – doing so liberally, accepting that we cannot predict the yield or the response of the soil. The one thing we do know is who is the Lord of the harvest. With all of this in mind we should be careful of how we think about seed sowing. "It's just not worth it in this factory, workshop, office, play group – nobody here has any interest in God." "This is a heathen environment, no seed could penetrate this soil – it's more like concrete than a garden." "I've been sowing for years and I'm still waiting for my first sign of life. The only effect so far is that I have been consistently by-passed for promotion." These are all understandable human reactions, but it's always worth sowing all the same.

Sometimes you have to wait a long time for any evidence of a harvest

Sometimes you have to wait a long time for any evidence of a harvest. But it's important to remember that it's not our harvest – it belongs to the Lord. A few years ago, at the twenty-fifth anniversary of a church plant that my wife and I were involved with in our mid-twenties, I witnessed the truth of that. A couple with two children spoke to me. The lady said that she was sorry she had never been able to meet me again to say that she had come to Christ after a talk I gave at a youth club over twenty-five years ago. This was wonderful news and very encouraging – but the Lord whose crop she was part of had known about it for years! One of the ways that I sow seed is by giving away Christian books. These can only be "sown" with prayer and a willingness to follow up as required. They are not, however, sown on the basis that I can calculate the returns. Some are welcomed, others are not well-received and some are not even acknowledged. But that is of no consequence.

Personal application Each Christian has to work out his own way of putting these lessons into practice. For many years, my approach has been to immediately tell people I am going to work with that I am a follower of Jesus Christ, including at job interviews. In my case, this involves a lot of people in many different organizations. I try to do this in the first meeting with everybody, regardless of standing or status. It's not a preach-in: it's just the first step. I do it for both their interests and for mine. It puts both of us on notice as to what to expect from each other – although the other person often does not know what to expect, and I have to help them. It also establishes a platform for my future behavior and trying to be salt and light. And their reaction? Well, it varies enormously. In most cases it's polite indifference, in some cases it raises questions and (quite often) it draws out a secret disciple or a lapsed one. People largely take the "if that's your thing, that's fine" approach – treating it as of little more significance than stamp collecting or hill walking. Building on that platform has had many fascinating consequences. For example, at my own university the Christian Union prepares an annual list for new students, citing the members of staff who are prepared to be known as followers of Christ. At one time, I was the only person out of a large faculty making this public declaration – although there were other believers. Because of this I had many conversations with students for whom my name being on the list opened the door. I had signaled that I was willing to talk about Christ. Sometimes that's all it takes at work – an initial, and early, signal. In quite a different context, I once had an earnest conversation with the chairman of a public company of which I was a director. He was deeply puzzled by the newfound faith and "enormous enthusiasm" that his daughter now had for the Lord Jesus. He was a very sophisticated, cultured and learned man, and he simply could not understand where this came from – having been a casual, ritualistic church visitor all his life. I gave him a copy of one of the late David Watson's books. At the next board meeting, he astonished me

I had signaled that I was willing to talk about Christ

(and everybody else) by introducing the agenda as follows: "Neil gave me an interesting book about Christian faith. Over the holiday break, I've read every word of it – I wish I could accept all of this; but he is going to tell us about his own faith before we start this morning". Opportunity sometimes knocks at unexpected times! I did this, of course – even though the cynics around the table thought that the chairman had lost the plot.

☑ **ACTION:** One way or another, you will have kept a record of your working life. It might be in the form of a biography or a C.V. Others might have less need for such formality because you are a homemaker, self-employed, in a family business, retired, suffering ill-health and so on. You might want to either look at your record or think about what you would put into it if you had to write it down. What does it show? What does it not show? Many aspects of our lives are not, of course, captured in such a document. Think about the spiritual dimension of your life and service, and ask what is likely to appear on God's version of your biography. Remember that all aspects of your work are of interest to him.

Having done all of that, contemplate the truth of this remark by Craig Blomberg, "Christians can live with integrity under virtually any economic system, but they can only do so by using their personal resources in accordance with scriptural principles".[11]

What difference has Jesus made so far in my work?

A central part of our normal work environment is the assessment of our progress. Few of us are exempt from someone measuring our performance and giving us feedback on how we are doing. In my own case, I am subject to many different ways of being measured – depending on the contribution that I am required to make. They range from the views of shareholders on company profits to the outcomes of research review processes in academic life to the evaluation of government agencies in terms of value for the spending of public money. The Bible clearly teaches that God will someday review each of us, based on an overview of our lives. Meanwhile, he is able by his Spirit to give us an ongoing evaluation of our discipleship. And he often does this through the Bible, teaching, pastoral advice, Christian books and so on. How do you react to these periodic reviews and private feedback? As the saying goes, "reputation is what men think you are; character is what God knows you are".

In the spirit of review, what follows is a method for self-assessment. In everyday life, Christian character at work shows itself in many different ways. Only a few of these manifestations are listed below, but they are the ones by which many people assess who we really are, and they are very practical. As you read through, ask yourself what progress you are making at work as a Christian in the following areas.

● *In your conversation*. What do you talk about other than work activities? How do the language you use and the way you speak reflect the fruit of the Spirit? Do your conversations convey what matters in your life? How much does God feature in what you say?

● *In your attitude to people*. Do you consistently show care, consideration and humanity? Does your behavior show evidence of love being translated into daily practice with all your fellow workers – independent of their relative standing and status in any organization?

● *In your attitude to work*. Is your attitude clearly in step with the Spirit in terms of ambition, cynicism, contentment, work-life balance, honesty and so on? Is your attitude clearly different from that of other, non-Christian, colleagues?

● *In your morality*. Have you established and expressed Christian standards? Have you observed them consistently?

● *In your overall behavior*. Would anyone that you work with, or for, be surprised to find that you were a follower of Jesus Christ? Sometimes people cannot hear a Christian word we say because of who we are.

Challenge No6

In reviewing the challenges contained in this chapter, we turn first of all to the succinct and direct challenge in our theme text.

1 In our working lives, to what extent do we "show ourselves to be his disciples"? Would those we work with be able to give evidence to that effect?

2 If you feel that such a question applies, what specifically is it that stops work being a mission field in your case?

3 Do you have a reputation for Christian integrity where you work? If you do, pray that the Lord will preserve it. If you don't, ask God to give you the strength to change your life – and be prepared to accept the consequences. Discipleship doesn't come cheap.

4 Attachment to the church without daily discipleship has been described as the husk without the kernel. Do you need to work to nurture the inner disciplines beneath the husk? What are some specific ways that you can show more of the fruit of the Spirit at work?

5 Apply the truth of William Barclay's remark about the disciple to your own situation. "Every single piece of work he produces must be good enough to show God." Is it?

Further reading

Anders, Max, *The Good Life: Living with Meaning in a 'Never Enough' World* (Dallas: Word, 1993).

Chewning, Richard C., Eby, John W. and Roels, Shirley J., *Business through the Eyes of Faith* (Leicester: IVP, 1992).

Hughes, Selwyn, *Christ-Empowered Living* (Nashville, TN: Broadman & Holman, 2001).

Thwaites, James, *The Church Beyond the Congregation* (Carlisle: Paternoster, 1999).

Endnotes

1 Col. 3:24.

2 1 Pet. 2:21.

3 Mk. 10:17-22.

4 Gal. 5:25.

5 For an excellent exposition of these characteristics, see Stephen F. Winward, *Fruit of the Spirit* (Leicester: IVP, 1981).

6 Christian character is a crucial part of Bible teaching. Should you wish to follow up other New Testament references, they include Eph. 4:2-3; Col. 3:12-14; 1 Tim. 6:11; Jas. 3:17-18; 2 Pet. 1:5-9.

7 Warren W. Wiersbe, *Galatians: Be Free* (Amersham-on-the-Hill: Scripture Press, 1986), p. 136.

8 Mt. 5:13-14.

9 Jn. 1:9.

10 Mk. 4:3-9, 13-20.

11 Craig L. Blomberg, *Interpreting the Parables* (Leicester: IVP, 1990), p. 309.

7
Working at the Moral Edge

"Since we have these promises, dear friends, let us purify ourselves from everything that contaminates body and spirit, perfecting holiness out of reverence for God." (2 Cor. 7:1)

Outline The material in this chapter follows very closely on the discussions concerning Christian behavior in Chapter 6. We focus here on one very visible and telling aspect of discipleship at work – namely the ethics by which we live. This chapter explores the way that our ethics affect the many decisions and moral judgments that we make each day in the workplace. It is often in this specific area that our Christian witness either stands or falls.

Why think of a moral edge?
Christians rarely have an ethical base that perfectly mirrors that of their employer. Christians find that peer groups and the observed lifestyle choices of their peers, job-related organizations of which they are members and the standards and practices of their industry or profession can all be sources of pressure to compromise biblical principles. Three Christian approaches to ethical behavior include followers, wanderers and dissenters.

What should a Christian focus on?
We turn here to look at God's character and foundational biblical principles to determine the Christian's focus. This section examines five important behavioral evidences – speaking the truth; treating people with respect; obedience to an alert conscience; behaving justly; and practicing Christian love – and some of the ways in which we are deflected from living these out.

▶

Everyday moral choices at work
In order to recognize how ethical choices quite literally surround us at work, this section examines four brief cases in the contexts of diverse careers.

What does divine power in action look like?
This final section explores the amazing, effective power that God has made available to us so that we can take these tasks on and be ambassadors for Christ.

Why think of a moral edge?   "As the sailor locates his position on the sea by 'shooting' the sun, so we may get our moral bearings by looking at God." This quotation from A.W. Tozer sets us on the right course for this chapter – in which we are much more interested in practical and personal Christian living than in debating moral philosophy. If our character perfectly mirrored that described in Chapter 6, and we effectively displayed the fruit of the Spirit, it would naturally follow that we put into practice the ethics that Jesus taught. That would constitute God-honoring ethical behavior. The Bible is neither a business nor an organizational manual. It does not spell out a specific code of ethical practice for every work situation – it does much more than that. As we read the Bible, God, through the power of the Holy Spirit, seeks to transform our hearts and therefore our characters. By so doing it equips us for every moral dilemma – and we all face many in our work. We are Christian from the inside out – so obeying the external laws and rules, important though they are, is only an outward manifestation of the conviction and power within us. Think about Peter's words to people going through some really tough persecution. "But in your hearts set apart Christ as Lord. Always be prepared to give an answer to everyone who asks you to give the reason for the hope that you have. But do this with gentleness and respect".[1] Indeed, we do need to be able to both practice and explain our Christian ethics. They are a product of a change of heart, a consequence of the reorientation of the center of our lives. Oswald Chambers expresses this idea very well: "Morality is not only correct conduct on the outside, but correct thinking within where only God can see". Your work colleagues have many different ideas about what is right and wrong; they may even query whether "right" and "wrong" are valid concepts or whether there is such a thing as right and wrong. People who work together do not usually swap lists of each other's moral principles or post them on the intranet or in the house newsletter. Neither do we spend much time discussing such principles as abstract concepts. Often people will only know what our ethical standards are by observing our actions and behavior. People know that we are Christians by the way we act. And some may already have formed their own opinion as to whose payroll we are on – and perhaps we would not be proud of their conclusions.

Figure 7.1 TWO VIEWS OF ETHICS AT WORK

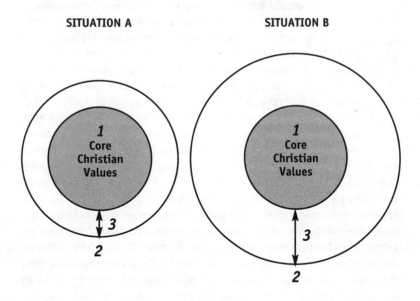

Notes:
2 – The value framework of our work environment
3 – The moral gap

The metaphor of the "moral edge" in this chapter illustrates a simple but vital point about Christian ethics in our work. Figure 7.1 will help us. The outer circle represents the overall mix of views of right and wrong in your place of work. These come from many sources – from the personal views of individuals, some of which may be derived from a faith; the application of professional standards and codes of conduct; the rules of the organization; the laws of the country and so on. The inner and smaller circle represents the ethics that Christians try to apply to work, based on their changed character. This circle is smaller because it has much clearer principles and should have fewer "gray areas". It does, of course, include laws, rules and codes. And it's based on what God commands for his people. It's smaller for another set of reasons as well. For many people, conversations about right and wrong often begin, "It all depends on the situation ...". A Christian would expect to have fewer of these conversations. Indeed, he may be unpopular because he sees things from a "black and white" perspective. Living out and explaining this counter-cultural set of values is a struggle, and we often fail. But John gives us a telling biblical picture in his reference to disciples "walking in the light". This is one illustration of the content of that inner circle. "But if we walk in the light, as he is in the light, we have fellowship with one another, and the blood of Jesus, his Son, purifies us from every sin."[2] Not one of us is without sin, and we are all capable of going over the moral edge. Therefore Figure 7.1 depicts two circles with a gap between them. Many Christians testify to the fact that this gap is growing in many different work environments. As it grows, the Christian is likely to be more out of step with the moral climate in which he works. The diagram distinguishes between work environments "A" and "B". In "A", the Christian may be in an environment where his values are understood and even welcomed – for example in a Christian-led company or ministry, or in an organization with high moral standards (from whatever source). Here the "gap" still exists, but it is much narrower. The gap still exists because of factors outside the organization and because of the fallenness of all the actors, but the Christian working in this environment spends less time and energy worrying about falling off "the moral edge". The work environment represented by "B" portrays a situation with which more of us will be familiar. Most Christians are very aware of some sort of gap – if you are

> *Not one of us is without sin, and we are all capable of going over the moral edge*

not, perhaps you might want to think more deeply about it. Some observe the gap growing in their present employment and feel increasingly uncomfortable as a result.

What happens when we allow ourselves to be drawn towards, or we fall off, the moral edge in our work? Among the many stresses associated with "bridging the gap" are the following types of push and pull pressures. These pressures are evident at all ages and phases of working life, although those in the earlier and more vulnerable stages of a career may feel them more strongly.

Peer group pressure You may be asked questions such as the following. "Everybody who went on last month's training course exaggerated their expense claims – why should you be different?" "We are all covering up on the time sheets for Jean, you know that her mother is ill – what's your problem?" "Including a porn show at one Christmas party wouldn't do you any harm. Surely your beliefs are not that shaky?"

We are all covering up on the time sheets for Jean, you know that her mother is ill – what's your problem?

Lifestyle pressure These personal pressures flow from observed peer group lifestyles. You may, for example, feel additional pressure from your spouse: "I don't want to be burdened by hearing about these moral problems you have at work – why can't you just ignore them? Everybody else seems to. After all, you're well paid and we need the money". Or you may find yourself thinking, "I am surrounded by dishonesty and corruption. My witness is a waste of time – but I will never get another job as good as this. I am trapped."

Organizational pressure "The kind of people we need here have to have that extra spark of creativity in all things – including creativity with the truth at times." "You may well find that the demands made by your customer on a night out go way beyond what you are happy with – but just remember that the customer is king in this organization." "Fine, you have your principles – as long as you don't put them before the company. I didn't hire you because of your principles."

Industry and professional pressures "I'm not sure that I can be a criminal lawyer and a Christian – I've almost lost a sense of what is true and what is false, given the people that I deal with all the time." "I'm selling insurance and savings products, and my salary is not related to what is best for my client but to what my best commission is. Sure it's a matter of judgment, but I'm struggling with my conscience." "Everybody cheats and cuts corners in the building industry, so forget your principles and get on with the job. All this stuff about health and safety is just bureaucracy."

The net effect of all of these examples – and they represent only the tip of a very large iceberg – is that Christians are pushed towards, and sometimes over, the boundaries of their principles into the norms that others are quite relaxed about. Fortunately, most of us do not face these issues every day. But every job involves some of these pressures and choices – somewhere, sometime. They usually steal up on you when you are least prepared, and they often center on everyday routine matters. We would do well to refer to our theme text from 2 Corinthians and remember that our behavior is to be "out of reverence for God".

As we examine the possible responses to these pressures more closely, it is important to remember also that God knows our hearts and has a unique insight into our motives at all times. The words of Thomas Aquinas both challenge and encourage us: "A man's heart is right when he wills what God wills". At the same time, we acknowledge that we exercise choice, we respond in different ways to pressures in the workplace, and at times we lose touch with where our hearts should be. On the basis of the picture in Figure 7.1, Christians can approach ethical behavior at work in any one of the following ways.

> *A man's heart is right when he wills what God wills*

● *A follower*. He finds out about, and sticks to, his core beliefs – as taught in the Bible and as practiced by Jesus. He makes no claim that this is easy, but he knows that it is right. He is regularly tested and his dependency on Christ is often pushed to even greater limits.

● *A wanderer*. He lives as close to the edge of his beliefs as he thinks he can. He presumes, mistakenly, that no one really notices or cares very much. He is very willing to experiment with what he really believes. He has occasional spasms of conscience.

● *A dissenter*. He likes the idea of a gap and is usually found in it, because there he can speak loftily about his moral principles and do what he likes in practice. He is rarely troubled by his position, because he has succeeded in separating work and faith. He once had an active conscience, but it's now gone. He buried it long ago.

☑ **ACTION:** Before we proceed any further with this subject, try placing yourself into one of the three categories above (or another, if you find you need a new category). Before you choose one, try to think of up to six choices or decisions that you have made at work over recent months that posed moral dilemmas (you weren't sure whether they were right or wrong). Were the decisions you made in character with being a follower of Jesus Christ? How have others responded to them? Have these choices helped or hindered your witness? Have you experienced any of the four types of moral pressure discussed above? If so, which ones have you handled best?

What should a Christian focus on?

We cannot, in this section, cover the entire canon of Christian ethics at work. Nor can we explore all the complexities associated with their application. Rather, we will focus on a few of the very telling moral dimensions of Christian character that require our detailed and consistent attention. Without these, our witness will be inhibited and our co-working with God will be blemished. It is important to note first, however, that it is possible to be highly moral without reference to Christianity or any other faith. Many atheists and humanists have a keen sense of right and wrong, are passionate about justice and show great care for people. And there is considerable overlap between Christian ethics and other human-centered ethical systems. Simply exhibiting behavior that is ethical is not enough. As Daniel Wilson wisely said, "Morality does not make a Christian, yet no man can be a Christian without it". The Christian practice of ethics has to come from a God who is at the center of our lives and who has transformed our outlook on the world of work (as well as our outlook on all other aspects of our lives). When we stray from our central relationship with Christ, our morality goes off-track soon after. The Christian's morality is built on a loving and obedient relationship with God. That relationship is its sole foundation. Paul's words are worth remembering, "Be imitators of God, therefore, as dearly loved children and live a life of love, just as Christ loved us and gave himself up for us as a fragrant offering and sacrifice to God".[3] How, then, do we keep ourselves prepared for life in a moral maze at work?

● *Remember God's character*. The three intertwined divine characteristics of holiness, justice and love have a direct bearing on all Christian ethical behavior. In determining our conduct, we can't choose between them. Although these qualities are not always easy to translate into a world of flawed humanity, they remain the bedrock for Christians. Jim Packer's words are stark: "We live in the age of God-shrinkers. For many, God is no more than a smudge".[4] We should make sure that Christians are not among them!

● *Remember the foundational principles*. The Ten Commandments are very relevant here, since God requires us to obey them. Unless we exercise this essential obedience, we will have no foundation for living a moral life.[5] The commandments ask us to build two basic things into our lives – reverence for God and respect for humankind. This two-directional focus is the very essence of Christianity. We dare not separate them, tempted though we may be by the pressures of work. Only by God's grace can we show the necessary respect for humankind in all types of work situations while at the same time regarding our work as part of our worship of God.

Only by God's grace can we show the necessary respect for humankind in all types of work situations

● *Remember Jesus' teaching*. It is very evident in the Sermon on the Mount, especially, that what Jesus was teaching was radical and far from the accepted norms. Nothing changes, does it? It has always been possible to claim to be "a great Bible student" and yet live in a way that is far removed from what we read in the pages of the New Testament. As has been wisely said, Christianity is obedience.

Our only effective weapons for spiritual warfare at work are the empowerment of the Spirit and prayerfully reminding ourselves daily of these three building blocks. Only with this divine help will we be able to exhibit Christ-honoring moral behavior. For our peers at work, this really is where the rubber hits the road. It's based on the following type of evidence that people form a view of the characters of Christians in the workplace. The five marks of Christian behavior cited below are all foundational.

Speaking the truth "The LORD detests lying lips, but he delights in men who are truthful".[6] These are very strong words, and we have to take them seriously. Honesty is perhaps the one personal characteristic that is most valued in both employers and employees. We are given many serious biblical warnings on this topic, including, "No-one who practices deceit will dwell in my house; no-one who speaks falsely will stand in my presence".[7] Not all Christians are honest, although many think they are and go into denial about what they say at times. It is not common that someone admits to lying. But evidence of lying is seriously damaging to the Christian cause. As Matthew Henry wrote many years ago, "There is nothing more offensive to God than deceit in commerce". This is a salutary thought for us all to absorb!

> "There is nothing more offensive to God than deceit in commerce"

Treating people with respect This quality is rooted in the love of God. Moreover, Christians believe that, in spite of sin, all men and women retain the image of God. Treating everyone with that in mind is a moral imperative. But it can be very difficult to put this into practice with some people in whose behavior it is almost impossible to see that residual spiritual core. I am at times appalled by how some Christians treat others with whom they work – and it's noticed. This behavior sometimes stems from arrogance and pride, which are impossible to justify on the basis of either God's love or his holiness.

Obedience to an alert conscience The area of conscience can be a dangerous one. On occasions we can find that our consciences are clear when they have no right to be. They have been deadened by the company we keep and by our own lack of faithfulness. Take some aspects of holiness at work, for example. One important consequence of following Christ is purity in conversations, intentions and in our attitudes to sexual immorality. Reflect on the directness of Jesus' comments to his disciples when he told them that it would be better to be blind or lame than to adopt lower ethical standards.[8] You might call that unreasonable, but he made his point with conviction. And we name him as Lord of our lives.

Behaving justly The complex issue of rights and duties is always an area of potential tension in the workplace. A Christian has to try to make decisions in an impartial way, free of conflicts of interest. The Christian needs a balanced approach, for example, to gathering evidence in a dispute, giving people the right to be heard and behaving with due process. Insisting unreasonably on our own rights can send very conflicting messages to our peers or employers. Applied without love, justice can be cold and dispassionate. So, for example, Christians making decisions in areas such as the implementation of alcohol policies and health-related absences from work need special wisdom.

Practicing Christian love Many of us would want to argue that this is the pivotal point of Christian ethics – not least because the Bible itself regards it as such.[9] In terms of relative ranking, Jesus expressed it in these terms. "'Love the Lord your God with all your heart and with all your soul and with all your mind.' This is the first and greatest commandment. And the second is like it: 'Love your neighbor as yourself'".[10] That instruction does not leave much room for doubt. Love has a great deal to do with relationships, creating as it does bonds between people. Many Christians blanch at the thought of having to translate love into the marketplace. Yet we cannot conduct our business and professional lives without effective relationships. But what ingredients distinguish Christian love? These include an ability to empathize with others, whatever their problem; not trying to settle scores or retaliate; being willing to go several extra miles with difficult colleagues; and being able to forgive, when that is very challenging.[11] Christian love really is *the* distinguishing mark of Christian life.

"Love the Lord your God with all your heart and with all your soul and with all your mind"

It would be very easy to diminish the weight and force of these principles by rationalizing that it is too difficult and complex to apply them in every situation. This sort of thought process often ends with a shrug of the shoulders – as if such challenges only give us a vision of what should be, but never quite is. Too many discussions about morality with Christians end with "this is all too difficult" types of phrases. But Christians should make every effort to apply these principles to the simple, everyday events at work – where it is only too obvious what the appropriate Christian behavior should be. This practice establishes the habit of focusing on the essentials of Christian ethical behavior. We then lean heavily on God for guidance in the really complex situations. My own problems with applying the Bible come not from the passages that I do not understand, but from those that I understand only too well. Perhaps you have a similar experience. And, ultimately, it is a matter of obedience. As Sinclair Ferguson asserts, "There is no such thing as genuine knowledge of God that does not show itself in obedience to his Word and will".

Alexander Hill, in his excellent book on this subject,[12] discusses three types of "false exits" whereby the biblical standards we have just discussed are diluted or avoided by some elegant (and not so elegant) arguments on the part of Christians in the marketplace. The first such "false exit" is the view that the culture in which the individual works defines what is acceptable – whether at an organizational or country level. So dual morality is born and justified – but the tensions persist, since it is virtually impossible to simply replace Christian morality with that of the prevailing culture. Second is the belief that compliance with the civil law is in itself enough to satisfy the Lord – irrespective of the quality of the legal system or its moral basis. In response to this view, we could safely say that legal compliance is a necessary moral duty for the Christian, but that it does not constitute ethical behavior in and of itself. The third "false exit" concerns the challenging question as to whether Christians are ever justified in lowering their personal moral standards when acting as agents for their employers. Unfortunately we cannot fully develop these crucial issues in this context, but it is important for us to think them through.

☑ **ACTION:** In response to the serious and demanding teaching here, first consider how you are currently displaying the five types of behavior discussed above in your workplace. Think very specifically here. If this review saddens you, ask God how you could change that and take him further into your work environment. Secondly, ask yourself if you are currently taking any "false exits", or versions of them, to avoid the force of biblical teaching on morality at work. If so, what would it take to get you back on to God's moral highway?

Everyday moral choices at work

J.A. Motyer has said, "To the Bible, history is the arena of moral decisions, moral conflicts and moral consequences". Life certainly feels like that. Often when a Christian interacts with others in a work context there is a moral dimension to that interaction. This is not something that should cause either fear or paranoia. Being aware of the moral dimension of our behavior in every aspect of life is a consequence of being ambassadors for Christ. Here are Paul's powerful words, "We are therefore Christ's ambassadors, as though God were making his appeal through us".[13] This is a telling observation – and part of God's appeal is the demonstration of the character of Christ through our ethical behavior. In what follows we will highlight the universality of these "touch points" (points of contact where we make decisions, consciously or unconsciously, about our moral response) for two reasons. First, we need to understand how much we need God in our life at work. Second, we need to think more carefully about the opportunities and threats to Christian witness that surround us. The four job examples below underscore these points.

First, we need to understand how much we need God in our life at work

● *George – Sales executive.* He is in a position of trust, and he is given much scope to do his job as he pleases – provided that his results are in line with the budget. Because George travels extensively, he has to take care as to how he uses his time in hotels and avoid the temptations that come from having spare time and being bored. These might include adjacent nightclubs, excessive alcohol and undesirable hotel videos. In his selling, he needs to be truthful about promises he makes, comparisons of product performance, prices, delivery dates – and avoid the temptations of financial and other kickbacks that prevail in his trade. On the financial side, he needs to take care in calculating expenses and commission payments. His business colleagues are very competitive and there is a strong materialistic culture in his organization. He wants to perform well yet avoid the trap of materialism in his life.

● *Ann – Social worker.* Ann is a pioneer in her profession and operates in a difficult inner city environment. Some of her moral challenges involve making honest and balanced judgments about problem families. She worries about how to see people professionally, yet through Christian eyes. She has some non-Christian colleagues who think that she spends too much time on individual cases making sure that she has it right. They criticize her in case-conferences for not being dispassionate enough. High profile and very public cases of professional failure by care workers make her more anxious. Issues of respect for people, a sense of injustice and personal integrity are all high on her agenda – and her compromise list, because sometimes it is easier to go with the flow.

● *Dave – Entrepreneur*. He has always been a car enthusiast. He has bought and sold them since he was at school – before he became a Christian. He is full of energy and ideas, and he knows that he is in an industry with a bad reputation. Among the challenges he faces are determining and communicating the true condition of cars that he sells and their reported mileage, as well as deciding the prices he pays his suppliers and those he charges his customers. Other challenges include his compliance with all the "nuisances" of taxation and accounting, health and safety legislation and employee conditions – things that some of his competitors ignore rather too often. He does regard much of this as "a bit over the top" – and he is tempted to cut corners. "What do these bureaucrats know about business?" is one of his common sayings. He faces challenges on other fronts, too – not least of which is how much time he has to spend with his family. He is great with customers, but he can be rough with his employees – and fortunately he knows it.

● *Norman – Equity salesman*. Norman just loves the cut and thrust of financial markets. It fascinates him intellectually and gives him a real buzz. He is a salesman in the stock-broking side of a major investment bank. Markets are down and business is not going well. Volume trading is needed as a matter of urgency. He is tempted to promote poor, high-risk stocks; to listen to in-house whispers from his colleagues that he is not supposed by law to hear; and to lure clients into trades just for the sake of it. It's a world of rumor and counter-rumor – where truth is not at a premium. Of course, it's all wrapped up in the formality of compliance and procedures. He recognizes the moral hypocrisy of many of his colleagues who are appalled by high-profile corporate scandals yet who display personal avarice on a grand scale daily. He has to try to stand free from it, or get out from under it.

☑ **ACTION:** While you might want to reflect on these four brief insights into the careers of others, try doing this sort of analysis on your own current job as well. Accepting that there are many "touch points" in each of our working lives, try to identify the ones that most frequently give you ethical problems at the present time. Which ones seem to offer you the greatest opportunities for witness?

We all feel at times that our working lives are like living in a moral maze. There are many ways ahead, but one ethical principle seems to clash with another as we try to discern the best path to take. I find that these clashes are sharpest when I am involved in something that could lead to the cause of Christ being held in disrepute. Although a situation may not have resulted from any wrongdoing on my part, it may lead to guilt by association. I can recall many such instances in my career, including the following three examples. At one point I had to deal with a colleague who had a serious, but largely hidden, alcohol abuse problem. Love told me to be all I could to this man and steer him to professional assistance. But fairness to others, poor performance and absenteeism led me ultimately to have to ask for his resignation. Although I would have preferred the route of love to prevail, I had to implement the latter one. In another context, where I was representing investors in a company, there was a persistent refusal by the executive directors to implement board policy after it had been agreed. It was a family company. Truth and openness had been abandoned, and relationships between family members were very strained. After many vain attempts to try to get good governance in the company, I had to insist on financial backing for this business being removed, to the risk of the jobs involved. I was torn between making the business decision with the most integrity and respect for the people concerned – the outcome was unpleasant for the management team concerned. In a third case, the police telephoned me. They wanted to meet to privately discuss a business unit whose parent company I advised. They approached me because they knew I was a Christian. It emerged that the police had uncovered a major criminal fraud involving the management, of which the owners had no knowledge. The police informed me about this and left me to decide what to do. Honesty and integrity required that I tell the (incredulous) owners immediately – although I could foresee the huge public scandal, the closure of the business unit, employment loss, damage to innocent people and potential prison sentences. All of these consequences did come to pass in the ensuing months. In this context, it was clear that I had no choice. It is virtually impossible to pursue the ethics of the Savior without bearing scars, and I have many of them myself. And so I lead you to the only possible way of living effectively at the moral edge – the power of God.

What does divine power in action look like?

When the word that we translate as "energy" occurs in the New Testament, it always implies effective action – namely, action that is strong and powerful and that leads to the desired and intended result. This word is used, for example, to describe the miraculous power that worked in the miracles of Jesus[14] and to the evidence of his power in the church. "Does God give you his Spirit and work miracles among you because you observe the law, or because you believe what you heard?"[15] But the word also refers to the power that works in the life of the Christian – and this usage is of special importance for this chapter and this whole book. Paul writes in the following very encouraging terms. "Now to him who is able to do immeasurably more than all we ask or imagine, according to his power that is at work within us, to him be glory in the church and in Christ Jesus throughout all generations, for ever and ever! Amen!"[16] It is that inner power alone that makes Christian life at all possible – not least in our testing work environments. As Joni Eareckson Tada once remarked, "The weaker we feel, the harder we lean on God. And the harder we lean, the stronger we grow." The Bible makes it clear that this effective power of God shows up in many ways. It is evident in the resurrection, in the church, in the defeat of sin – but it also shows up through love, in our evangelizing and in personal morality. It's part of our daily challenge. Aren't you glad that we are not expected to do any of this in our own strength? The question at the beginning of this section is, "What does divine power in action look like?" And the answer? It looks like you and me! At least that was the designer's intention.

Challenge No7

Would you honestly say that you are living out the designer's intention through your ethical behavior at work?

1 How would you respond to the view that there are no general principles for Christian morality and that to imply there are merely leads to legalistic Christianity?

2 Think about ways in which Paul's message to Christian leaders might apply to your position where you work. "He must also have a good reputation with outsiders, so that he will not fall into disgrace and into the devil's trap."[17]

3 Are Christian morals for Christians or for all others where you work?

4 Think and pray about the ethical impression that you have left with all those with whom you have interacted in your last working week.

5 Reflect on the saying that God does not call the prepared, but he prepares those he calls.

Further reading

Barclay, William, *Christian Ethics for Today* (San Francisco: Harper & Row, 1971).

Ryken, Leland, *Work and Leisure in Christian Perspective* (Portland, OR: Multnomah Press, 1987).

Vardy, Peter, and Grosch, Paul, *The Puzzle of Ethics* (London: HarperCollins, 1994).

Williams, Oliver, and Houck, John, *Full Value: Cases in Christian Ethics* (San Francisco: Harper & Row, 1978).

Endnotes

1 1 Pet. 3:15-16.

2 1 Jn. 1:7.

3 Eph. 5:1-2.

4 Packer, *Rediscovering Holiness*, pp. 68-69.

5 One very thoughtful treatment of the Ten Commandments is to be found in William Barclay, *The Plain Man's Guide to Ethics* (Glasgow: Fontana, 1973).

6 Prov. 12:22.

7 Ps. 101:7.

8 Mt. 18:7-9.

9 1 Cor. 13:13.

10 Mt. 22:37-38.

11 Mt. 5:38-42.

12 Alexander Hill, *Just Business: Christian Ethics for the Market Place* (Downers Grove, IL: IVP, 1997). See in particular Part 2, on 'False Exits'.

13 2 Cor. 5:20.

14 Mt. 14:2.

15 Gal. 3:5.

16 Eph. 3:20-21; see also Col. 1:9-14, esp. v. 11.

17 1 Tim. 3:7.

8
Living through a Work Crisis

"For I know the plans I have for you, declares the Lord, plans to prosper you and not to harm you, plans to give you a hope and a future." (Jer. 29:11)

Outline   All of us, at some point, face circumstances that take on crisis proportions, and these can often be work related. When we are in the midst of these crises they disrupt our lives in a most unwelcome way, even though we may subsequently see them in a different light. We will explore a number of these crises in this, the final chapter in Part 3 on our practice at work. After examining the feeling of exclusion associated with such situations, the core of the chapter considers four groups of work-related crises. Throughout the chapter, experiences from the lives of different Christians illustrate and help to clarify the discussion.

Working for God – but feeling excluded
This introductory section considers the type of events that can lead us to disconnect our lives from some of the foundational principles discussed in Chapters 1 to 3. These events can be divided into four general categories.

What do I do when the world of work bypasses me?
Here we look sensitively and practically at selected cases within each of the categories – getting into work; staying in work; leaving work involuntarily; retiring from work. The aim is for all of us to try to better understand these experiences and therefore to make us more able to assist and support friends and colleagues living through such circumstances.

Learning from Elijah's crisis
Elijah's work crisis highlights some widely applicable principles. His journey through the stages of being in the grip of fear, in the eye of God, in a state of ignorance and in the path of God has much to teach us all.

Working for God – but feeling excluded

Many different events and situations make it very difficult for individuals to give the correct Christian answer to the question, "Whose work is it anyway?" because they have short or long-term difficulties in relating to, and connecting with, the world of work. People experience these dilemmas for a whole host of reasons. Sometimes these difficulties arise out of the mistaken belief that we can only be co-workers with God if we are in paid employment. Nothing could be further from the truth. We need to approach this topic with sensitivity and humility, since many of us have had no direct personal experience of these circumstances, and indeed few of us will even be aware of them all. But many of us will have observed their effects and witnessed their devastating impact on other people – including on Christians. For example, although I have never been laid off, I have worked with and tried to help many who have been. Many of us have not experienced the trauma of persistent illness that excludes people of all ages from the gainful employment that they so much desire – but some of us have witnessed its effects by caring for those who have. Allan Chambers said that "Crises refine life. In them you discover what you are". This process of discovery is often a painful and private one. I have used the word "crises" – decisive moments or turning points – as the collective noun for the topics covered. In reality, crises are often characterized by intense stress, extremity, trouble and disaster – so it's hard to describe them with a single word. For clarity, we will divide work-related crises into four general categories. The groups are quite diverse and include a variety of life experiences – not all of which will be covered in detail in this chapter. But many Christians face each kind of situation below.

TABLE 8.1 CRISES CONNECTED WITH WORK

● *Getting into work.* Finding employment can be a problem for many different people – for those whose upbringing and family circumstances have led to them being socially excluded, an exclusion which is often extended by a limited education; for those who are highly trained at school or college but can find no suitable employment following that training; for temporary workers seeking permanent posts; for those wanting to re-enter paid employment after a lengthy absence; for the long-term unemployed and, in many cases, for those who are physically or mentally disadvantaged.

● *Staying in work.* Similarly, it is difficult for many people to sustain employment. Those with recurring and debilitating health problems or with outdated skills, people who have reached a level where, for various reasons, the career routes ahead are all blocked, as well as those in organizations where there is extreme pressure to reduce numbers employed due to changes in technology, ownership or markets, all experience this difficulty.

● *Leaving work involuntarily.* People at all ages and stages in their working lives, and for various reasons, experience lay offs. Many of them go on to suffer short or long-term unemployment thereafter.

● *Retiring from work.* While some people leave work at the contractually specified age, others leave earlier, or by agreement due to reorganization, mergers and takeovers, or ill-health and so on.

A fifth category, *Prospering as a Christian at work*, is not included in Table 8.1 because, although this situation also has crisis dimensions for many people, the book as a whole addresses this issue. There are several reasons for including a chapter focusing on crisis. The primary reason is to affirm that the work of Christians in all of these situations matters to God and that work for God and being employed are not necessarily linked. The second reason is to remind those of us who are engrossed in our own employment that Christians in these situations need both counseling and pastoral care. And, thirdly, each one of us could find ourselves in a similar situation someday – and some forward thinking about how we might react would be well worth our time.

The same basic principles that we saw in Chapters 1 to 3 apply in these crisis situations, because they are for all Christians at all times. But such crises often produce conditions that make it difficult for a Christian to make sense of the world of work. Because most of our peers assume that employment is a synonym for work, being without regular employment often results in a profound feeling of being excluded. Telling a Christian who finds himself in any of the four categories in Table 8.1 that he is still in God's employment can be interpreted as trite. "Easy to say when it's not you that finds it so difficult to get a permanent job. I have now been on short-term contracts for 15 years." "Can you possibly explain to me why I am unemployed three years after graduation? I was confident that I chose the course God wanted me to take." "I've been forced to retire at age fifty, and I have no idea what to do with the rest of my life – my primary reason for living for the past 30 years is now gone." "I was out of the labor market for 12 years while I was bringing up my family – all the re-entry training has so far come to nothing." These are just a few typical responses from wounded and grieving Christian people. In such situations, a huge spiritual effort is sometimes needed to feel fulfilled through the tasks currently open to them; to have a sense of continuing to serve both humankind and God; and to maintain their calling (using John Stott's phrase) "to make (the Lord) visible, intelligible and desirable". Bitterness, disillusionment and distressed personal circumstances can all be enemies of that calling. Conversely, a positive attitude in such crises can be a powerful witness. The Bible is full of examples of career uncertainties and perplexing development paths in which the outcomes were not obvious to the passive observer. Think of Ruth and Naomi as refugees in need of basic income; of Moses with many career switches and breaks, and his final role being the product of long-term development and much retraining; or of Daniel and Joseph, who both had fulfilling and challenging jobs but would rather have had them back home. Generations of Christians living with uncertainty of all kinds have clung to the promise in the theme text. "'For I know the plans I have for you,' declares the LORD, 'plans to prosper you and not to harm you, plans to give you hope and a future.'"[1] This promise is reassuring, robust and refreshing. We need to be thankful that God is concerned with every detail of our lives and remember, as D.L. Moody said, "God never made a promise that was too good to be true".

☑ **ACTION:** Look again at Table 8.1, taking different perspectives on it. For example, do you find your own particular situation there? You probably know Christians in some of these categories. Consider what help and advice you might offer to them. Whatever your relationship to the world of work, think carefully about how this poem by Annie Johnson Flint applies to you.

Christ has no hands but our hands
To do his work today;
He has no feet but our feet

> To lead men in his way;
> He has no tongues but our tongues
> To tell men how he died;
> He has no help but our help
> To bring them to his side.

What do I do when the world of work bypasses me?

There is no easy answer to this question, so I won't try to give one. But, for the reasons mentioned above, let's look at a few of the many situations faced by Christians within each of the four groups in Table 8.1 and look to the Bible for advice that will benefit all of us – whether our experience of these difficulties is direct or indirect. Over the past 30 years, I have spent time discussing career changes with many different people – not as an expert, but as a concerned person. I have done this in part because I am interested in career paths, and in part because I am a Christian. Most of these people have not been Christians, and so these discussions have resulted in many witness opportunities. For Christians in these positions, the challenge is to maintain a sense of purpose and mission in their lives. While some people show great strength and are able to lean on the Lord throughout such crises, many really struggle. Most of the illustrations that follow are based on real people in real crises within my broad circle of Christian friends over recent years.

Getting into work

The six different people in this category described below all feel excluded from work and cannot find a way to break into it. They suffer because society associates work with success, material wealth and status. People in the first subgroup of this category, however, may lack skills and not have the inclination to acquire them – in part because they have never been encouraged so to do or have no family role models. They may have been nurtured in a culture of dependency on state social provision for any number of reasons. Some are new to the Christian faith and therefore have few role models at home or in the church. It is helpful for those lacking skills to get involved in some form of disciplined activity, even if it is voluntary, and take all the advice and training they can get. These people often do not have a good network of support and contacts and need help to do this – and they may need such help at many different times. Biblically, we are to find and develop God-given aptitudes within his people, be good stewards of what

We will be able to witness to God's transforming power in our own lives

we have, foster order in our lives and establish good relationships, in the context of which we will be able to witness to God's transforming power in our own lives. Cases like this are far from easy. They are often quite frustrating and require a lot of persistence. Dan, for example – a man with many of the above characteristics – once told me that he did not want to work. "People like you get heart attacks from working – there's no way that's going to happen to me!"

This attitude was difficult to comprehend and, I suggested to him, not a good starting point for a Christian. But if work continues to pass such people by, cynicism, bitterness and a sense of being rejected – even by other Christians – often follow. Some people are able to overcome such trials and witness to God's transforming power in such circumstances, but most need help to triumph over these struggles.

The next subgroup includes those who are highly trained but cannot find appropriate employment. Maria, for example, had always planned to be a primary school teacher – since her days in Sunday club. Her involvement with primary-age church groups and various camps throughout her teenage years had confirmed this. Everyone who saw her work with small children regarded her as a "natural teacher". She was rather like the Pied Piper, followed by little children. She was convinced, through prayer, that God was calling her to this profession. She passed through college with flying colors but, when she completed her studies, there were 35 students in her graduating class and only four jobs in her locality. Her mother had a severe stress-related illness, and so she was reluctant to move any distance from home. She continued to interview and work voluntarily as a classroom assistant, but two years later she still had no teaching post. By this time she had worked in many temporary and unfulfilling jobs. Maria had moved from disappointment to distress and then to disillusionment as her dreams failed to materialize. There are many people like Maria, and when speaking with them my approach is to ask the Lord to reaffirm his apparent specific direction for their lives – if this is really the Lord's purpose, there will be an opportunity ahead. If they truly feel that this chosen profession is their calling, then they should find work (paid or voluntary) that is as closely related as possible to what they want to do to demonstrate their worth and gain experience. I usually also tell people in this situation that career paths are rarely in straight lines – something that is news to them, and to many others as well. I also encourage them to be flexible about when and how this calling will be realized, on the grounds that they are better to be in the world of work than out of it and that God may not always have exactly the same plan, or method of implementation, as we expect. Part of the process of helping such people is to gently guide them to consider what God is teaching them through this experience.

The most difficult subgroup of those trying to get into work is the long-term unemployed. Yet among this group are many contented Christians who know that their work belongs to the Lord. While some of them would prefer to be earning a living in traditional ways, any number of reasons, including health problems and involvement in long-term care within their families, preclude this. They are willing and committed Christian workers who would put others with apparently greater resources to shame. There are, of course, many others who cannot seem to come to terms with their situation. They show all the classic symptoms: a sense of failure, loss of self-esteem, insecurity, depression and despair – and therefore they often need professional counseling. It is often very difficult for people in these situations to rethink their lives – they often do not have either the energy or flexibility to do that. Although we may not always realize it, Christian ministries of all kinds provide many such people with routes to fulfillment. For example, many contribute in a major way by caring, praying and offering a wide range of practical help within a Christian community. We should support the church in taking a lead in this area and encourage people to take these opportunities – even while waiting for employment. Involvement in ministry to others can provide excellent therapy, and it's a great way to put the Bible into practice. As Paul wrote to the Romans, "Therefore, I urge you, brothers, in view of God's mercy, to offer your bodies as living sacrifices, holy and pleasing to God – which is your spiritual worship".[2] For people in such situations, the link between their work and their worship can so easily be broken simply because there is an aching gap in their lives.

It is often very difficult for people in these situations to rethink their lives

Staying in work   While this section explores some of the subgroups mentioned above in Table 8.1, the heading will also sound all too familiar to many others. Recent years have seen heightened levels of risk and uncertainty about the quantity, quality and duration of work in many countries. Meanwhile, work brings conflict to many, as seen in Chapter 5; while others feel threatened by its complexities and the directions of change, as we saw in Chapter 3. Part of the general work-related anxiety of many Christians is worry about staying in work. Oswald Chambers remarks that "worry is an indication that we think that God cannot look after us". Many of us would have to plead guilty to this. All of us need to learn from Jesus' powerful words. "Look at the birds of the air; they do not sow or reap or store away in barns, and yet your heavenly Father feeds them. Are you not much more valuable than they?"[3] If you are in this state of worry, ask God to remind you of your value to him. Start by looking again at the cross of Christ.

The first subgroup from Table 8.1 that we will explore here consists of those who feel that they have, or are about to, hit a brick wall in their careers. They may feel this way for any number of reasons, including their lack of qualifications, outdated skills, attitudes, discrimination or performance. They feel undervalued and often change jobs regularly to offset one or other of these difficulties. There are many Christians for whom staying in work is a problem, and I have tried to help some of them – with varying degrees of success. People in these situations often know verses like, "I have learned the secret of being content in any and every situation, whether well fed or hungry, whether living in plenty or in want".[4] But they cannot, or will not, apply this verse to their work situation. For whatever reason, they will not be content to accept things as they are. Let me tell you about one of them. Walter had never been that interested in studying. He hated school and had no desire to take the extension classes that his employer demanded. The first seven years of his work in an accountant's practice went reasonably well. He was good with numbers and worked hard. But, now married and in his late twenties, he became more and more irritated by the new and fully qualified recruits being promoted above him. "They know nothing about this business – all theory and no experience. It'll tell in the long run." However he looked at it, he was a partly qualified accountant going nowhere in this office. Rather than do a serious career review, or return to studying,

There are many Christians for whom staying in work is a problem

he decided to stay and be a critic. (A good Christian critic, of course!) By the time he was thirty-five, Walter was so resentful, bitter and twisted that he was bad company, a poor employee and an ineffective witness for Christ. One of the biggest problems in trying to advise such people is to get them to recognize that the real employment problem lies in their attitude; and how it is linked to bringing God glory. Invariably, people in these circumstances exhibit a streak of vigorous denial. If they honestly review their true position before God with some gracious but direct practical help, they can move to another track. Many are not prepared to think in a sufficiently radical way about their employment. The cause of Christ suffers because many Christian people have this "chip on their shoulder" attitude to work. How can people with such attitudes glorify God?

The next subgroup, of those with debilitating health problems, is difficult for different reasons. Many are the heroic achievements of people who struggle to stay in work in such cases. One Christian friend, who worked in the same organization as I did, had suffered from chronic fatigue syndrome for a long time. Jeremy's colleagues were very supportive over an extended period. They shared his workload, covered during his unpredictable absences and were generally very helpful. One day he surprised me by telling me that he felt that, as a Christian, he had to resign because he had not been pulling his weight. He was under no organizational pressure to do so, but he felt the pressure internally. "The problem is", he said, "I can't handle everybody being so nice to me – I'm so grateful to the Lord, but I just have to go away and think about my future in a new way." In spite of my advice to take a career break and maintain his employment links, he did leave and subsequently recovered. I cite this case because I found it profoundly humbling. It showed me how little I really knew about the way people in these situations feel – and how impossible it is to generalize. Another group seriously affected by health problems includes those who have to leave work in order to become full-time carers for close family members. I have one particular Christian friend in that category who left a senior post in industry several years ago to care for his wife. His tender love and gentleness towards his wife in very trying circumstances have demonstrated the love of Christ to all who know them. He may be absent from the world of work, but he is right at the

I can't handle everybody being so nice to me

frontier of the work of Christ. He reminds me of the great truth in the words of A.W. Tozer, "the call of Christ is always a promotion".

Leaving work involuntarily   Some Christians tend to think that being laid off and unemployment are the only two work-related problems that concern Christians. We have seen that this is not the case at all, yet there is little doubt that for all concerned such events are very traumatic and arouse a whole series of emotions that can disrupt a Christian's life.[5] The process of coming to terms with being laid off is often a harrowing one. Initial shock is accompanied by loss of self-esteem, status, income, security, friendships, career prospects and so on. Optimism and pessimism, in different measures, often follow thereafter. New opportunities, new beginnings and a belief that the threatened redundancy might not happen are tempered by a loss of a sense of being valued or even of having any value in the current work environment. Feelings of failure, loss of confidence, anger, resignation and mental and physical distress are all part of the process as well. All of this involves much stress, sometimes depression, and a sense of despair. I would never belittle any of this or be critical of Christians or others who are experiencing it. For most people this is a truly dreadful experience. And many have to repeatedly suffer being laid off through no fault of their own.

Having seen people in these circumstances over many years, I have concluded that sympathetic listening is crucial. It is essential to allow time for grieving, to be realistic about the options and to offer help to pursue them. People need to be personally and proactively engaged in the process of coming to terms with the situation and finding a way forward – especially since they often see themselves as victims. Since I am not a counselor, there are many cases that I would not attempt to handle – my own area of expertise is in offering practical help to take the next steps in rebuilding a career. The one thing that we can all do is to encourage those in this situation. And our theme text from Jeremiah is a vital part of that, when it feels that God has no such plan for us. The three examples that follow remind those of us with plenty of work opportunities that we are all capable of giving substantive help in such times of special need.

I have concluded that sympathetic listening is crucial

Donald, a Christian businessman and managing director of his company, was laid off without warning after 25 years of service. Although I did not know him well, he called my office one evening in desperation. "I have to talk with someone away from my family and friends. Someone who will listen, understand and be honest with me." He was a self-starter, but he was totally shocked that this could happen to him. Apart from the usual concerns about his wife and young family, he had one other surprising worry. "I know no one outside my business and have not written a CV for over 25 years." We worked together for some months and he changed direction in his career to good effect.

James was a proud man with some business experience. When his company went into voluntary liquidation, his job went with it – as well as his lifestyle. His health was not good, and his one concern was that his business problems would not sully a lifetime of Christian witness. In this case I was able to give him some practical help with the realization of assets. It was helpful to be able to share with him about the God-given ability to be still and know God (see Chapter 3).

Quite often, I have been able to encourage people who have made false starts in their careers or who have tried in vain to make career changes. Many people are in the wrong jobs with regard to their aptitudes. Not all of them find this out by being laid off, although Douglas was one who did. He was in a cut and thrust commercial environment that did not suit him. A reorganization led to his finance role being terminated. We discussed, prayed and explored options for many months. Given his gentle personality, I encouraged him to actively pursue different directions, including self-employment. After many trying and testing months, he is now happily working in educational administration. There were many times when he needed to get through the uncertainty by clinging on to the Lord – not least in matters of faith. As all of us need to accept, "faith is being sure of what we hope for and certain of what we do not see."[6]

Many people are in the wrong jobs with regard to their aptitudes

Being laid off does not always have negative outcomes, in either the short or long term. There are many stories of longed-for career changes being finally made possible by financial settlements associated with being laid off. Time out for retraining, traveling and radical thinking is often ultimately welcomed. New businesses in some countries result from such initially painful situations. Similarly, there are many Christians who only hear God's call on their lives when they are disrupted from pursuing their own course by a seemingly disastrous event.

Retiring from work   For many Christians, this final category holds no terror or elements of crisis. Happy indeed is their lot in the eyes of many! If the individual is in good health, has taken time to plan purposeful activity and done some prudent financial planning, retirement can be a very desirable state. For some others, the transition associated with retirement is clearly difficult. Many, who have been almost exclusively defined by their work, fear their loss of standing and are sure that they are leaving their employer with so much still to offer. As a consequence, they can suddenly feel old, bored and useless. Many people manage this transition by tapering their activity – as they move, for example, from executive to advisory roles. But such alternatives are not open to everyone. And many retirees also have serious financial concerns. Many Christians approach retirement with anxieties about finding a purpose in life – especially when they are in posts that are very demanding of their time. They often do not have a well-established pattern of Christian service in their lives and wonder if it will be possible to find one. Churches need to take an active interest in promoting resettlement training for retiring Christians. Those who are retiring need to make a renewed effort to distinguish between "work" and "employment". Retirement is only an end to our employment by human beings. For the Christian, there can be no question of retiring from active service – but clearly there are different forms of service open to those in their mature years. The church and many charities are greatly blessed by people who realize all of this. Scores of retired Christian people have an infinite number of skills that can be used for God – from former nurses sorting medicines for shipment to needy countries to the utility engineer who manages a charity warehouse and the retired headmaster who has built and maintains a charity's computer system. I meet many Christians approaching retirement who do not know where to look for such opportunities – and I am happy to point them in the right direction! But not all Christians take a fresh look at their stewardship as they approach this stage in life. And that is to the detriment of the Christian cause. Woodrow Wilson once remarked that, "the princes among us are those who forget themselves and serve mankind". Perhaps that is one of the special challenges of retirement with which God can help us.

Whether we are, or have been, experiencing any of these crises or whether we are encouragers along the way, Paul's words apply to all of us. "There are different ways God works in our lives, but it is the same God who does the work through all of us."[7]

☑ **ACTION:** For some of you, this section may have made difficult reading. The wounds are too fresh and the experience too current, recent or painful. While paid employment may pass you by, God never does. Nor does he exclude you from his work plans. You are on his roster, and a vital part of his resource inventory. Pray for those known to you who are within the groups in Table 8.1. Ask God precisely what you can do to help them – no matter how preoccupied you are with your own working life. The more connected and knowledgeable you are, the more you may be able to help others.

Learning from Elijah's crisis It is impossible to find one single biblical parallel for the diversity of circumstances considered in this chapter. One particular work crisis in the life of the prophet Elijah, however, brings out many relevant principles that apply to crises that so often surround us. The context of 1 Kings 19 is important here. Here was a man with a sterling record of work for God. He had on three occasions been kept alive by a special divine supply of food – by ravens, through a widow's store and by an angel. That he was still alive to experience this crisis was in itself amazing. In his work he had fearlessly rebuked kings, shown great power in prayer and had been honored on several occasions by God. Elijah was an achiever of the best kind. His life had been threatened many, many times. And a further threat from Jezebel sparked off this particular crisis. One perhaps surprising feature of this crisis was that it came soon after one of Elijah's greatest triumphs. God had just vindicated his servant in a test of strength between himself and the prophets of Baal and Asherah. Sometimes we are at our most vulnerable when we think that we are strong.

> ☑ **ACTION:** Read 1 Kings 19.

● *In the grip of fear.* Fear for his life had sent Elijah running into the desert. He sat down under a tree and prayed that he might die. "'I have had enough, LORD,' he said".[8] Most of us know that feeling – and similar words may have crossed our own lips on occasion. Elijah was in a depressed state of mind and very vulnerable. He had had enough of threat, tension, stress, loneliness and uncertainty. He had had enough of life under a curse of imminent death. This point came after his long experience of God, recent evidence of God's blessing in his work and years of good service – and yet Elijah, like us, had his weak spots. It's easy to say that he should not have been afraid, but he was. Many of us have been there ourselves, even when we know of instruction such as, "Fear God and keep his commandments, for this is the whole duty of man".[9] Elijah's problem was that his fear of a woman temporarily conquered his fear of God. William Gurnall once said, "We fear men so much, because we fear God so little". In this situation, God came to Elijah through an angel with a wake-up call. God gives him food, rest and instruction – the three ingredients that God invariably brings to us when we are in a crisis. Our first priority should be to let go of the fear and find a place where we can hear God again.

We fear men so much, because we fear God so little

● *In the eye of God.* Now some distance away in Horeb, the mountain of God, he spent a night in a cave. The Lord appeared with a startling and penetrating question, "What are you doing here, Elijah?".[10] Of course, God knew very well why Elijah was there – as he knows the background to any parallel situation in our lives. Perhaps the import of the Lord's repeated question was that Elijah was in the wrong place to do his work and in the wrong condition – in terror rather than at peace. But there was more – he was working under false assumptions. He told the Lord that he was alone, the only true follower left in his nation. In his mind, he had known many times that he was never on his own, but his heart said otherwise in this crisis. Sound familiar? There was something else. As he recounted to God just how dire things were in the world around him, he needed to be reminded that he was trying to carry the wrong burdens. The work belonged to the Lord, not to Elijah. So that day the Lord showed himself to Elijah in a fresh way – not in the wind, earthquake or in the fire, but in a gentle whisper. We need to listen carefully – God may be speaking in a gentle whisper. But, however he speaks, listening is essential.

● *In a state of ignorance.* We all have our own view of the world, and Elijah was no exception. His was a dangerous and troublesome view, and one that damaged his spiritual health. He responded to God with these words, "The Israelites have rejected your covenant, broken down your altars, and put your prophets to death with the sword. I am the only one left, and now they are trying to kill me too".[11] Like us, his judgment was suspect under intense pressure. We rarely see with any real clarity in such situations – except with the Lord's help. When he thought that he was on his own, Elijah discounted both God and 7,000 others who had not bowed their knees to false gods. We see Elijah in the agony of self-pity. Into this crisis God spoke. We could paraphrase his words as follows – "Experience my presence again. As you and I meet, and I display my power before you, recalibrate your life and answer my question again – what are you doing here?". Once more we can see something of great relevance to us here.

● *In the path of God.* "Go out and stand on the mountain in the presence of the LORD, for the LORD is about to pass by."[12] In this particular situation, Elijah was off God's path for his life – something that can easily happen in a crisis. God comes and does three things. He removes Elijah's personal burden of assuming that he was the sole agent of God; he corrects that and the other false assumptions that led him to be in the desert; and he gives him a totally new direction. Elijah received all the much-needed reassurance that only God could provide. He was still part of God's team – in our terms, he was still on the payroll. God had many things for him to do. We find this same man divinely honored, appearing at the transfiguration talking with Moses and Jesus.[13] Elsewhere we are also assured that, "Elijah was a man just like us".[14]

Elijah was a man just like us

> ☑ **ACTION:** Give some thought as to how these five principles apply to your own situation. Whether or not you have had a "crisis" with work like those considered in this chapter, you might find a need to recalibrate your life to God's power again as part of knowing the answer to the question, "Whose work is it anyway?". Indeed, as you have read the story of Elijah, you might feel that you are in some sort of desert, well off God's path, and in need of redirection.

Challenge No8

As you ask God for help to sustain you or a Christian friend through such a crisis, think about the following points.

1 How would you describe your current awareness of God's plan for you? In what ways has that awareness changed through present or past crises? There may be both positive and negative elements in your response – but keep in mind God's positive intent, as illustrated in the theme text from Jeremiah.

2 What have the various crises in your working life, whether great or small, taught you about how your work matters to God?

3 P.T. Forsyth said, "You must live with people to know their problems and live with God in order to solve them". How can you apply this principle to your own situation?

Further reading

Cymbala, Jim, *Fresh Faith* (Grand Rapids: Zondervan, 1999).

Hybels, Bill, *Making Life Work* (Leicester: IVP, 1999).

White, John, *The Fight: A Practical Handbook of Christian Living* (Leicester: IVP, 1977).

Yancey, Philip, *Seeing in the Dark: Faith in Times of Doubt* (London: Marshall Pickering, 1988).

Endnotes

1 Jer. 29:11.

2 Rom. 12:1.

3 Mt. 6:26.

4 Phil. 4:12.

5 This is a subject on which there is much good Christian literature. See, for example, Peter Curran, *Handling Redundancy* (Grove Ethical Studies 99; Cambridge: Grove Books, 1995). There is also a large volume of secular literature for those with a further interest in this area. See, for example, Michael Argyle, *The Social Psychology of Work* (London: Penguin, 2nd edn, 1989).

6 Heb. 11:1.

7 1 Cor. 12:6 (NLT).

8 1 Kgs. 19:4.

9 Ecc. 12:13.

10 1 Kgs. 19:9.

11 1 Kgs. 19:10.

12 1 Kgs. 19:11.

13 Mt. 17:3.

14 Jas. 5:17.

PART FOUR

PROGRESSING IN OUR WORK WITH GOD

9
Working in Line with God's Plan

"Jesus said, 'Go home to your own people. Tell them your story – what the Master did, how he had mercy on you.'" (Mk. 5:19, The Message)

Outline   These final two chapters are all about making progress in our work with God at our side – working together towards joint goals and empowered by his Spirit. Making progress in any journey depends on our point of departure, and earlier chapters have guided each of us to better understand where we are starting from. In this chapter we ask three questions, learn about being on God's payroll and explore a case study from Paul's experience.

Do I understand my call and its consequences?
After determining that we are approaching this question with the right attitude, we investigate what it means to be on God's payroll. Then we explore the importance of telling our own stories after going through a checklist about Christian testimony.

Do I create and take my opportunities?
Having considered our own approach to witnessing, we see that we can learn a lot from the example of Paul, who seized the opportunity with which he was presented in Athens.

How much progress I am making?
We find both reassurance and challenge in assessing our own progress, acknowledging that we need God's answers to our own nagging questions about our work and faith.

Do I understand my call and its consequences? As we begin to consider whether our work is within God's plan, it may be helpful to pause for further reflection. What you get out of this exercise depends on the attitude that you bring to it. First of all, are you convinced that it is right to view your work as a part of God's plan? That is certainly the way he sees it. Secondly, if your work is "outside his plan", because you pursue it purely for your own ends, do you want to change this? And are you ready to pay the costs and face the consequences, as well as to receive the peace and the blessings? As you think about this, consider these astonishing words spoken by David Livingstone (the pioneering nineteenth-century Scottish medical missionary) about his life. "I never made a sacrifice. We ought not to talk of sacrifice when we remember the great sacrifice that He made who left his Father's throne on high to give Himself for us." Unless we catch something of that spirit, we will arrive at the wrong answer to our central question, "Whose work is it anyway?" As we consider how our approach to work fits into God's plan, this chapter follows a simple, logical sequence paralleling the four basic stages in our relationship with God.

● *We hear God's call*. And in hearing we believe, and then we have a "story" to tell the world around us.

● *We follow God's purpose*. When we are open to his direction, we ask for his plan to be shown to us, and the power to implement it.

● *We look for opportunities*. We constantly ask God to guide us to individuals with whom we can share our faith and to circumstances in which we can show our faith in action, always praying for his strength and wisdom to make the most of these opportunities.

● *We pray about our progress*. We ask that all we do will be to God's glory, in his time and to his standards.

The Bible teaches that God calls men and women to work with him

The Bible teaches that God calls men and women to work with him.[1] A working definition of a Christian is someone who has responded to God's call – initially to repent and believe, and then to worship and serve. But we can be guilty of wanting to accept the privileges of that calling while we ignore the responsibilities that it entails – including the call to serve God in, and through, our work. We need to have discernment in order to hear God's call, and he often has to call many, many times before we hear him. In order to respond, we also have to have the courage to take risks. Why is it that we are often prepared to take risks with our health, careers or even our lives by taking part in hazardous activities of various kinds, yet we are not prepared to go in faith with God's plan for our work? Christians will sometimes say, "I will risk my reputation if I am too up-front about my faith at work. What if I fail? Where would that leave my credibility?". Or they may say, "I may not progress in my place of employment the way I should if I show too much of some of God's qualities. People don't understand these things today". The first quote, at least, purports to come out of a godly motivation. But the truth is that God is sovereign, and he will take us through any such failures if we are truly working for him. The second quote is sad, but it is a sentiment that many Christians often tacitly display. Either way, in the wise words of Erwin Lutzer, "God calls us to live a life we cannot live, so that we must depend on him for supernatural ability. We are called to do the impossible, to live beyond our natural ability". Unless we start there, we will get nowhere.

Throughout this book we have used the metaphor of being on God's payroll – an accessible, yet challenging, way of looking at our working relationship with the Lord. As we turn now to think about it a little more deeply, we must have confidence that God is the world's best possible employer.

Lessons from God's payroll

I'm on a payroll, because somebody hired me. My employers thought that I was worth recruiting, and they saw my potential even when I didn't see it myself. They accepted the responsibility to mentor, develop and train me for tasks initially beyond my capability. My employers understand that people need to be encouraged and supported in order to reach their full potential in their jobs. Some of the things that they ask me to do really stretch me, and I'm not always as conscious as I should be that my boss knows that I feel stretched. I have discovered that I thrive in this "no blame" culture, in which this heavenly employer picks me up, dusts me off and keeps me going. There is no hierarchy in this business – all of us report directly to the top. Access is instant and assured. And nobody measures worth by money. There are millions of others in this great enterprise. It's the original family business, and all the employees are held together in a bond of love. Nobody gets fired – but some employees seem to take long sabbaticals away from the front line of his work. Members of this corporate family come from every cultural group on the planet. Most have never met, yet when they do meet they instantly know each other. Sound incredible? Yes, it does. And you and I are on God's payroll, solely through his divine initiative. We all got here by responding to a call. Part of the joy of being part of this great enterprise is working together towards a common goal and recruiting others. All of those on his payroll sing a song of celebration and attribution to Jesus Christ our Lord. It scans the whole of history and finds only one person worthy of praise:

"And they sang a new song: 'You are worthy to take the scroll and to open the seals, because you were slain, and with your blood you purchased men for God from every tribe and language and people and nation. You have made them to be a kingdom and priests to serve our God, and they will reign on the earth.'"[2]

Everyone on this payroll keeps a record of their experience somewhere in their hearts. Each person has his or her own story. You have yours, and I have mine.

A story worth telling   The above theme text from Mark, especially as it is translated in *The Message*, is a powerful lesson from the deranged, disturbed and then restored man from the region of the Gerasenes. He cried out to Jesus in desperation from his home among the tombs. His life was then transformed. He knew it, and so did everybody else who met him. There was no doubt about it. He was immediately commissioned to go and tell. So are we. Working as part of God's plan often involves going "home" to where we are known – to the places where we live and work, to the people who know us, warts and all. God calls us to live and to tell our unique story. All Christians have a story, but some are not absorbed or excited enough by it to want to tell it. Many think that their story is simply a modest one and of no great consequence to anyone. Some of us may have forgotten just how much of God's mercy was involved in our rescue – and how much is still involved in keeping us on track. Others have never thought long enough about their experience to compose their story. If our lives do not tell the same story as our words, telling the story is a waste of time. Helen Keller was once asked if she could think of anything worse than being blind, "Yes," she replied, "to be able to see, but to have no vision". There are few things worse than telling a story that does not match the life. Those who call themselves Christians signify by this very name that they have a wonderful story to tell of God's grace in their lives. But not all Christians tell this story in the context of their work. That's why I wrote this book.

I am a fan of both biography and autobiography – mainly of those relating to the lives of major historical and political figures. There are some great Christian books of this genre, too, that have inspired generations of Jesus' followers. The Bible itself is full of life stories. I am often amazed at the appetite that people have for ghostwritten accounts of some of the most prominent figures in contemporary life – whether in art, culture, sport or politics. In some ways their popularity is indicative of a desire to share in some of the glamor and excitement of celebrity experiences – often because the readers have a lack of purpose in their own lives. Some of these celebrity autobiographies contain a high degree of fantasy, display worrying levels of personal obsession, give insight to inconsequential lives and do not present good role models. Because we are not rich and famous and do not live wildly exciting lives, we may feel that our personal Christian story is not important. This is not God's opinion – and we should remember that. Each one of us is part of the great weight of evidence to the power of the gospel. We need to remember, too, that it is personal testimony that initially attracts many converts to Christianity to explore the faith.

As we have seen, we cannot be co-workers with God if our character is devoid of any of his features. The family of God has to display the family likeness. These godly characteristics, and the way we apply them to everyday situations, add up to our testimony as Christians – namely, the extent to which we demonstrate that Christianity works in our lives. The Christian author Robert Cook was correct when he observed, "Witnessing is not an effort, it is an overspill". So, in order to work together to God's plan, we need to ask what is spilling over from our

> We cannot be co-workers with God if our character is devoid of any of his features

lives. Every Christian has a testimony. As you go through the following checklist, consider what your testimony looks like.

● *Who knows that I am a follower of Jesus Christ?* We need to ask this question in several spheres, and your (honest) answer might be different in each. These spheres include: home and family; the neighborhood; the workplace; the broader realms of influence into which work takes you. Many Christians do not want their profession of faith to be known in all of these circles. I've heard few good explanations for this silence, and the Bible is clear that God hasn't heard any. If you have kept such a silence in one or more spheres of your life, I encourage you to think about this afresh, in light of what we have learned thus far. Sadly, I have come across several situations in which work colleagues were astonished to find out that people they had worked with for years were actually Christians. In a studied and calculated way, they had managed to avoid making that explicitly known – by missing opportunities to witness, by not exhibiting Christian character and even by denying the existence of their Christian commitment and activities. This sort of behavior will take a bit of explaining to the Lord at the judgment seat. There is no hiding from the truth that everybody has to know.

There is no hiding from the truth that everybody has to know

● *What do they know?* Those who know that you are a Christian will either know a little or a great deal. This depends to some extent on how closely you work with a person, especially in a large organization. At one extreme, our peers may observe our different lifestyle without understanding why we live this way – and plenty of people have alternative lifestyles for entirely different reasons. "Difference" in itself, therefore, is not enough. It is only through establishing good relationships with our peers that we can both show and explain what it is to be Christian. Many, of course, will not be interested in knowing more or, indeed, knowing anything at all. I am constantly challenged by this and regularly ask myself, "After years of working with me, how often have my colleagues seen a signpost pointing them to Christ?". "Are the people I work with better informed or more misinformed about Christ by knowing me?" You might want to ask yourself similar questions.

● *What are the consequences of their knowing?* There are many such consequences for us, living as Christians. People will look for godly qualities of character and standards of behavior in us and will regard us as a resource in times of need. We need to be prepared to apply Peter's advice, "Always be prepared to give an answer to everyone who asks you to give the reason for the hope that you have".[3] (If you don't have a ready answer, think afresh about your "reasons".) We do, of course, have to ask ourselves a rather pointed question, namely: "Am I prepared for these consequences?". Sadly, some Christians are not – so they live as spiritual hermits, running for cover whenever they are required to represent Christ. Some do this out of fear, anxious that they might not be able to help with appropriate advice or concerned about their scant Bible knowledge. Such people need every ounce of help, prayer and encouragement that we can give them. Others, alas, live this way because standing up for Christ might diminish their standing, status or authority in their job. The latter are often self-assured and confident people in every other regard. For some reason, it is identifying with the Christ of the cross that seems to bring them offense. None of this is what God intended, and we can only imagine the sorrow that it brings him.

● *What happens when they know?* Ultimately, this is in God's hands. But as Paul wrote concerning the witness of slaves in a Christian community "... so that in every way they will make the teaching about God our Savior attractive".[4] This is the result of Christian witness at its best – people want to have what we have. This is the substance of what we considered in Chapter 6, and the essence of all that underpinned Chapters 1-3. If our testimony brings glory to the Lord, then we are ready to move ahead in his plans. If it does not, there will be little salt and light associated with our work lives. There is great truth (and challenge) in the saying that every Christian occupies some kind of pulpit, and preaches some kind of sermon, every day.

☑ **ACTION:** These truths are very challenging. As you consider the above four questions about your present witness to the power of Christ, be quite specific about how they apply to your present work situation – whatever it is. With James, we are taking a careful look in the biblical mirror here.[5] There are several ways to regard this biblical mirror with reference to our reputation at work – the cornerstone upon which we build our witness.

Never look at it. What it shows is too painful and embarrassing. Far too many Christians do this – and they rarely read the Bible. The other danger is thinking that it doesn't tell you much. There is no looking here, because it is assumed not to add value. The Bible is discarded as being immaterial – even to Christian lives.

Give it a casual glance. As we do when rushing to an urgent appointment, both the looking and the learning are only superficial. I call this "the 5 a.m. look" – the attention my mirror gets as I leave to catch a red-eye flight heading for a distant city.

Study what it shows. Wanting to really think through the consequences, you relegate this to whenever you have a spare moment. This is the "I must get around to it sometime" look. Such moments rarely come without a crisis.

Point to the reflections. We do this in the belief that this teaching is for someone else – because they need it much more than you do. Here we give ourselves little more than "observer status". This is the critic's look, distinguished by its own myopia.

Look, think and take remedial action. This is the only truly biblical reaction to the two-edged sword that is God's word. This is what the Lord wants. It is the only look that is consistent with his Lordship over our lives.

Which of these best describes the time you spend in front of the biblical mirror? And what do you plan to do about it?

Do I create and take my opportunities? I have never met a Christian who thinks that he has always been faithful in both creating and seizing opportunities for witness and service at work. I have, however, met some people with a rare talent for engaging in conversation and winning the confidence of others, who are able to create openings that many of us would never see. Equally, I have known some outstanding individuals whose personal quality of character just radiated Christ, yet who were men and women of few words. Many faithful

Christians have a sense of guilt about the extent to which they are able to speak about God to their work colleagues. We need to begin by recognizing our diversity and accepting that the Creator knows about this. But we do also need to distinguish between our relative share of interpersonal skills (which differ dramatically) and our God-given ability to emulate Christ by the power of the Spirit. So as we try to answer this question, "Do I create and take my opportunities?", reflect back to Chapter 6 on discipleship at work. How can we create opportunities? You might be inclined to reply that we simply can't – that only the Spirit can stir the spiritual interests of others. To a large degree that is true, but we need to remember that he may use our example to do some of the stirring! The one thing that we are all empowered to do is to display the beauties of Christ in our workplace. There are no biblical grounds for saying that each and every human being is not capable of this by God's Spirit. Who could ignore such behavior where you work? Would that sort of behavior not, in and of itself, create a wealth of opportunities? Is our behavior not therefore the best place to start?

Most Christians have a lot to learn about understanding their non-Christian work colleagues. We need to pray that God will give us such insight. The following considerations contribute towards the creation of opportunities:[6]

Our colleagues at times sense barriers between us and them, and some of that division is of our making. Some of this comes from having different lifestyles and priorities, but some of it results from our tendency to be judgmental.

Jesus spent time engaging with people, breaking down barriers. The ruling religious elite of the day consistently criticized him for this – but he never stopped doing it.

For a variety of justified and unjustified reasons, some people have very negative attitudes towards Christianity. Some have baggage from their own pasts, and so do we. Whatever else we do, our care, passion and enthusiasm for both God and our colleagues have to be clear.

People need to trust us first, and that takes time – as does building up cumulative evidence of trustworthiness. There is no substitute for the power of example. We have to show people that Christianity relates to real issues in life like loneliness, fear and anxiety.

Many of us need to learn to be silent where necessary, and patience is essential. If we show Christ to people, opportunities will come.

After a while, a diverse torrent of needs often pours out of people – even reserved people. We have to take their needs seriously. Their expectation is that we can help in some way – because our lives have implicitly shown that we are part of God's help team. And so we are.

People often don't have a lot of time to listen. We need to practice summarizing the gospel in few words – perhaps using a verse, parable or personal experience to demonstrate the key principles.

We should be confident that our colleagues need God – although they often do not understand that. Blaise Pascal said that there is a "God-shaped gap" within each of us. This often shows in forms of dissatisfaction with life that create opportunities for witness.

In recognizing our need to understand our colleagues, let's not forget the prior need to understand our own faith – making sure that we have a firm grasp of the fundamentals. How else can we move from building bridges to winning converts? With these observations about opportunity in mind let's examine a specific case about seizing opportunities.

The case of Paul in Athens Only you can identify all the opportunities open to you in your place of work, and some further and important biblical principles may help you in this task. During Paul's visit to Athens, he was able to witness to a whole city. The principles for witnessing to our peers in a work situation are the same. Athens, a cultured city with many idols, is not all that dissimilar from the environment in which many of us work. Such a context combines elegance with weakness; intellectual wealth with poverty; security with fear of the future. We find Paul walking through the city with a very observant eye – looking, assessing, searching for opportunities. Similarly, we need to pray that God would help us to be alert and keen observers. As we reflect on this incident, we will see that there are a series of events, attitudes and observations that collectively characterize Paul's seizing of this opportunity for the Lord.

☑ **ACTION:** Read Acts 17:16-34.

● *A distressed servant*. What was upsetting Paul? "While Paul was waiting for them [Silas and Timothy] in Athens, he was greatly distressed to see that the city was full of idols."[7] Paul was provoked, vexed and stirred by what surrounded him. Both the atmosphere and the people disturbed him. Unless we have the same attitude about those with whom we work and unless we feel the love of Christ constraining us, we will not be able to do God's work effectively. Athens was an impressive city. Its architectural splendor was legendary and its cultural attainments renowned. The prevailing attitude there was a mixture of superstitious idolatry and enlightened philosophy. However, the things that others thought remarkable when they visited this city did not impress Paul. He had quite a different perspective – not because he was a philistine in cultural matters, but rather because he was a man totally focused on his calling. As Campbell Morgan describes it, "But all the man-made things he saw reminded him of man's capacity for God, and the degradation of that capacity".[8] While God can work with distressed and broken servants, he can do very little with indifferent ones.

● *A city full of idols*. In Athens, Paul was surrounded by the riches of four centuries of art and philosophy, with altars and temples all around him. A Roman satirist once said, "it is easier to find a god in Athens than to find a man". That about summed it up. The idols came in all shapes and sizes. They were made of stone, brass, gold, silver and ivory. Rarely have there ever been more options for worship. This sounds remarkably like the twenty-first century. We have to live in this environment, be aware of it and bring Christian testimony to many people who worship a multitude of God substitutes in one way or another. And many of these idols are associated with work or its products of wealth, success and ambition. As D.L. Moody wisely said, "Satan doesn't care what we worship, as long as we don't worship God".

"Satan doesn't care what we worship, as long as we don't worship God"

● *A lot of confused listeners*. Paul's message was for everybody. So we find him reasoning with Jews and God-fearing Greeks, then with the self-indulgent Epicureans and the cold, proud Stoics. The mix of people, philosophies and locations may be different in today's world, but the variety is similar – and so too is the confusion. The people did not give Paul's words a lot of credence. "What is this babbler trying to say?"[9] they asked, using the slang word for a seed-picker or a loafer who trades in scraps of learning. Not exactly an overwhelmingly positive response from his audience! On the face of it, it was not a good platform upon which to proclaim his message. Rather like the people of Athens, our work colleagues listen to lots of the latest ideas about the meaning of life – and they often see the gospel as only one contribution among many.

● *An unknown God*. Paul found an altar with this inscription on it, the very wording of which was itself an acknowledgment of their ignorance of this god. "Now what you worship as something unknown I am going to proclaim to you",[10] Paul declared. We have much to learn from Paul's tone here. He was not harsh or condemning; he noted their interest in religion and their evident need to worship; and he even quoted their own respected poets. He displayed both courtesy and kindness in large measure as he tried to build a relationship with his confused, yet learned, audience. Paul was clear that he had to bring the message of Christ, but he did it in a Christ-like way. If we could always remember that, people would receive our words so much better.

Paul was clear that he had to bring the message of Christ

● *A clear witness*. As he spoke to the audience on Mars Hill, Paul was tuned into God's purpose. The material he covers here is noteworthy, and a model of what we have to try to communicate – albeit often over a longer time scale and in various conversations. The antidote to idol worship (both then and now) was to tell them of the living and true God – as creator, sustainer, ruler, father and judge. But then came the crunch – as he fully discharged his responsibility to the Lord. "In the past God overlooked such ignorance, but now he commands all people everywhere to repent."[11] We often get to the point where people switch off and want to hear no more. Paul reached this point by mentioning the resurrection of the Lord Jesus. Such certainty was associated with judgment – and that is never popular. Ultimately people need to know the facts of the gospel.

● *A mixed reception*. Paradoxically, this reaction is encouraging for us. Some sneered, some postponed and some followed. At first glance, this was not a dramatic outcome – but the first response is not always indicative of the whole harvest. Indeed, in the case of Athens, church history tells us that there were subsequently excellent results from the preaching of the gospel in Athens. Those who sow seed have to learn to sow, and then wait. The verse from John Greenleaf Whittier sums this up to perfection.

> *"Thine is the seed time; God alone*
> *Beholds the end of what is sown;*
> *Beyond our vision weak and dim*
> *The harvest time is hid with him."*

☑ **ACTION:** You have walked through Athens with Paul and observed how he handled this opportunity. Use this framework to compare how you are handling similar situations at work. What have you learned from Paul? In what area do you most need God's help? We all need to pray that we will share Paul's attitude: "We proclaim him, admonishing and teaching everyone with all wisdom, so that we may present everyone perfect in Christ. To this end I labor, struggling with all his energy, which so powerfully works in me."[12]

How much progress am I making? One of the interesting characteristics of this militant secular age in which we live is the growing interest in the concept of "meaningful work". This concept implies that work should be both satisfying and something that calls for commitment, and that it should also give the worker a sense of wider purpose in his tasks. The cynic (or someone more interested in having a job than in metaphysical debate) might argue that any work that someone is willing to pay someone else to do must be meaningful. Yet many people are evidently looking for a dimension in their work beyond money – for some measure of autonomy and independence, for personal development opportunities, for ways of expressing their personality and so on. Part of this is finding a work environment that encourages, challenges and ensures that individuals give of their best. Christians readily relate to these desires.

More than that, Christians know the creator of "meaningful" work. God puts our work back into a right relationship with him, as expressed in passages such as "And whatever you do, whether in word or deed, do it all in the name of the Lord Jesus, giving thanks to God the Father through him."[13] The Bible is clear that the same God who has transformed us by his grace can extend this grace to all aspects of our life and work. Reflect on the specific work dimensions of this passage: "Therefore, if anyone is in Christ, he is a new creation; the old has gone, the new has come!"[14] This sounds like a radical new type of worker. Each of us needs to ask, "Am I that type of worker?"

The Lord intends that our joint work with him will be meaningful

The Lord intends that our joint work with him will be meaningful. But does it always feel that way? No, it doesn't. Do we always think that we are making progress in our witness to our colleagues? No, we certainly don't – unless your experience differs markedly from mine. Do we always have a feeling of job satisfaction in our work with the Lord? Sadly, not always – and sometimes there are long gaps between periods when we have that sense of satisfaction. Taking God into the workplace is a bit like moving up to the front line in a battle. Staying back in the reserves is a lot easier – but it does not fulfill our call. When we move forward we get closer to the enemy, and he can see us coming. Our intentions are clear to him, and his intentions should also be clear to us. We need to expect this battle and commit it to prayer. We sometimes forget to do that. We should never forget that it is only by engaging with the enemy that we get near those for whom Christ died. Neither should we forget that we are on the side of the victor! Alan Redpath's keen observation is very helpful here. "There is no winning without warfare; there is no opportunity without opposition; there is no victory without vigilance." The following, one of my favorite Bible verses, fills me with hope, gives me a great sense of the potential that God sees in each of us and leaves me breathless at the power of the risen Christ working through his people. "But thanks be to God, who always leads us in triumphal procession in Christ and through us spreads everywhere the fragrance of the knowledge of him."[15]

It is in our nature to want to see progress – both in the short and long term. While God may allow us to see such progress, he may not. Chapters 3 through 7 have laid out some of the biblical prerequisites for progress –

both things to do and things to avoid. To be able to achieve the Lord's goals, we need to ask for the empowerment of the Spirit to apply these. While we are applying these truths, it is very likely that we will need to ask for double measures of patience, grace and love. We will also need to learn from each about different approaches to workplace ministry and seek to develop skills in this area. But, above all, we need to learn to listen to and respond to the promptings of the Spirit as opportunities are opened up to us. Paul was a person who was driven by goals. He uses an interesting phrase as he describes his own progress, "but I press on to take hold of that for which Christ Jesus took hold of me".[16] While Paul was pursuing Christ-likeness, he knew that he was not there yet and that there was much scope for improvement. We should ask the Lord to confirm why he "took hold of" us. William Barclay caught the thought behind these words beautifully when he said, "Every man is grasped by Christ for some purpose; every man is a dream of Jesus."[17] The Lord saw something in you and me that we may not yet have seen. May he use these pages to help us find that purpose and deliver on that vision of our potential. Since we often have many questions for God about our role in his work, we end this chapter with some encouragement from one of Paul's lessons to the church at Colossae.

Every man is grasped by Christ for some purpose

Asking questions, getting God's answers   "Let the peace which Christ gives settle all questionings in your hearts" (Weymouth).[18]

Following are some of the "questionings" that cross our minds.

● *Too good to be true*. Sometimes the very message of salvation by God's grace and Christ's sacrifice seems just that. "If God only knew what I was like" – but he does, and he always has. Remember, he chose the team. Think about the message that the angel gave to Zechariah – the good news that Elizabeth was to have a child, John the Baptist. Zechariah didn't believe it and was unable to speak until the words came true.[19] We have to believe God's good news in Jesus for ourselves and for others to whom we witness.

● *Too afraid to follow*. There are times when the challenges of the work environment are so daunting and the opposition so substantial that fear takes over. Jesus called Peter to leave the boat and follow, but the wind and the waves caused him to panic.[20] Jesus rescued him immediately – and queried his faith and weakness. He has to mount many similar rescue missions for us. He alone can keep us from losing our nerve – thus we learn lessons about heaven's buoyancy and earth's gravity.

● *Too weak to stand*. Most of us show weakness quite regularly. Listen to the ringing words of the prophet Jahaziel spoken to the king Jehoshaphat. "Do not be afraid or discouraged because of this vast army. For the battle is not yours, but God's ... Take up your positions, stand firm and see the deliverance the LORD will give you."[21] This advice occurs regularly throughout the Bible – precisely because we really need to hear and heed it. We need to stand firm in order for God to work through us. When we forget, we are much the poorer for so doing.

● *Too dark to navigate*. There are many times at work when we make this judgment call. The way ahead with people and situations is far from obvious. At times life could be said to be quite like Paul's commentary on a ship to Rome in very heavy weather. "When neither sun nor stars appeared for many days and the storm continued raging, we finally gave up all hope of being saved."[22] But Paul saw an angel who alleviated his fear, showed him the way ahead to Rome and gave him assurance of their survival. We, too, need promises and illumination – and both are available for the asking and for the believing.

Challenge No9

We have only touched on a few aspects of our lives in this chapter concerning whether or not our work is in line with God's plan. There are many other aspects to this question, some of which are considered in earlier chapters, especially Chapter 2. With all of what you have learned in mind, think and pray through the following issues.

1 Do you feel that you understand the consequences of your call to serve the Lord in your work?

2 Do you feel that you are equipped and ready to give an account of your faith to the different audiences you encounter at work?

3 If you were to choose one thing (above all others) that you wanted to put into practice regarding seizing opportunities in your workplace, what would that be?

4 Pray that God will help you to measure progress in your witness in his terms and empower you to respond to his timetable.

5 We all have unanswered questions about our Christian faith, not least because there are great mysteries underlying it. Pray that God will strengthen your grasp of the fundamentals and use this as a platform for witness through your work.

Further reading

Chalke, Steve, with Penny Relph, *Managing Your Time* (Eastbourne: Kingsway, 1998).

McGrath, Alistair, *Bridge-Building: Communicating Christianity Effectively* (Leicester: IVP, 1992).

Ortberg, John, *If You Want to Walk on Water You've Got to Get Out of the Boat* (Grand Rapids: Zondervan, 2001).

Roberts, Vaughan, *Distinctives: Daring to be Different in an Indifferent World* (Carlisle: OM Publishing, 2000).

Endnotes

1 This is a vital issue, considered in some detail in *Whose Life Is It Anyway?* (Carlisle: Authentic Lifestyle, 2002), Ch. 7, "Lordship, Grace and the Call of God".

2 Rev. 5:9-10.

3 1 Pet. 3:15.

4 Tit. 2:10.

5 Jas. 1:23-25.

6 Mark Greene makes a number of illuminating points on these issues in *Thank God It's Monday*, as do Michael Green and Alistair McGrath in *How Shall We Reach Them?*

7 Acts 17:16.

8 G. Campbell Morgan, *The Acts of the Apostles* (London: Pickering & Inglis, 1946), p. 321.

9 Acts 17:18.

10 Acts 17:23.

11 Acts 17:30.

12 Col. 1:28-29.

13 Col. 3:17.

14 2 Cor. 5:17.

15 2 Cor. 2:14.

16 Phil. 3:12.

17 William Barclay, *The Letters to the Philippians, Colossians, Thessalonians* (Philadelphia: Westminster Press, 2nd edn, 1959), p. 82.

18 Col. 3:15.

19 Lk. 1:18-20.

20 Mt. 14:29-31.

21 2 Chr. 20:15-17.

22 Acts 27:20.

10
Weighing My Work in the Balance

"Now glory be to God! By his mighty power at work within us, he is able to accomplish infinitely more than we would ever dare to ask or hope."
(Eph. 3:20, NLT)

Outline The goals of this final chapter are to review what we have learned and to encourage you. While our past or present relationship with work may leave much to be desired, if we will apply these biblical principles to our work it will open up immeasurable potential for the Christian church. After tackling two important questions, we examine some matters to help us set a course for the way ahead.

Whose work is it anyway?: Conclusion
This opening section revisits the core question as it reviews central themes from the previous chapters and offers some conclusions. Our focus here is on the opportunities that God can open up through us, illustrated by the call of Mary's master at the resurrection.

Whose scales am I using?
There are three different scales we can use: namely our own, those of our peers, or God's scales. Using God's scales requires some spiritual exercise, and we see that several stumbling blocks are put in our way.

Setting the course for the way ahead
Some searching questions set out here help us to review our past and set a different course for the future. Out of this, we will explore some dimensions of a Christian's career based on Paul's writings to Corinth. Finally, we consider the matter of our will to please the Lord.

Whose work is it anyway?: Conclusion

We began our study of this question by acknowledging that this question is an awkward, difficult and demanding one. It is probably no less so now that we have reached the final chapter and can confirm that it is the Lord's work we do every day. Having accepted that we are indeed doing his work, we need to recognize and accept all of the help God gives us. We can do this by making this exciting theme text from Ephesians 3 our own. It's the "mighty power" that makes the glory possible.

If we surrender our work to him, God will achieve things through us that are way beyond our imaginations – outcomes that we would not dare to either ask or hope for. But there is a condition – I need to bring my work to the altar and lay it before the Lord. And we must live our lives in a way that will allow God's power to accompany us at work. Only then will it become God's work. Harry Emerson Fosdick said that "democracy assumes that there are extraordinary possibilities in ordinary people". Christianity also makes that assumption. Jesus Christ knew that long ago, and it's the essence of this theme text from Ephesians. Remember that this is your work and mine that we are discussing – with all of its problems and challenges. God sees it as full of possibilities for his glory. This is not some ideal job in a uniquely favorable environment with especially receptive colleagues. It's none of these – it's the job you left the last time you closed the office, classroom, factory, surgery or bedroom door. It's the job with that unhelpful boss, the cynical colleagues, the unyielding client and the difficult customer. It's that job that fills you with anxiety, fulfillment, hope and frustration. That's the job that the Lord wants to join you in doing every day – thereby bringing glory to his name.

> *If we surrender our work to him, God will achieve things through us*

"Expect great things of God – attempt great things for God" was William Carey's great declaration of faith. Throughout the book, we have explored many different aspects of Bible teaching that are of relevance to the subject of work. The pages of this book have set out challenges and opened up the possibilities with passion and directness. Why? Because this is a major issue for the Christian church. But only God's Spirit can empower us to take these truths and apply them in each of our lives.

As we have seen, the answer to this central question involves much more than our lips. To make our work God's work we need to have changed attitudes in our hearts and we need to fully engage our minds and wills. Some of us need to set radically different patterns of behavior and new sets of priorities. All of this is counter-cultural and far removed from what many of us experience in our work environment. And this will be far from problem-free – quite the contrary. It is helpful to remember here the courageous words of Peter to a persecuted and despised group of disciples. "However, if you suffer as a Christian, do not be ashamed, but praise God that you bear that name."[1] In that environment, many people regarded the name "Christian" with contempt. There might be a higher general level of tolerance in our postmodern world, but the Christian's popularity is no more guaranteed, and many of our audiences are no less hostile at heart. As we face up to this challenge, it's worth recalling that the standard New Testament word for a member of the early church was not Christian, but "saint". This name had connotations of both holiness and being different – essential elements of our representation of the Lord, as we saw in Chapter 6. So to properly represent the Savior in our work, we will need to be firmly rooted and robust in our belief as to whose work it is. Table 10.1 summarizes some of the principal lessons of earlier chapters. In addition to being a useful review, this table might be used as a personal prayer list as we ask God to both reinforce the principles and enable us to implement them.

TABLE 10.1

Principles (Chapters 1 and 2)

Faith and work cannot be separated. To do so is to flaunt God's design for his people.
God presumes that our work involves us as co-workers, disciples with a calling, as we exercise stewardship of his resources and offer our work as a service. We do all of this in a way that brings glory to him.
My personal work is uniquely special to God – through it he expects me to be a witness, to be shaped to his ends as a person, to demonstrate his love and to bring glory to his name by my behavior.

Perspective (Chapter 3)

I will not understand whose work it is without having God's perspective on my work – all of us need to ask for this on an ongoing basis. God alone can give us this vital perspective.

To make sense of all the paradoxes of the work environment now and in the future, I need to find (and keep finding) stillness for deliverance, instruction and restoration.

Practice (Chapters 4-8)

The world of work holds particular dangers for Christians, and we need to recognize these. These dangers include being captured by the spirit of the age, failing to be a witness and regarding work as an idol to be worshiped. The antidote to all of these lies in a right relationship with God. Do I have one?

As we face up to the existence of conflict at work, we need to keep our (spiritual) eyes open. Conflicts with our colleagues will occur, and we need to handle them with grace and love. We also need to acknowledge and resolve conflicts with our owner on a daily basis.

God wants us to be his disciples at work, displaying integrity, character and the fruit of the Spirit. This is the best testimony that any of us could bring to our work. The mandate is to be salt and light and to engage in seed sowing. The challenge remains to ask what difference Jesus had made so far in our work – in our attitudes to people, work and morality and in our overall behavior.

Some aspects of our work take us to the moral edge. At all times, we need to respond to such challenges with the help of the Spirit as we find our way through the moral maze in matters of truth, respect for people, alertness of conscience, just behavior and practicing Christian love.

Many Christians feel excluded from the world of work and face different types of work-related crises – including finding work, staying in work, leaving work involuntarily and retiring. God does not exclude any of his disciples from his work, but those of us in regular, paid employment have a role to play in helping others who suffer from the discouragements that surround such work-related crises.

Progress (Chapter 9)

In order to make progress, I need to sense God's call and its consequences in my daily work. I need to tell my personal story of God's grace, and my behavior at work is the foundation for all my efforts to witness. The Lord looks for progress (and provides help for us) as we seek to create and take opportunities for witness. I need to honestly review just how much progress I am making in this area on a regular basis.

The missing link in all of the above is that each of us needs to hear the Lord call our name in order to make us personally aware of both the challenges and opportunities that stem from our work situation. Even in a family where there are many children, the father knows them all by name. He connects a task, advice or instruction to one of these children by using his or her name. So it is in the family of God. When, if ever, have you heard God's call by name? If you have, did it make you aware of a task that was yours and yours alone to accomplish? God calls us in diverse ways – through Scripture and advice from others; in times of praise and worship; through personal challenge from a preacher; in special circumstances of need and so on. The following is a biblical illustration of this personal touch, and its impact, when it comes from God. Although this is not a work-related scene, we have seen repeatedly that we need first to work on true discipleship and thereafter apply it to the work context.

Mary's master

The setting is the morning of Jesus' resurrection. The atmosphere is somber. Mary Magdalene, who owed so much to Jesus, is weeping at the tomb. There is a whiff of despair in the air, the tomb is empty and the cause is apparently lost. The disciples have dispersed, optimism and hope for the future are gone. The prospects for life ahead are grim, and persecution looms. Mistaking the Lord for the gardener, Mary asks where the missing body has been taken. With devastating effect, Jesus said to her "Mary".[2] What an extraordinary difference it made to hear that voice speak her name! Joy, triumph and pleasure overflow in her reaction – Jesus is alive! This difference has at least three dimensions.

● *The difference in the name*. He used her name, personally and exclusively. It stirred her memory, because she had clearly heard that voice before. Its tender use opened her eyes – the man at her side was definitely not the gardener. When she heard the unexpected voice, she was finally able to see what had been there to see all along.

● *The difference in the response*. Her formality goes and she responds in a very personal way because he was speaking to her alone. Her tears turn to joy and she feels new purpose, fresh direction and enlivened hope. She wants to grasp hold of Jesus and confirm the reality of his presence. She gets a fresh mandate, to go and tell his brothers, and she is reminded of a promise.

● *The difference in the news*. This is the heart of the matter. Jesus is no longer reported missing, his work stalled, his mission unfulfilled. Mary rushed to the disciples with the news "I have seen the Lord!".[3] Undoubtedly, this moment in Mary's life will hereafter be the key aspect of her story – the very foundation of her own witness. Few would query whose work Mary was doing after that experience! She now had the "good news" of the gospel. So do we.

Our contemporary setting is very different, but there are parallels in all three of these dimensions. Perhaps it has been some time since we listened for our name or recognized it when it was called. Maybe it has been even longer since we affirmed our response to it or took stock of the commitment we once made to spread the good news in and through our work.

☑ **ACTION:** As you have read this book and reviewed your own work situation, what have you identified as the biggest challenges in making your work the Lord's? Having read and prayed about the material in Table 10.1, what's the first step you now need to take to put your relationship with God and your work on a biblical footing? If you are already there and have put these principles into practice, think about ways in which you can mentor other Christians with regard to their approach to faith and work. Then go help them!

Whose scales am I using? You have probably paused to think and take stock at many different points throughout this book, particularly in response to the challenges at the end of each chapter. In this final overview of our work-faith relationship, we need to ask whose scales and system of measurement we are using in our self-assessment. Three of the basic options include:

● *My own.* By this standard, you may be just fine. Work is deemed (by you) to be in balance with your faith and with all other priorities – that is, until you ask someone else (perhaps your partner or your family, or indeed your pastor, minister or vicar). Your own scales are good, high quality and durable – indeed, they may have lasted a whole (Christian) lifetime, without ever being at the repair shop for a service. Why? Because you designed them, built them and calibrated them, and you are their prime user. On their own they stand up, but read on ...

● *My peers'.* By this standard, you may again seem in excellent shape – just because there are likely to be so many excesses in this reference group. In many cases this is like setting the hurdle level a few centimeters above the ground – getting over it is not a serious problem. Some of your colleagues may even think that a work-life balance is a new module on the multi-gym at the sports club. Others have no interest in achieving it and may even take pride in talking about it but never changing. It's a macho thing. But have you noticed that, if they are not Christians, their standard is automatically flawed? They have chosen not to be answerable to God. So their standards are not much use to you – even though you are tempted (or even at times obliged) to use them. And if you see Christian peers living according to their own standards rather than God's – and there are lots of them who do – don't copy them. Lift your sights higher. Don't go for the soft option.

● *My Lord's.* Now prepare yourself for a shock. The following are the standards for the citizens of heaven. It was Jesus who said, "If anyone would come after me, he must deny himself and take up his cross and follow me. For whoever wants to save his life will lose it, but whoever loses his life for me and for the gospel will save it. What good is it for a

> *If anyone would come after me, he must deny himself and take up his cross and follow me*

man to gain the whole world, yet forfeit his soul? Or what can a man give in exchange for his soul?"[4] Dietrich Bonhoffer, referring to discipleship, rightly commented that "salvation without discipline is cheap grace". The following four spiritual exercises, based on each of these four verses from Mark 8, are designed to help us reflect prayerfully on Jesus' profound and demanding words.

> We are to deny ourselves as objects of worship — even as candidates for respect

(i) Listening (v. 34). What is Jesus asking? He is looking for an act of renunciation from each of us. We are to deny ourselves as objects of worship – even as candidates for respect. The positive action is, then, to shoulder our "cross" – with all its connotations of pain, disgrace and contempt. Jesus asks us to follow him – not in some general sense of offering service, but rather in the specific sense of imitation. Disciples follow masters.

(ii) Hesitating (v. 35). This so often describes our state of mind. To save our lives is to lose them; to lose our lives is to save them. Such is the paradoxical teaching of Christ. Losing our lives might involve losing literally everything, or not advancing in our careers, or radically switching our priorities, or something else altogether – but, if it is for his service, at his command and involves spreading the gospel, therein lies great gain. It is worth noting just how often this teaching about saving and losing features in the words of the Lord.[5] He clearly thought that it would be a major issue – and he was right! In order to make progress, we have to get past the hesitation stage.

(iii) Counting (v. 36). Here Jesus uses the language of ordinary secular business. What will be the surplus (or profit), applying the normal principles of value and exchange, even if the whole world, literally all that is material and visible, could be attained? This thought embraces all intellect, ambition, finance – everything that would attract us. And what's the potential loss? The soul is ruined and forfeited. In the rush and tumble of our work lives, much of which involves counting, this is one sum that we cannot afford to get wrong. We need to learn what to count and how to count it.

(iv) Thinking (v. 37). The final paradox is here in verse 37. It stretches to the incredible and sounds like a contradiction – "just suppose a man could give something for his soul". We know very well that there is no equivalent value – no one else could ever redeem it. No one, that is, apart from Christ the Lord. And it is he who calls us to give our work to him, because he has already redeemed our souls.

☑ **ACTION:** Reflecting on these four spiritual exercises will take some time and some peace and quiet. Try applying them to real situations in your life and working environment just to test the variance between the first two scales or standards (your own and those of your peers) and those of the Lord whose name you claim. Having done that, consider the weight of F.R. Maltby's remark, "Jesus promised the disciples three things – that they would be completely fearless, absurdly happy and in constant trouble".

As we ponder these words from Maltby and face the challenge of measuring our lives by the Lord's standards, we turn to consider Peter and John speaking before the Sanhedrin. This incident, as told in Acts, assures us that God can take ordinary people and enable them to do extraordinary things. Measured by the standards of the world around us, we may or may not feature in anybody's pecking order or be noticed by those in influential positions. While following the Lord does not guarantee us either one, neither does it exclude these possibilities. This passage is a great leveler. "When they [the Jewish leaders] saw the courage of Peter and John and realized that they were unschooled, ordinary men, they were astonished and they took note that these men had been with Jesus."[6] This text makes some interesting points about how people perceive us. John and Peter's backgrounds were not impressive, but their courage was. They were "unschooled" in the sense that they were not deemed qualified to engage in theological debate – that required rabbinical training – but they did know the presence of Jesus, and it showed! They were "ordinary" in that they had no standing in public affairs or noteworthy professional status. Their reason for being was simply expressed. "For we cannot help speaking about what we have seen and heard"[7] – back to the quality of their "story". William Barclay once said, "the most unanswerable defense of Christianity is a Christian man". Peter and

John's audience was astonished. How many people do we astonish with our witness and worship through our work and service?

The startling words from the pen of C.S. Lewis are worth considering here, "There are no ordinary people. You have never met a mere mortal ... But it is immortals whom we joke with, marry, snub, and exploit – immortal horrors or everlasting splendours". You might want to think about this statement as you reflect on what God can do with ordinary people. Ask him to give you insight into how he could use you to make a greater impact on others through your work.

We encounter many stumbling blocks in our paths as we try to apply this teaching to our work. Let me suggest three such stumbling blocks I have seen many times in my own experience and in observing others wrestle with their work. You might add others as well.

● *Milestones unobserved.* Many Christians don't quite know how they got into their present relationship with work – but they are very unhappy with it and know that their faith-work balance is not in line with God's plan. Was it one particular job or career change that brought them to this present state? Or working in an environment especially hostile to witness? Or were they influenced by peer group pressure? Was it not coping well with a new environment and new, strong-willed colleagues? Have they missed so many opportunities that they no longer know how to respond in a godly way? Was it a run of bad, unchristian behavior? Or a major personal moral failure? Whatever the balance of cause and effect, something crucial has happened – perhaps even by stealth – and it is difficult to undo its effects. The great message of the Bible is that you can start again – but doing this requires confession, will and courage. Learn, for example, from Peter's denial, David's moral failure and the frailty of Elijah.

The great message of the Bible is that you can start again

● *Idols not burned.* We have observed in earlier chapters that work itself can become an idol, and that it can generate many attendant "mini-idols". During Paul's witness in Ephesus, Luke reports that "A number who had practiced sorcery brought their scrolls together and burned them publicly".[8]

This, and similar responses by new Christians, had a major impact on the way the word of the Lord spread in that city. You may not favor public burning, and our idols may have low calorific value – but we still need to let go of them if God is to use our work. We may need to participate in a very specific act of renunciation – perhaps concerning relationships, time-shaping priorities, behavior patterns or anything else that is the baggage of a past that we are supposed to have left for something far better. Each of us knows what our idols are.

● *Enemies not understood.* Work is such a blessing at one level, but we also know that it has its hazards. While work itself is not an enemy, we all wrestle with work at some time or another. And, for some of us, representing the Lord on earth through our work is a constant challenge. The following words should ring in our ears – even though many of us rarely think of them as applying to our work. "For our struggle is not against flesh and blood, but against the rulers, against the authorities, against the powers of this dark world and against the spiritual forces of evil in the heavenly realms."[9] There are definitely forces working against the Christian church taking the Christian message to the marketplace. We need to understand that it is a battle and daily equip ourselves accordingly. As Billy Graham said, "Jesus invited us not to a picnic, but to a pilgrimage; not to a frolic, but to a fight".

> ☑ **ACTION:** On balance, do you regard your present overall relationship with your work as a threat to, or as an opportunity for, Christian witness? Is that relationship consistent with what God asks of you? Honestly identify and assess your own stumbling blocks – and ask the Lord either to remove them or to remove you from them. Most of those listed above will only change at our initiative!

Setting the course for the way ahead

Setting this course implies that we must undertake personal review and consideration and, above all, make choices. While we may be very constrained as to where we work and what we do, all Christians have a choice as to how we work. It often comes down to whether or not we are prepared to let Jesus Christ be the Lord of our work. I would be the last person to claim that integrating work and faith is easy. I have far too many bruises, I have let God down in too many situations, I did not seize the opportunity in too many incidents, and my behavior was not Christ-like in too many contexts to claim that. Yet I passionately believe that the fact that so many Christians (by their own confession) have a flawed faith-work relationship has created great damage to the advance of the faith – for all the reasons we have discussed. Too few of our colleagues have seen Christianity in action – we have introduced too few of them to Christ by our actions and words. This creates a new issue of stewardship – we need to be good stewards of our opportunities within an activity that takes up a great proportion of our lives. The personal question is, will your stewardship of this area of your life change? And will studying, knowing and praying about whose work it really is make a difference in your life?

God needs men and women who will powerfully represent him in the workplace and who clearly see that it is his purpose that they work for his glory where he has placed them. Gordon MacDonald has also wrestled with this problem of how to bring the kingdom of God to a place of work, and the questions he poses are very thought-provoking. As we reflect on what we have been learning together, we can all profitably ask them of ourselves.

● Are you maximizing your past experiences?

● Are you an asset or a liability?

● Are you managing the routines?

● Do you know which issues you are prepared to stand for, no matter what?

● Are you in a position to spread Christ-following values?

● What is the nature of your influence on key relationships?

● How do you handle your power and success?

- Are you maintaining life's balances?

- What do your spiritual disciplines look like?

- To whom have you made yourself accountable for personal and spiritual growth?

- Do you practice disciplined stewardship?

- Has your real-world faith helped some people to become Christ-followers?

- Where are you going?[10]

The Christian's career   In order to look more deeply at these questions and root them in the Bible, we conclude by looking at the Christian's career through Paul's words in 2 Corinthians 1-5. Paul's words here reflect many issues concerning his Christian life and his apostleship, both of which were subject to some sharp criticism at the time he wrote this letter. This passage is a useful summary of many of the points that we have considered, and it also presents the challenge to apply what we have learned to our own specific circumstances.

☑ **ACTION:** Read 2 Corinthians 1-5.

- *Finding context.* While you may not think of it in these terms, every Christian has a career. When God called you, he guaranteed that you would have one. But you will have noticed how few secular careers go in straight lines. While there are people who do the job they were trained to do, and in the same place, for their whole working lives, they are few and far between. For example, many engineers become managers, lots of nurses become administrators and some classics graduates become merchant bankers! Only God knows the path that each of us will travel. In each individual's career there are both milestones and crossroads – times of critical and life shaping decisions. Sometimes these points of decision are obvious, while at other times changes around us subsequently affect us in ways we could never have predicted. You may be experiencing such a time of uncertainty as you read this book. I pray that it may help bring a new context to your life and work.

● *Setting targets.* Some people are very target-oriented. They have very clear career goals – expressed in terms of earnings, status, advancements by a certain age and so on. Indeed, for most of us, contemporary business and professional life is filled with goals and targets. It's possible that we know much more about our employer's objectives for us than we do about God's. If this is so, we need to lift our sights a little. Thinking of how he had survived in the past, Paul's advice was profound. "On him we have set our hope that he will continue to deliver us."[11] Much of what we have been discussing requires us to set additional (and perhaps very different) targets for our life at work. In order to achieve the goals that God has for us, we need to place our hope in him alone. But listen to the encouragement that comes with the call to be faithful. "For no matter how many promises God has made, they are 'Yes' in Christ."[12] Many years ago, I worked with a very wealthy and unhappy man. His family life was a mess, and he was very disappointed in his sons. He once told me that he would never trust anyone with his bank account. Yet God, through Jesus Christ, makes a totally open-ended commitment to us – to answer our core question, "Whose work is it anyway?", and respond in a Christian way to its implications, setting our targets with God.

> *Yet God, through Jesus Christ, makes a totally open-ended commitment to us*

● *Defining the job.* While God created each one of us with unique abilities and calls us to varying roles, he also equips us all with everything necessary to fulfill our calling as Christians. This passage points to several of these requirements for the Christian, one of which we touched on in Chapter 9. Namely, it is our responsibility that "through us spreads everywhere the fragrance of the knowledge of him".[13] A fragrance is a beautiful and appealing odor. We are also asked to show that we "are a letter from Christ"[14] – and to accept that this letter is open and read by all we meet. Whether we like it or not, as Charles Colson says, "Holiness is the everyday business of every Christian". Holiness is certainly a central requirement in the only version of our job specification that counts – the Lord's.

● *Seeking qualifications*. Some verses give us a lift – a sense that the Lord has been where we are before and knows all the issues that arise from trying to put into practice what we have been learning. The following verses impart just that sense. "Not that we are competent to claim anything for ourselves, but our competence comes from God. He has made us competent as ministers of a new covenant – not of the letter but of the Spirit; for the letter kills, but the Spirit gives life."[15] In addition to all the skills and energies that we bring to our working lives, we need this added gifting from God. By any standards, Paul was a highly trained man – but that was not enough in itself. Neither is it for us. And we need to be better at admitting that fact.

● *Being motivated*. Many aspects of every job are routine and lack glamor. We have all experienced them, and sometimes this dimension of our work diminishes our motivation. Tiredness and despair often follow. And our performance falters. Paul had his own share of pain with his mission – both physical and mental. He went as far as to say, "for I bear on my body the marks of Jesus".[16] While few can claim to parallel Paul's experience, most of us have an equivalent set of marks that remind us just how tough living for Christ can be. Paul's encouragement and motivation came from knowing that he had a mission to fulfill: "Therefore, since through God's mercy we have this ministry, we do not lose heart".[17]

● *Keeping real*. Status and position matter to people. Sometimes they matter too much – even to Christians who should know better. Paul's teaching here calls for a new level of humility – regardless of how much or how little we attain in the career stakes of this world. Some of the most arrogant Christians I have met are not those in positions of great authority in their careers, but others who have fallen in love with authority while in lesser positions – and who regularly abuse it. There is no scope for any of this in God's eyes. As Paul writes, "For we do not preach ourselves, but Jesus Christ as Lord, and ourselves as your servants for Jesus' sake".[18] The Servant-King himself calls Christians to servant status. As if to reinforce all of this and

> *The Servant-King himself calls Christians to servant status*

reassure us, Paul then writes, "But we have this treasure in jars of clay to show that this all-surpassing power is from God and not from us".[19] Only God would link clay and power!

● *Maintaining perspective.* Various things cause us all to lose perspective at times – both in our daily tasks and in our Christian witness. Sometimes success and failure cloud our vision, or the apparently trouble-free lives of those who do not follow the Lord, periods of radical change and disruption, ill-health, family problems and so on. Paul notes that God's message of reconciliation has been passed to him and to all believers. If anything was ever designed to give us a proper perspective on how we all fit into God's plan, it's that very message. So, Paul concludes, "We are therefore Christ's ambassadors, as though God were making his appeal through us – we implore you on Christ's behalf: Be reconciled to God".[20] Of course, we need God's help to remember that and not to be overwhelmed by it. But, whatever we do, we must not hide from representing God as his ambassadors where we work.

A final word God makes all things possible for us in Christ, but he needs us to do our part – not least to surrender our own will to his. As Frederick Wood wrote, "The will is the deciding factor in everything we do. In every sphere of life it settles alternatives". Indeed it does. I leave you with a poem introduced to me by my late father, whose testimony in his community and workplace always honored God. In that he showed me a fine example, and I am most grateful for that. I know that he would have found much to praise God for in this book – not least in its highlighting the potential for Christians to better link faith and work.

The will of God
My will is not my own
Till Thou has made it Thine
If it would reach the monarch's throne
It must its crown resign;
It only stands unbent, amid the clashing strife,
When on Thy bosom it has leant
And found in Thee its life.
          – George Matheson (1842-1906)

Challenge No10

1 Is your answer to our core question, "Whose work is it anyway?", any different now than when you started this book?

2 Take time to chart out the various twists and turns of your relationship with the world of work and the Lord of your life. Pray about the challenges that this assessment reveals.

3 After looking at the Christian's career through the biblical lens of 2 Corinthians 1-5, what do you need to review and reassess in your own situation?

Further reading

Griffiths, Michael, *Take My Life* (Leicester: IVP, 1967).

Hood, Neil, *Whose Life Is It Anyway?* (Carlisle: Authentic Lifestyle, 2002).

Silvoso, Ed, *Anointed for Business* (Ventura, CA: Regal, 2002).

Tozer, A.W., *The Pursuit of God* (Milton Keynes: Authentic Media, 2005).

Endnotes

1 1 Pet. 4:16.

2 Jn. 20:16.

3 Jn. 20:18.

4 Mk. 8:34-37.

5 It is mentioned in all of the Gospels. See, e.g., Mt. 10:39; Lk. 17:33; Jn. 12:25.

6 Acts 4:13.

7 Acts 4:20.

8 Acts 19:19.

9 Eph. 6:12.

10 Gordon MacDonald, *Forging a Real World Faith* (Crowborough: Highland, 1989), pp. 266-70.

11 2 Cor. 1:10.

12 2 Cor. 1:20.

13 2 Cor. 2:14.

14 2 Cor. 3:3. This metaphor is developed in some detail in Hood, *Whose Life?*, Ch. 2, pp. 32-33.

15 2 Cor. 3:5-6.

16 Gal. 6:17.

17 2 Cor. 4:1.

18 2 Cor. 4:5.

19 2 Cor. 4:7.

20 2 Cor. 5:20.

God's Wealth

Whose money is it anyway?

Neil Hood

In memory of my late parents,
Andrew and Lizzie Hood,
who made sterling efforts to
ground me in Christian faith
and who showed me a fine example
of quiet devotion to the Lord
in adverse circumstances;
and of my sister Jean,
whose premature death had
such a profound and lasting
effect on my life.

Contents

Preface

Money plays a vital role in all of our lives – whether we have a lot or a little, whether we love it or hold it loosely. We spend a lot of time both earning and spending money. We either enjoy its presence or bemoan its absence. Christians generally don't like talking about money, nor are they overeager to understand and practice God's advice on money and possessions. But God's views on this subject are much more extensive and much more clearly explained than we might imagine – or indeed than we might like. It's quite astonishing how rarely the topic of money features in church teaching – yet the Bible frequently addresses the issue, and Jesus talks about money and possessions in almost half of his parables. As you read this book, you may find that you are much more in tune with the prevailing worldview on money than you are with God's teaching on the topic. For example, God sees his disciples as channels of money, rather than as banks in which to keep it. And while we may use money as a measure of whether or not we are winning in the game of life, God certainly does not. Money attracts many worshipers, and there are a lot of Christians among them. But few own up to being either a disciple or a worshiper of money. In fact, many of us are both. For all of these reasons, expect to be challenged by the issues covered in this book. I have been challenged as I have written it, even though I have wrestled with putting these biblical principles into practice for many years now.

Because I trained as an economist, money has been central in my career. I have lectured about money, earned money for shareholders, managed money for investors and grown and protected money for pension fund members. Along the way, I have worked closely with and advised some very wealthy individuals. I have had the opportunity to observe both the good and bad consequences of serious wealth. My work in many different contexts to raise money for Christian ministries has taught me a lot about the prevalent attitudes to money within Christian communities. I have no great interest in possessing personal wealth and regard it as a resource that is held in trust for the owner, to be deployed as he instructs. But my stewardship of money and possessions still concerns me, as it should concern each one of us. This book asks the central question "Whose money is it anyway?" If we were to take the biblical answer to this question seriously – reading, thinking, praying and acting in response to it – we would all be changed people.

Why this book? That which receives the best of our time, energy and attention is our god. Money is that god for most people today. People focus on acquiring, accumulating and spending money with almost religious devotion. Shopping malls are our cathedrals, the latest products the objects of our worship and desire, and the barrage of advertisements the voices that we heed. This thinking seeps even into the minds of Christians, restricting our service and weakening our discipleship. It seems natural and right to regard what we own as ours. After all, did we not strive, work, save and train for it? Over the years I have found it very hard to discuss the "Whose money is it anyway?" question with Christians. Words like "personal", "private" and "difficult" occur more often in these conversations than do biblical words like "stewardship", "tithing" and "accountability". Is money not also an area in which Christians are called to hold one another accountable before God? How are Christians to live distinctively in a society that espouses an economic form of religion? We will explore the biblical answers to these and many other related questions throughout this book.

This book concludes a trilogy on the practice of Christian living in the market place. In August 2001, after over thirty years of secular writing, I began to bring my faith and professional experience together to write for the benefit of fellow Christians facing similar challenges. I have experienced a profound sense of conviction as I have written on these three related, practical and cutting-edge issues – namely busyness and service; work and faith; and money and eternity. Churches do not generally teach on these topics, yet the Bible itself is very concerned about them. In many ways these subjects chose me, simply because I have wrestled with them throughout my Christian life. I wanted to address them honestly and in a way that could guide others facing similar pressures and challenges. I have been both encouraged and humbled by the feedback from both Christian and non-Christian readers of the first two books,[1] who have said that these are challenging and thought-provoking books. The three books are designed so that they can be read independently, although there are occasional cross-references in the second and third volumes. The three books complement each other and are presented in the same style for continuity. The first two books are being widely used for both personal and small group study in many different parts of the world, and for that I readily give the Lord all the glory.

Who is it for? This book is for every Christian, everywhere. It contains as much about discipleship as it does about money and possessions. Materialism can thrive in the midst of both wealth and poverty – it just takes different forms. It is not, therefore, valid to say that "a book about money has nothing to teach me, since I have no money". As we will see, "problems with money" take many forms in God's eyes. The lifestyle we choose, how we respond to God's instructions on money and stewardship, how (or if) we are able to distinguish between greed and need, how desires for money and possessions affect our worship, are all crucial issues we need to consider biblically.

I am acutely aware there are many millions of Christians in the world who are poor by all the standard economic measures of poverty. In my experience, many Christians with little physical wealth are noted for their abundant love and generosity and have much to teach the more affluent members of their Christian family across the world. People like me, and many other readers, need to recapture the faith and dependence upon God that characterizes the lives of such materially poor Christians. They may be poor in money and possessions, but they are often truly rich in the "hidden manna".

This book is designed to make you think afresh about your relationship with money, and how that measures up against the relationship that God requires. For most of us that process of evaluation will highlight a discrepancy (and perhaps a serious one), which should lead us to prayer and a substantive reassessment of our behavior. Honestly struggling with God's expectations in this area might be painful, and the outcome radical. Most people assume that earnings and lifestyle should be closely related. This may be the first time that you have seriously considered what the Bible teaches about money and possessions. Just think of what God's people could achieve if we held the financial resources he has given to us less tightly, and if we all understood and acted upon the biblical answer to "Whose money is it anyway?"

Style and sources Like the others in the series, this book is firmly rooted in the Bible. I have no other source of wisdom to offer you. The aim is to examine its teaching so that its principles challenge us. This is not a book that tells you how to make money or that sets out ten easy step to follow

God's plan for your money – there are already many helpful books in these genres. This book focuses on the basic biblical principles concerning money and possessions – principles that, if we applied them, would be life changing. The fact that we find them radical is a reflection of how much we have discounted and discarded the Bible's teaching on this subject. This book is written to be accessible – the reader can dip in, take a thought, illustration, case or a challenge and go away to think about it. On occasion, I refer to some of the many other writers who have influenced my thought processes. Wherever possible, they are acknowledged. In addition, I have illustrated various points using relevant quotations from some standard sources.[2]

Structure The book is divided into three parts. Part One, *The Foundations*, asks some uncomfortable questions about the Christian perspective on money and possessions and introduces the predominant biblical principles. Chapter 2 considers the treasure and the heart. How open are we to Jesus changing our hearts on money matters? Part Two, *The Hazards*, examines various potential snares including how money occupies our minds; spiritual warfare; Christian expectations regarding prosperity; the missing link between money, earthly possessions and eternal values; Christian stewardship; and the importance of putting Jesus first. Part Three, *The Outcomes*, looks at the profound implications of taking God's advice about money and helps us to take stock and measure the impact that this teaching will have on our lives.

Acknowledgments With the completion of this trilogy of books, I acknowledge the great encouragement that so many readers have given me to continue to write on practical theology. I also recognize the many different people who have helped form my Christian views on money and possessions. Then there are those who have kindly endorsed this book. Once again, my personal assistant Irene Hood has worked with me through this project with her usual thoroughness and attention to detail. Finally there is the team at Authentic. Mark Finnie and his colleagues have helped to shape and develop this series and have also been a constant source of stimulus and encouragement. Many of my readers have commented favorably on the excellent work done by Peter Little on the design and production of the books. Meanwhile, my editor Tara Smith has worked with me throughout and has been a considerable help in clarifying my language and refining my writing style. All of them deserve my sincere and unreserved thanks – and a warning that there may be more to come!

Neil Hood
December 2003

Endnotes

1 Neil Hood, *Whose Life is it Anyway?* (Carlisle: Authentic Lifestyle, 2002); *God's Payroll: Whose Work is it Anyway?* (Carlisle: Authentic Lifestyle, 2003).

2 These quotations have come from a range of reference works, including: *Gathered Gold*, compiled by John Blanchard (Darlington: Evangelical Press, 1984); *Sifted Silver*, compiled by John Blanchard (Darlington: Evangelical Press, 1995); Edythe Draper, *Quotations for the Christian World* (Wheaton, IL: Tyndale, 1992); F. B. Proctor, *Treasury of Quotations on Religious Subjects* (Grand Rapids, MI: Kregel Publications, 1977); *5000 Quotations for Teachers and Preachers*, compiled by Robert Backhouse (Eastbourne: Kingsway Publications, 1994).

PART ONE
THE FOUNDATIONS

1
Money in the Christian's World

"For you know that it was not with perishable things such as silver or gold that you were redeemed from the empty way of life handed down to you from your forefathers, but with the precious blood of Christ, a lamb without blemish or defect." (1 Pet. 1:18-19)

Outline

Introduction
What kind of language do we use about money? What does this reveal about our attitudes to money?

Whose money is it anyway?
What is money and what kinds of problems does it bring? Seven different types of people answer this question.

Why do we ignore the Bible's instruction about money?
While the Bible has a lot to say about money, many Christians seem to neglect this teaching. We look at four reasons why this might be the case.

Five biblical principles on money
We examine these five principles and consider the extent to which we have applied them to our lives.

The obedience that comes from faith
Faith and obedience are both integral to being a disciple of Christ. We cannot understand God's perspective on money until we accept that it is Christ we heed, in faith and total obedience.

Introduction The verses above from 1 Peter place money in its proper context. Great or small, nothing that we possess is capable of our redemption. Why is it, then, that the perishable seems so attractive to many of us? Should Christians regard money differently than those in the world around them? After all, we work for the same salaries, use the same currencies, go to the same banks and buy from the same stores. "Money is money", we hear people say. "Life is just a routine cycle of earning, saving and spending. I keep hoping that there will be enough money to keep the cycle in motion. That's the way the world works." Indeed it is, but is that a biblical perspective? "Money is only a means to an end," others say. That's fine, provided we remember what the means and the end really are. The question that lies at the heart of this book is this: what is the nature of the difference between the world's view of money and the Bible's view of money? Difference is in the eye of the observer, a product of perspective and experience. We live in a world that is both consumed by, and preoccupied with, money. The biblical view is radically different.

☑ **ACTION:** Jot down some of the words that you use when thinking and talking about your finances and Christian giving. Then look at Table 1.1 to see if your vocabulary fits more with Column 1 or Column 2. What do you learn from this comparison?

TABLE 1.1 TWO PERSPECTIVES ON CHRISTIAN GIVING	
Column 1	**Column 2**
"Giving is ... difficult ... personal ... private ... a matter of conscience ... historical ... confidential ... problematic ... demanding."	*"Giving has to do with ... accountability ... mission ... ownership ... stewardship ... challenge ... change ... eternity ... generosity."*

In their proper context, there is nothing wrong with the words in the first column of Table 1.1. There is much about giving that is both personal and private. But sometimes "difficult" means "impossible to change", or "my mind is closed on this subject". Equally, "conscience" is a word that we should use with some care. It's just possible that your conscience is clear on the subject of giving when it has no right to be – were you to compare your actions to Jesus' teaching.

"I am persuaded that there is nothing upon which the Christian conscience is so ill-informed as the subject of Christian giving" – Samuel Chadwick

The careless use of "historical" is often a handy defense against tithing, because "this was for another age and not for the twenty-first century". The biblical evidence is quite clear that tithing is indeed a command to us in the twenty-first century.

We will be looking at the implications of the words in the second column throughout the book. The parables, for example, challenge us repeatedly on issues of accountability, ownership, stewardship, challenge and generosity. One of the most difficult concepts is the association of money with eternity. Most of us would never mention the two in the same sentence.

Whose money is it anyway?

This is a really tough question for most Christians. We work for our money and we need it. We also like it and want to keep it and make our own decisions about it. We assert our independence through the power that money gives us. For many of us money is personal and private, rarely discussed in polite company – at least overtly. The possession of money is a source of power, and those who don't have money tend to assign power to those who do. So because we feel that money is personal, private and powerful (and much more besides), few of us talk to God about it. Surveys show disturbingly low levels of Christian giving in many western societies. This would suggest that few Christians have seriously considered the question "Whose money is it anyway?"

"Being oblivious to eternity leaves us as experts in the trivial and novices in the significant" – Randy Alcorn

In almost all modern societies, life revolves around money. A lot of people have problems with money – problems that come in many different forms, including the desire for wealth and all its trappings; the inability to manage money within a household budget; the mismatch between earnings and needs or desires; the desire for money without wanting to work for it; selfishness when confronted by the needs of others; the tendency to stratify society and evaluate a person's worth according to their wealth; the sadness of being caught in a poverty trap because of social, physical and psychological difficulties, and so on. Christians are not exempt from any of these problems. You probably know people facing all of these difficulties, and it is likely that you are dealing with some of them yourself. But you may not be able to see your own situation clearly enough to identify your particular difficulties with money.

What is the root of these problems? We may accept that money is merely a tool of trade, a convenient and necessary means of payment, and that its value is ascribed rather than inherent. Our relationship with money, however, cannot be defined in these neutral terms. The world around us is not morally neutral, and money is a force for both good and evil. In principle money is neutral, in practice it is not. The power, worship and control of money seep into our thinking. Jesus saw that danger when he told his disciples, "You cannot serve both God and Money".[1] Jesus saw money as a rival. We cannot let money, either by its presence or absence, rule our lives.

"To escape the error of salvation by works we have fallen into the opposite error of salvation without obedience" – A.W. Tozer

Christians rarely seem to make a connection between money and obedience. Some might want to take issue with the title of this book – "God's wealth". After all, if we concede ownership to God, some uncomfortable decisions might follow – and we might be required to radically change our perspective. At its heart, this is a question about obedience.

Although the call to obedience applies to every dimension of our Christian faith, financial matters do present some unique challenges to obedience. While at one level it is only a medium of exchange, money is also a proxy for influence – even among Christians. Money fosters deep (and often unrecognized) desires to own more of it and induces self-deception. Some people offer remarkable rationalizations concerning the decisions they make about money. "I must maximize my earnings at this stage of my life, whatever the costs to my family and my health." "I am skilled and able but I'm not looking for employment because the state will always provide for my needs – I want to enjoy my time without the stress of working." "This is my spending phase of life. I'll think about giving later – when I get older and start thinking about retirement."

TABLE 1.2 "WHOSE MONEY IS IT ANYWAY?"
Some answers from ...
1. **Dodgers:** "Don't ask me this question. My life is complicated enough. The Bible probably does talk a lot about this – but that's not where I'm at right now."
2. **Cynics:** "Since I have so little money, the small amount I do have must be mine. Giving is not my problem. But I could give you the names of plenty of others who should really look at this issue."
3. **Spenders:** "What money I have is totally committed at my present level of giving. There is no scope for changing it – at least not now. Ask me in 20 years. You might think it sounds feeble, but I am not going to change my lifestyle."
4. **Calculators:** "I already give quite a lot by my standards – and by the standards of my peers, I might add. I can't think of anything that would make me want to give any more – especially not a book about Christian giving!"
5. **Donors:** "I don't give systematically. It doesn't really fit my spending habits, and I'm not very organized in money matters. But some appeals (and some people) break my heart – and then I'm quite generous. I confess this doesn't actually happen very often."
6. **Hoarders:** "I'm saving to donate, and I'm a good steward of what I have. The time will come to pay it out – but maybe not while I'm still alive. I give a little, although it's only a fraction of what is possible. There are lots of other people just like me."
7. **Givers:** "The Bible asks me to give myself first, and then answer the question – but the likely answer bothers me, and I doubt if my present attitude to giving matches up to it. I hope that I have the faith and courage to put what I learn into practice."

☑ **ACTION:** Read through the seven categories in Table 1.2 and try to identify yourself. You might find that you have different attitudes at different times across several of these categories. Alternatively, and only if you have to, develop another category that more accurately describes your position.

Why do we ignore the Bible's instruction about money?

About fifteen percent of Jesus' recorded words are on the subject of money. Sixteen of his thirty-eight parables talk about how to handle money and possessions. The Bible contains many more verses about money than it does about other foundational subjects such as faith and prayer. The New Testament mentions contentment seven times, and six of those are set in contexts about money. Why, then, do many Christians spend so little time weighing up the consequences of that teaching? Consider the following four reasons.

"If a person gets his attitude towards money straight, it will help straighten out almost every other area of his life" — Billy Graham

Neglected and rejected: Many Christians are not regularly taught about money and possessions. When the subject is taught, the Bible's message is often seen as too demanding, too "other worldly", and irrelevant for today. If our lives revolve around receiving and keeping money, it is just too big a shift to see that money is really about giving and sharing. As a result, there is a marked disparity between biblical principles and contemporary Christian practice.

Hijacked: Since money is the god of this age, and many of our institutions are part of its worship, one way or another we are sucked into its sphere of influence. This hijacking of our minds and hearts can be subtle, but it is pervasive. Only the Spirit can break us free from the bondage of greed. Think, for example, about how little of the time that you spend thinking about money is spent thinking about giving.

Deflected: It's Satan's business to try to dull our sensitivity to the biblical challenge regarding money and possessions. Money and possessions are in enemy territory. We don't want to hear God's radical challenge. We want just a little bit more, we have other priorities, and we're defensive about our capacity to help.

Redirected: Whom do we serve? Our practice with regard to money and possessions goes to the very roots of our discipleship. We will serve God or money, not both. Jesus confronted converts or seekers with this fact numerous times. He told the rich ruler, for example, "You still lack one thing.

"He who has God and everything has no more than he who has God alone" — C.S. Lewis

Sell everything you have and give to the poor, and you will have treasure in heaven. Then come, follow me".[2] The rich man found this to be both unwelcome and unpalatable wisdom. We would be wise not to redirect our allegiance as he did.

✔ **ACTION:** If you were not entirely satisfied with your assessment of yourself against Table 1.2, ask whether (and how) these four reasons have played a part in your attitude to money and possessions. What it would take to change your behavior? If none of these apply to you, rejoice and think about how you could help others that are misguided in their attitudes about money.

Five biblical principles on money

What are the Bible's overarching principles concerning money and possessions?[3] There are at least five key principles against which we need to measure our attitudes and behavior. We will look at each of these principles in greater detail throughout the book.

1. A design for good: From its very first pages, the Bible views material possessions as good gifts from God, intended for our enjoyment. God declared the whole creation "good", and the people of Israel received blessings in kind for covenant obedience. People such as Abraham, David and Solomon enjoyed wealth and were also godly men. The book of Proverbs regards wealth as a reward for good and God-honoring work. The New Testament tells us about wealthy Christians hosting churches in their homes and funding missionary activities. There are no grounds for arguing that the Christian ownership of money and possessions is wrong. Nor does the Bible suggest that poverty is desirable.

2. An inherent capacity to distract: But – and it's a substantial exception – the Bible is clear that while they were designed for good, material possessions are also one of the major distractions that divert human hearts from the worship of God. This theme recurs again and again. From early on in humankind's history, God placed limits on the accumulation of wealth.

Many of the prophets recognized that vast wealth was often the product of both social injustice and the worship of false gods. Moreover, there was lots of tension between those who were faithful to God and those who simultaneously became both rich and wicked. Hosea, for example, quotes the Lord, "When I fed them, they were satisfied; when they were satisfied, they became proud; then they forgot me."[4] Possessions can lead to amnesia – both then and now. Paul's strident words of warning ring in our ears, "For the love of money is a root of all kinds of evil."[5]

3. A transformation in stewardship: One of the signs of new life in Christ is life-transforming stewardship of money and possessions. This concept of stewardship surfaces often in the Old Testament in the form of tithes and taxes designed to support the priesthood and the poor. Equally evident is God's concern for the "widows, fatherless, aliens and the poor". In the New Testament, stewardship is a consequence of the transformation that comes from salvation. Jesus makes this very clear in the Sermon on the Mount – as we shall see in Chapter 2. Luke's Gospel also includes many examples of Jesus' teaching on discipleship and material possessions. In the context of the parable of the shrewd manager, for example, Jesus said, "So if you have not been trustworthy in handling worldly wealth, who will trust you with true riches?"[6] There is no hiding place from this teaching.

4. A redistribution challenge: Scripture points to many different situations in which the extremes of both wealth and poverty are equally unacceptable to God. It is easy for us to divert the force of this teaching into a debate about relativities in different economies and times in history. But the clear teaching of Scripture is that God wants his people to take steps to distribute wealth more equally. Economic injustice is a major theme of the prophets, for example, and false worship was closely linked to the economic sins of the nation. Several passages in the New Testament contain savage critiques of the rich oppressing the poor. In the words that James addressed to such people, "Your wealth has rotted, and moths have eaten your clothes. Your gold and silver are corroded."[7] One important element of redistribution is mobilizing the resources we possess to extend the kingdom of God. Thus the talent parables all urge us to put our resources to work until the Lord returns.[8] These parables also remind us that the talents belong to God and are therefore his to command. "Again, it will be like a man going on a journey, who called his servants and entrusted his property to them."[9] In effect, the challenge is not just to redistribute resources, but – in the first place – to deploy them. In that regard, some Christians never even get to first base.

5. An essential spiritual link: While we may wish to contain the material and the spiritual dimensions of our lives in separate watertight compartments, the Bible rejects this approach. In God's eyes, the two are inseparable. New creatures in Christ make (and keep making) new decisions about wealth and possessions – for spiritual reasons. We cannot follow Christ without our faith affecting this area of our lives.

"Money has never yet made anyone rich – Lucius Seneca (a secular contemporary of Jesus)

We will return to this complex and challenging principle, looking at links between the spiritual and the financial made by some and not by others (as, for example, in prosperity theology). The New Testament never promises material wealth as a reward for spiritual obedience. There will be blessings, but not necessarily material ones. Of the many compelling passages that discuss general links between the material and the spiritual, Jesus' temptation is perhaps one of the most striking. We ignore at our peril this warning against the seduction of possessions and the desire to protect our physical life at the expense of our eternal destiny. Jesus spurns Satan with these words: "Man does not live on bread alone, but on every word that comes from the mouth of God".[10]

☑ **ACTION:** Have you ever taken the time to think these issues through and formulate your own view on money and possessions according to biblical principles? Do you find that money – either having it or desiring it – distracts you from your focus on God? What is your particular weakness with regard to money and possessions? How would you rate yourself as a steward of that which God has given you? Are you hiding your talents? Squandering them? Or investing them wisely? Would you say at this point that you have separate compartments for the spiritual and material in your life? If so, what steps could you take to integrate them?

The obedience that comes from faith

The answer to our "Whose money is it anyway?" question is fundamentally a matter of obedience. In his letter to the Romans Paul refers to, "Jesus Christ our Lord, through whom we have received grace and apostleship to bring about the obedience of faith for the sake of his name among all the nations."[11] The key words here are "obedience", "faith" and "name". We need to take these three words with us as we consider some of the radical teaching of the Bible on money and possessions in the chapters that follow.

"Things alter for the worse spontaneously, if they do not alter for the better designedly" – Lord Bacon

What kind of name?: We are all free agents – there is no meaningful compulsion to obey, apart from the Spirit in our hearts and our love for God. His is the only name that should be powerful enough to command our obedience. But is it? The motivation for obedience is faith. If we believe what God says, we will obey him. "If you love me, you will obey what I command. And I will ask the Father, and he will give you another Counselor to be with you forever – the Spirit of truth."[12] But in this passage, as Andrew Murray noted, "The Saviour claims obedience as the condition of the Father's giving and our receiving the Spirit." Our obedience is always and only "for the sake of his name".

What kind of faith?: We do not obey out of general credence or broad consensus. We obey, rather, because of our confident trust in God and in his purposes for our lives. Why? God requires our commitment. There is simply no known biblical substitute for it. Jesus makes the following great fellowship promise: "If anyone loves me, he will obey my teaching. My Father will love him, and we will come to him and make our home with him."[13] The picture of the tree and

"I had rather obey than work miracles" – Martin Luther

the fruit also poses this question of faith. Jesus said, "Not everyone who says to me 'Lord, Lord,' will enter the kingdom of heaven, but only he who does the will of my Father who is in heaven."[14] What does my kind of faith produce? Adherence? Activity? Too much noise? Or nothing much at all? Is obedience on the list of its outcomes?

What kind of obedience?: Although Jesus expects total obedience from his disciples, it is possible to place parts of our lives beyond obedience to God. Are money and possessions in that category for you? Phillip Keller talks of "pathway people"[15] in whose gardens, or lives, places have been beaten as hard as rock by the effects of other people and other influences. So the seed falls on such pathways and dies. This simple but powerful metaphor might help to explain where you are regarding money and possessions. Your receptivity to obeying God in the area of money and possessions may have been beaten down by peer pressure, by personal ambitions, by thinking that the Bible is not an authority in these matters or by occupying your mind with other priorities. God's intentions for his disciples are clear, as illustrated in the doxology in Romans:

> Now to him who is able to establish you by my gospel and the proclamation of Jesus Christ, according to the revelation of the mystery hidden for long ages past, but now revealed and made known through the prophetic writings by the command of the eternal God, so that all nations might believe and obey him – to the only wise God be glory forever through Jesus Christ! Amen.[16]

Taking stock

The subject of money really matters to God. Think about how much it matters to you. Do you want to be on the same wavelength with God about money? What would it take for you to get there?

How much time and attention have you given to considering whether your giving matches God's expectations?

Identify any inconsistencies between your values and behavior. Are the values that you hold about money and those you actually put into operation the same? If not, why not?

Can you recall a situation in which, faced with a financial need that you felt God wanted you to meet, you were not obedient? What were the consequences of your disobedience, and what can you learn from the experience?

Look again at where you are within the categories in Table 1.2 as you leave this chapter. We will return to it at the end of the book.

Further reading

Blomberg, Craig L., *Neither Poverty nor Riches: A Biblical Theology of Possessions* (Downers Grove, IL: IVP, 1999).

Hollis, Allen, *The Bible and Money* (New York: Hawthorn Books, 1976).

Tondeur, Keith, *Your Money and Your Life* (London: SPCK, 1996).

Wilson, Michael, *Managing Your Money* (Leicester: IVP, 1994).

Endnotes

1 Lk. 16:13.

2 Lk. 18:22.

3 For a masterly review of the whole of Scripture relating to poverty and wealth, see Craig L. Blomberg, *Neither Poverty nor Riches: A Biblical Theology of Possessions* (Downers Grove, IL: IVP, 1999).

4 Hos. 13:6.

5 1 Tim. 6:10.

6 Lk. 16:11.

7 Jas. 5:2-3.

8 See, e.g., Lk. 19:13.

9 Mt. 25:14.

10 Mt. 4:4.

11 Rom. 1:4-5 (RSV).

12 Jn. 14:15-17a.

13 Jn. 14:23.

14 Mt. 7:21.

15 Phillip Keller, *A Gardener Looks at the Fruits of the Spirit* (London: HarperCollins, 1991).

16 Rom. 16:25-27.

2
The Treasure and the Heart

"For where your treasure is, there your heart will be also." (Mt. 6:21)

Outline   How we answer the question "Whose money is it anyway?"
                 is ultimately a reflection of whether or not we are willing to
totally surrender our hearts – the spiritual center of our lives – to Jesus.
What is the relationship between our treasure and our hearts? What does it
mean to see life from a kingdom perspective?

The kingdom perspective
How do we find heavenly perspective in the routines of earthly life?
Why is it important?

Where is your treasure?
Five "treasure inventories" help us see, clearly and biblically, where
our hearts are.

Finding the treasure
In the treasure hunt of life, where do we look? Here we compare and
contrast some biblical and contemporary views of treasure.

Where is your heart?
On the premise that the treasure and the heart cannot be separated, we
ask three questions based on 1 Peter 3:15.

God's wisdom on the treasure and the heart
Four biblical perspectives on treasure conclude the chapter.

The kingdom
perspective

Bill Gothart observed that "wisdom is seeing life from God's perspective". By that standard – and with all of our knowledge – few of us would claim to be wise. Every day we try to see things from a range of perspectives. We might observe, for example, that "The weather was bad yesterday, but it was much better than last week." "My sick friend's health is still not good, but compared to the condition she was in before her surgery, she is a living miracle." "This job isn't great, but after months of waiting I'm glad to have any job that uses my skills." "I wonder how the families of the earthquake victims face each new day?" We use all of our faculties as we stand back, appraise progress and get a fresh perspective. This exercise helps to give us a sense of time, preserve our sanity and establish our place in the world.

We need to get perspective in our spiritual lives, too – particularly because as Christians we have been introduced to some very radical ways of viewing our world. These views are so radical and counter-cultural that it would be very easy to deny their existence or water down their importance. For example: "Since, then, you have been raised with Christ, set your hearts on things above, where Christ is seated at the right hand of God. Set your minds on things above, not on earthly things."[1] Most of us feel a sense of shame when we try to measure our thoughts and activities against that standard. While these verses do not constitute an invitation to other-worldliness, they do call us to recalibrate the way in which we view our world.

I have spent a lot of time traveling long distances by air. People cope with these types of tedious journeys in many different ways. I take lots of books of different types – and end up sleeping for much of the time. One of my long-standing habits is to adjust my watch to the time zone of my destination as soon as I enter the departing aircraft. Why? It gets me thinking about where I'm going, the time at which I will arrive and the condition I will be in when I get there. While this exercise takes seconds, adjusting our lives to heavenly conditions takes much longer. But it's much more necessary. If heaven is our destination, what are we doing to acclimatize ourselves?

I also have business friends who make concerted efforts during long and complex journeys across time zones to never adjust their watches. They want to keep thinking of, and relating to, their "home base" – just like Christians who don't tune in to where they are going. Their "treasures on earth" are much more appealing to them than "treasures in heaven". We will not find the biblical answer to the question "Whose money is it anyway?" without buying in to heavenly values.[2] In the passage from the Sermon on the Mount where the verse above is found,[3] Jesus implicitly asks his followers to do some arithmetic. While it is a simple concept, it is a fundamental exercise I call counting by twos.

TABLE 2.1 COUNTING BY TWOS: AN EXERCISE IN SPIRITUAL ARITHMETIC	
2 locations:	We need to be aware of the reality of both heaven and earth
2 preoccupations:	Life in the here and now, the life to come in heaven
2 choices:	To either see clearly or walk in blindness
2 loyalties:	Decide whether to be loyal to God or money
2 kingdoms:	Live by the rules of this world or by God's law
2 securities:	Acquire treasure that can be stolen, or treasure that is eternally secure

True disciples of Christ need to see money and possessions according to God's perspective. This perspective is necessarily different from that of the Christian's colleagues, peers and contemporaries.

> ✔ **ACTION:** To what extent does your life reflect a kingdom perspective? What "time zone" is your life set to – the earthly or the heavenly? Where does your ultimate loyalty lie? Where is your security?

"I have held many things in my hands and I have lost them all. But whatever I have placed in God's hands, that I still possess" – Martin Luther

Where is your treasure?

What does Jesus mean by "treasure" when he talks about your heart being with your treasure? He is not just talking about money, and he is talking to everyone – even if you think you have no "treasure". Jesus is not saying that it is wrong to have treasures – but it is essential to identify both *what* and *where* these treasures are. The heart follows the treasures – not vice versa. Take the following five simple "treasure inventories", writing down your answers as you go.

Value: What do you value most? Rank the top ten things that are most important to you according to their relative value. This is a difficult exercise, since most of us would prefer not to rank people and relationships. Few of us are able to wholly identify with John Wesley's remark – "I value all things only by the price they shall gain in eternity" – and claim that this principle drives our lives at all times.

Energy: Where do you consistently spend the best of your energies? At work? With your family? Pursuing pleasure? If you are in poor health or stressful circumstances, just surviving might require all of your energy (and you may not feel that life contains much treasure). Most of us, however, can quickly see the connection between our effort and our treasures – and we are not always happy with the priorities that this connection reveals.

Loss: What do you have that would be most painful for you to lose? Your answers to this question will probably overlap considerably with the list of things you value most. Health, family and possessions of some sort may be in most lists. Try thinking about loss in heavenly terms. What is missing from your list? Spiritual peace? An awareness of being loved by God? An assurance of salvation?

Mind: What occupies your mind most often? Many of us don't like probing what goes on there. You might answer, "it depends on all kinds of things beyond my control". And indeed it often does. Turn the question around to consider where your mind comes to rest most often. Where does it settle when it is "on idle"? When you know the answer to that, you may be getting close to where your treasure is.

Pleasure: What gives you the greatest pleasure? Your answers here are likely to be the outcomes of things on your other lists. The smile of your child or partner, the joy of vacation time, the result of a soccer game, a beautiful spring garden, time to read a favorite author or good news from a friend are all among the myriad of possibilities. But are there any spiritual pleasures on your list? Such pleasures might, for example, include an answered prayer, a sense of God's blessing on you, a friend pointed to Christ, a rich time of fellowship.

☑ **ACTION:** Compare your lists from each of the five "inventories" above. Which items appear most often on these lists? What is or are your treasure(s)? If you're not sure, what clues do you have?

Finding the treasure

There are lots of Christians who seem to enjoy taking part in life's treasure hunt but who never find the real treasure. They enjoy searching for clues, playing the game, debating and philosophizing as to where it might be, but they never get there. They often find other, proxy treasures along the way and become totally absorbed by them. They might catch a glimpse of the real treasure – but life is too busy, and they don't take the time to stop and really look. The consequences of such behavior for the cause of Christ and the witness of the church are grave indeed. Jesus treated this treasure hunt with great seriousness and he gave detailed clues, including the following, to all of us.

"Treasures in heaven are accumulated by our attitude to our treasures (or the lack of them) on earth" – Edwin Lutzer

1. The treasure in the field: "The kingdom of heaven is like treasure hidden in a field. When a man found it, he hid it again, and then in his joy went and sold all he had and bought that field."[4] By the standards of this parable, when a seeker finds special treasure, nothing else is of any real value. With no doubts or regrets, the finder sells everything else. If this is a metaphor for making Christ our Lord, why is it that many believers value other things so much? Blindness, preoccupation, partial commitment and laziness are among our many excuses. Do we know what it is that we are looking for?

2. The eye as the lamp: "The eye is the lamp of the body. If your eyes are good, your whole body will be full of light. But if your eyes are bad, your whole body will be full of darkness. If then the light within you is darkness, how great is that darkness!"[5] Most of us have regular medical checkups or "physicals". When did you last have a "spiritual" – to test your spiritual vision? Jesus spoke of those who missed the treasure as being shortsighted, blind or foolish.

"Our theology tells us that this life is the preface — not the book; the preliminaries — not the main event; the tune up — not the concert" — Randy Alcorn[6]

3. The widow's coins: "'I tell you the truth,' he [Jesus] said, 'this poor widow has put in more than all the others. All these people gave their gifts out of their wealth; but she out of her poverty put in all she had to live on.'"[7] There would have been plenty of observers beside the temple treasury that day – most of them impressed by the apparent generosity of the rich. But Jesus draws attention to only *one* offering. The anonymous widow's two copper coins were on no one else's radar – but they were on his. Why? Because Jesus could see into the hearts of all the givers. And there was a spirit of real sacrifice in only one of them. This widow had discovered heaven's view of treasure. Have you? It's little wonder that she has gone down in history – and we're still talking about her.

☑ **ACTION:** What do these three examples have to say to you about your attitude to earthly treasure? Read 1 Timothy 6:19, which tells us that Christians need to have a correct attitude to wealth "so that they may take hold of the life that is truly life". How does this take us to the heart of the matter?

In Table 2.2, five Christians articulate their attitudes to treasure. As you read their responses, note how confused and uncertain some of these people are.

The things we treasure can control and consume us – occupying our thoughts, demanding our constant attention and influencing how we measure everybody and everything else. While they may be legitimate in and of themselves, we fool ourselves if we insist that treasures like this are not aggressive and invasive. If we value them *above everything else*, the values of the kingdom cannot shape our lives. Don Carson identifies the challenge for all of us when he says, "our whole lives drift relentlessly toward the spot where our treasures are stored, because our hearts will take us there. To follow Jesus faithfully entails therefore a consistent development of our deepest loves, to train ourselves to adopt an unswerving loyalty to kingdom values and to delight in all that God approves".[8]

TABLE 2.2 FIVE CHRISTIANS RESPOND TO THE QUESTION "WHERE IS YOUR TREASURE?"

MICHAEL: "I'm not sure I like what your question implies. It's not that simple. My treasure is both on earth and in heaven. I'm self-made and self-sufficient. I know that I spend too much time earning money – but if I don't earn it, I can't give it. I'm not storing up treasure – I'm thinking about heaven – at least most of the time. What's that about my heart? I have clearly separated my heart and my treasure. They are not connected, I can assure you. And I can handle my own life, thank you."

PATRICK: "It's quite simple – my family comes first, and then my business. I have a lot of responsibilities in both. You see, I've lost a fortune on the stock market in recent years, and somehow I have to make up for this. What else can I pass on to my family? God probably doesn't really approve of my priorities – but I haven't thought about it much. Anyway, heavenly treasures are a bit intangible, aren't they? How would you even know what they are? My motives are pure, and surely that's all that matters."

MARY: "I suspect that my treasure is where I've spent most of my time and effort over the years. Excelling in academic life is difficult – endless research and publication pressures, peer group reviews, and the administrative and teaching burden is heavy. However, I really love my work and have no regrets. So my treasure must be buried deep in my career somewhere. I'm not sure how that happened. I didn't really intend my heart to be there – but it is. Life used to be much simpler. I'll have to fix it of course, but I'm not sure when or how. I do know that life doesn't go on forever."

JOAN: "My heart is in my sport. I haven't made much money in it yet, but it's the most important thing in my life right now. I suppose it has all kinds of consequences that I'd rather not think about. There isn't much else to say here, is there? If I don't focus completely on my fitness, I just won't make it. Yes, people tell me I'm obsessed – but so are all great athletes. There can't be anything wrong with that. Heaven? What about it? Great prospect, fantastic promises, but can I get back to the track now?"

WILLIAM: "My heart is in this great Christian charity that I run. It's all that I ever wanted to do, and it consumes me. I confess that sometimes I get really lost in the mechanics of it and in the operational detail. I'm not in this for the money, obviously, but its success is very important to me. So I suppose that is a kind of treasure. Am I investing enough in heavenly treasures? I do sometimes wonder about that. The cause is heavenly, but I can lose the plot. I need to keep thinking about what is of real value. You wouldn't think that this would be an issue in a job like mine – but it is!"

☑ **ACTION:** What are the different attitudes to treasure found in Table 2.2? What do you see of yourself here? Reflect on the quotation from Don Carson on page 214 and jot down two things you could begin to do to develop and train yourself to follow Jesus more faithfully.

Where is your heart? Try as we may, we cannot separate our treasure from our hearts. If we think more specifically about money and possessions as forms of earthly treasure, what we do with them determines where our heart is. And while as Christian disciples we may have both God and money, we cannot *serve* both God and money. When we responded to the call of Christ and made him Lord, we entered into an exclusive relationship with him. When we focus our hearts on something, our priorities reflect that focus and our behavior communicates it to others. The following quotation from one of the most moving pieces of persecution literature in the Bible illustrates this vital point. It was written shortly after Nero's persecution of Christians around the middle of the first century. "But in your hearts set apart Christ as Lord."[9] These words set out the where, what and who of focusing our hearts on God.

"When the centre of one's life is rightly related to God, he is able to respond properly to the vicissitudes of life" – Edwin Blum

Where? The Bible makes clear that the heart is the religious center of a man or woman. In the context of the difficult environment in which 1 Peter was written, this verse constitutes a remarkable statement.

When we ask what our treasure is, we are really asking what is at the *center* of our lives. We might struggle to find (or admit) where our center lies, but God knows exactly where it is – and where it should be. Did he not say "that all human history shall be consummated in Christ"?[10]

"For the Christian the one supreme test for the present soundness and ultimate worth of everything religious must be the place our Lord occupies in it" – A.W. Tozer

For us, therefore, the challenging question is this: "What is going on at the center of my life?"

What? What do we need to do to "set apart" Christ as Lord? "Setting apart" in this context means to sanctify, hold in reverence, give honor to, be consecrated to. It is an intentional act, requiring focus and discipline. Many Christians treat their relationship with God casually, occasionally hearing his words and seldom acknowledging his lordship in all aspects of life – not least with regard to money and possessions. The Bible consistently emphasizes how essential it is to place God alone at the center of our lives. It would not be an exaggeration to say that the aim of salvation through faith is to lead us to apply this verse to our lives. Augustine's observation of the disciples' reaction to the ascension of Christ is incredibly poignant. "You ascended from before our eyes, and we turned back grieving, only to find you in our hearts." That is exactly where Christ has to be if we are going to serve him.

Who? Jesus is Lord – no one, and nothing, else. Why? God the Father has already exalted him. "Therefore God exalted him to the highest place and gave him the name that is above every name, that at the name of Jesus every knee should bow, in heaven and on earth and under the earth, and every tongue confess that Jesus Christ is Lord, to the glory of God the Father."[11] If we believe this, then we evaluate our "treasures" and determine our priorities with reference to him. We also recognize that the affections of our hearts are dissipated when not directed towards him.

"If Christ's lordship does not disrupt our own lordship, then the reality of our conversion must be questioned" – Charles Colson

If Christ is central to God's plans, where is he in our plans? How we answer that question, and how we live in light of that answer, will be one of the best guides to where our heart is. Many Christians deny having heart problems – especially with regard to money and possessions. The confidence and self-assurance that come with affluence (even a little affluence) lead us to think that we can manage and control everything – including how we present our hearts to God. Although you might be in denial about where your heart is, God knows. Moreover, if you asked him, he would show you and willingly put it right.

> Give me the greedy heart and the little creeping treasons,
> Give me the proud heart and the blind, obstinate eyes;
> Give me the shallow heart, and the vain lust, and the folly;
> Give me the coward heart and the spiritless refusals;
> Give me the confused self that you can do nothing with;
> I can do something.
> – *Dorothy L. Sayers*

God's wisdom on the treasure and the heart

The following four cameos of biblical wisdom have helped me see more clearly where my treasure is some of the time – and where I know it should be all of the time.

1. Poor, but bringing riches? Paul faced many hardships in his life, and he commented that he was, "sorrowful, yet always rejoicing; poor, yet making many rich; having nothing, and yet possessing everything".[12] How can we reconcile the paradox here? Paul did not make his outstanding contribution to the kingdom from a position of earthly wealth. Yet the message of the gospel that he so effectively championed brought unimaginable spiritual riches to those who received it. God can enable us to do the same in our generation.

2. Wealth, but from where? The one message that Moses could never stop preaching to the nation of Israel was not to forget the Lord. "You may say to yourself, 'My power and the strength of my hands have produced this wealth for me'. But remember the LORD your God, for it is he who gives you the ability to produce wealth."[13] You might have good reason to be proud of your achievements and of the way you have used the talents you have to maximum effect. But who gave the talents to you? Wealth can tempt us to assert our independence, thereby denying our dependence on God.

3. Possessions, but is this life? Jesus taught the crowd, "Watch out! Be on your guard against all kinds of greed; a man's life does not consist in the abundance of his possessions."[14] Many of the people you know would probably dismiss this statement as wrong. "That was fine for first-century Palestine, but not for the consumer age of the twenty-first century." "I assess people by what they are worth." "Society determines its pecking order according to what people possess. And I suppose I do the same." This attitude, whether implicit or explicit, is everywhere. For many Christians, it's implicit because we don't like to admit the truth about how we rank people. Possessions do not equate with life, however – at least not on God's scales.

4. Gold, but from what source? "Here is what I want you to do: Buy your gold from me, gold that's been through the refiner's fire. Then you'll be rich."[15] The church in Laodicea to whom these words were written was evidently affluent. Yet it was described as tepid in its attitude to the risen Lord. There was ample gold – but was it the right gold?[16] Here, then, was the Spirit's investment advice to make sure that these Christians bought gold from the true source. They were rich, but their souls were impoverished. Does this sound at all familiar?

"God wants no man to be more prosperous than his soul" – Vance Havner

"Jesus differs from all other teachers; they reach the ear, but he instructs the heart; they deal with the outward letter, but he imparts an inward taste for the truth" – C.H. Spurgeon

Taking stock

Is your perspective on life predominantly earthly or heavenly?

Have you found Christ, God's treasure, or are you still engaged in a "treasure hunt"?

What would we overhear if you were to answer the question raised in Table 2.2? Would you be comfortable with other people hearing your honest answer to this question?

Further reading

Olford, Stephen, *The Grace of Giving* (London: Lakeland, 1972).

Packer, J.I., *God has Spoken* (London: Hodder & Stoughton, 1979).

Rosner, Brian, *How to Get Really Rich: A Sharp Look at the Religion of Greed* (Leicester: IVP, 1999).

Vogt, Virgil, *Treasure in Heaven* (Ann Arbor, MI: Servant Books, 1982).

Endnotes

1 Col. 3:1-2.

2 We will return to this theme in Chapter 6.

3 Mt. 6:19-24.

4 Mt. 13:44.

5 Mt. 6:22-23.

6 Randy Alcorn, *Money, Possessions and Eternity* (Wheaton, IL: Tyndale, 1989), p. 131.

7 Lk. 21:3-4.

8 D.A. Carson, *Sermon on the Mount* (Carlisle: Paternoster, 2001), p. 85.

9 1 Pet. 3:15.

10 Eph. 1:10 (J.B. Phillips).

11 Phil. 2:9-11.

12 2 Cor. 6:10.

13 Deut. 8:17-18.

14 Lk. 12:15.

15 Rev. 3:18 (The Message).

16 See Chapter 5 for more on the church in Laodicea.

PART TWO
THE HAZARDS

3
Money on our Minds

"Give me neither poverty nor riches, but give me only my daily bread. Otherwise, I may have too much and disown you and say, 'Who is the LORD?'" (Prov. 30: 8-9)

Outline What are the hazards associated with money and possessions? This chapter identifies these potential pitfalls in order to help us avoid them.

Money, money, money
How does money influence our thinking? How much should it occupy a Christian's mind?

Attitudes to money and materialism
Four case studies examine the following attitudes to money: it's mine by design; it's ours to spend; it's yours to ask; it's yours Lord – take it.

God's design: A change of mind
What is God's plan for renewing our minds? How have our minds been dulled by contemporary attitudes to money?

Rejecting God's design: The effects of materialism and consumerism
How do these two dangerous and pervasive attitudes corrode our perspective?

Money, money, money How much time and energy should a Christian devote to thinking about money? You might say that to pose such a question is an unreasonable intrusion and that it depends on many things according to individual circumstances. And that is true. Health problems, intermittent employment, family and social concerns are only a few of the reasons why a Christian may be more preoccupied with money than he or she might otherwise choose to be. However, many of us could not give such justification for the role that money plays in our thinking. Paradoxically, people who have too much money and those who have too little experience similar stresses. Perhaps the better question to ask is whether the Christian's mind should be less engaged with money than those in the world around us in similar circumstances? In light of what we learned in Chapter 2, the biblical answer is undoubtedly "Yes". But is that a realistic expectation?

Because money controls the thought patterns of many around us, this thinking seeps into our minds almost by osmosis. Money exists because we believe that we have a future here on earth – otherwise no one would hold on to it as a way of storing value. Money means a great deal to most people. They work for it, spend it, worry about it, borrow it, dream about it, hoard it and want more of it. Some even lie, cheat or kill for it. Money constitutes power, security, freedom and comfort. It binds societies and families together and it splits them apart. Money is one of the major causes of domestic strife – even among the very wealthy.

Money may not buy happiness – but it can dull the pain of unhappiness

The opportunity to get more money can often override other principles and practices that would otherwise govern a person's life. When people build their lives around getting and spending money, it becomes a trap. In some societies people tend to be secretive about money, regarding it as a private matter. In others, the possession of money leads to opposite forms of behavior and conspicuous consumption, with lifestyles that far exceed earning capacity. There are Christians in all of these categories.

While you might not wholly agree with Tolstoy's perspective here, it is thought-provoking. Like so many other things in our world, money is a force both for great good and great evil – even in the hands of Christians. And the temptation to love it is inexplicably powerful.

"Money is a new and terrible form of slavery, and, like the old form of personal slavery, it corrupts both the slave and the slave-owner, but it is even worse because it frees the slave-owner from personal relations" – Leo Tolstoy

I confess that I think about money a lot. There are several reasons for this, and some of them are legitimate. As a director of public companies, as a trustee and adviser to pension funds and as chairman of a private equity company, for example, I have an obligation to look after the financial interests of shareholders and others. Value for money, performance and financial probity are high on the agenda in my role within a large economic development agency. The challenges are similar in my work for Christian charities, in addition to raising money for Christian causes. The need and scale of this fundraising have sometimes been quite substantial, and so money was very much on my mind – as was continuous prayer! You could take two views of the above synopsis. You might say, "Fine, he's a Christian who knows about money, so he'll be able to keep it in its proper place in his mind." Or you might wonder, "It must be a bit of a problem to stop thinking about all of this when it comes to where money fits into his personal life". In fact it is a bit of both – but more of the latter. While I have no personal interest in owning and retaining wealth, the challenge for me is to remember what is eternally real and lasting. Much of what I do every day feels very "real" and immediate, and it affects a lot of people, so I need to treat it seriously. But I have to keep all of this in context in my personal life, and I cannot allow it to dominate my mind. God wants me to regularly focus my mind on other things. My own case is but one example of our constant need for God's assistance in keeping an occupation from becoming a preoccupation.

☑ **ACTION:** Pause and assess your own situation. Some surveys suggest that, on a scale of one to ten, money is roughly in the middle of life's priorities for most people. Where would you place money in your list of priorities? As a Christian, are you content with where it is? Would you be content, with the author of Proverbs, to say "Give me neither poverty nor riches"? Why or why not?

Attitudes to money and materialism   Studying the way other people behave can be very beneficial – provided that we do so with open minds, prepared to learn from what we observe. The following four case studies introduce some people with very different attitudes towards money.

It's ours to save Avril and David are married and in their early thirties. They are both professionals – a corporate lawyer and a financial analyst, respectively. Life for them is mainly about earning money and achieving success through their work. They have many peers with the same outlook – and the pressures, divorces and broken relationships to match. Avril and David have no children, and they'd like to keep it that way. When they take time to relax they spend it in the sports center, occasionally taking extravagant trips to exotic locations. And they go to expensive restaurants – "just to catch up after our hectic week". By any standards, Avril and David are affluent. "After all, we need to earn a lot of money to justify all our years of training and to sustain our lifestyle – there has to be some reward!" The couple met at a Christian campus event. Since then, their enthusiasm for Christian matters has waned a lot. Nowadays, they visit church about as frequently as they visit the dentist. But they like the connection. "It adds another dimension to our life, and quite a few of our clients like a bit of faith in the mix." They earn a lot, but give little. Videos on poverty and famine in Africa sometimes touch their hearts – but not too much. "After all you wouldn't know where to begin to solve these problems." They are big on savings, money management and personal financial security, but they get a bit annoyed about appeals for money for Christian causes. "Why doesn't everybody else keep their financial affairs in good order?" Responding to God's love through giving, stewardship and tithing is simply not on their agenda. "Our priority at this stage in life is saving – after all, you never know what the future might bring. At some point in the future we'll set up a tax efficient trust for good causes." Avril and David are self-contained; they have found a way to keep their consciences clear; and they have put God in a box of their own design. And it's quite a small box. Their money and all of their other resources belong to them. For them, Christian faith is at the margin – but still a good thing to have. And it has nothing to do with *their* money.

It's ours to spend Brian doesn't often get really stirred up by his pastor's teaching. In fact, what Joe the pastor has to say rarely makes much of an impression on Brian. Brian gets fired up every day by his business, sometimes by a good ball game on TV and, rarely, by a great iron shot from a bunker. But this time he was fired up by church – and he was mad at Joe. Joe had just given his third talk in a month on money and possessions, and it was too much for Brian. "I come to church to forget about work and money. I can think about these things any day of the week. Why can't this guy stick to some good Bible stories? That's the kind of thing the kids need to hear." Joe got the brunt of this anger when he greeted Brian leaving church. But Joe was an experienced pastor, and he knew precisely what to expect when he preached on this unpopular and often sensitive subject. "Brian, maybe the fact that you're hurting means you need to learn more about how important this topic is to God." That was the last straw. Brian ranted and raved all the way home. And Joan agreed with him. "Why in the world should we try to figure out what God might think about the way we allocate our money? That's taking Christianity too far." Brian and Joan had been very successful in the insurance business. They were both great at sales and customer service. As partners, they had made their first million by the age of thirty. Now, at forty-two, life was good – very good. They had vacation homes on the beach and in the mountains (although it was getting difficult to find time to enjoy these luxuries). They saw their biggest needs being more time for holidays (they only managed six foreign vacations the previous year) and memberships in better country clubs. It wasn't easy to fit church into all of this, but they did give regularly. "I don't know what Joe's problem is – we give our dues to the church. We could give more – but not under that kind of pressure!"

It's yours to ask Mary and Bill Neilsen struggle with both employment and money. Mary is a homemaker who has devoted her life to her family and to caring for everyone around her. "We know we can call Mary if we have a crisis", her neighbors would all say. Mary and Bill have two teenage girls, Madge and Gill, who share their mother's concern for others. As a family, they regularly provide a foster home for disadvantaged teenage girls and take disabled children on vacations with them. The girls both work as volunteers in local children's homes. Many friends observe, "If you want to see Christian love in practice, visit the Neilsen home." Bill has recurring health problems, and as a result it has been very difficult for him to hold down a regular teaching post. He has no thought of promotion – only of surviving, maintaining his modest income and supporting his family. Saving is something he hears about other people doing, but he has little personal experience of it. He does know about tithing – because he read about it in the Bible, and because he and Mary have practiced it since they were married as graduate students. The Neilsen family is not wealthy. Their neighborhood is not grand. Their home is very modest. Indeed, most things about them are unremarkable – except their generosity of spirit. Mary and Bill are generous with their time, love and money. Mary often says to needy people, "Whatever we have is yours." And she means it. She assures them, "Don't worry about us, we have more than enough." She doesn't realize that she is speaking the language of Jesus of Nazareth. But she does know who owns her money. This family can give you endless illustrations of how it is more blessed to give than receive. To meet them is to be humbled. Their faith has everything to do with their money.

It's yours, Lord – take it John Legrange astonished everybody when he became a Christian. The transformation was remarkable. "God and Legrange are a new couple" and "Smooth John takes to religion" were among the more printable headlines in the popular media. John had always been in the public eye, and he was regularly associated with scandal of one sort or another. Broken marriages, the use of soft drugs and allegations concerning the illegal use of firearms were among the more colorful parts of his bio. He often appeared in tabloid magazines, usually pictured in one of his own nightclubs. He never seemed to be far from the rich and famous, and his contributions to good causes were legendary. Everyone admired his charity – except the local police, who had good reason to be suspicious about where some of his wealth had come from. But now things were different – very different. "My journey to get to know Jesus has been long and painful. There's so much in my life I now need to put right." So he set about doing that. He contacted everybody that he knew he had cheated and paid them back. He put his nightclubs up for sale, pledging the proceeds to mission work in rundown urban communities. He tried, and failed, to put his marriage back together – the trust had gone. He prayed that time and his changed behavior would bring healing there. He wanted to know what he should do with his money. He really believed that it belonged to God, and that he should offer it all to him. "Isn't this what Christians do?" he asked his pastor George. "It depends. Some do, but most don't. You take the Bible a bit literally, John. Maybe you should think this through for a while." John was rather confused by this advice, but he was determined to press ahead anyway. He was also vulnerable, since there were so many people who were very willing to take his money – and not always with Christian intentions. His lifestyle as a Christian was very different, and so much of what he owned was not important to him anymore. "Why are other Christians not thinking along the same lines?" He received so many different answers to that question that he thought that he might write a book about it sometime. "Whose money is it anyway?" was his working title.

☑ **ACTION:** Consider the following questions:

1. What, if anything, in Avril and David's situation helped you to see your own attitudes more clearly? How will you act upon what you have learned?

2. Do you ever resent challenges to your giving by your pastor or other Christian teachers? What is at the root of such feelings?

3. What could you learn from the Neilsens' lifestyle and choices?

4. If John were on your prayer list, how would you pray for him?

God's design: A change of mind

The Bible makes it clear that God wants to renew our minds – to shape us to his thoughts, ways and purposes. While we might maintain that we can be "neutral" thinkers, this is an unsustainable claim. Neither can we say that our behavior does not reflect our thoughts. Striving and pushing ahead, as well as the desire to possess, are part of human nature. Paul sees this with great clarity. "Those who live according to the sinful nature have their minds set on what that nature desires; but those who live in accordance with the Spirit have their minds set on what the Spirit desires."[1] The critical issue is what we set our minds on, since that determines all of our activities. Paul sees that "mind setting" requires divine intervention. "And the peace of God, which transcends all understanding, will guard your hearts and your minds in Christ Jesus."[2]

"The Christian mind has succumbed to the secular drift with a degree of weakness and nervelessness unmatched in Christian history" – Henry Blamires

FIGURE 3.1 GOD'S DESIGN: A CHANGE OF MIND*

DULLED

Depraved   Darkened   Unspiritual

CHANGED

Salvation and the
entry of the Spirit of God

Understanding

Discernment

OPENED

Enlightenment

Obedience

CHALLENGED - - ➤ The Mind of Christ

*Based on Rom. 8, Phil. 2, 2 Cor. 10

Figure 3.1 describes the process by which God, through his grace, transforms an individual's mind from darkness to light. This change is mystical and practical, wonderful and challenging. Part of God's whole design is to change our minds about money in particular. How does this work?

Dulled: In this natural condition people earn, spend and save money to achieve personal ends. While these people may apply some "spiritual" and moral principles when considering how to allocate their money, these principles are not necessarily Christian. If they do have vaguely Christian ideas, these don't influence their behavior.

Changed: The Spirit enters the heart and mind of the new Christian. As a result, the changed person may be prompted to ask questions about money – possibly for the first time. What and who is it for? What does it mean that Jesus is now Lord of my money and possessions? How should I change my behavior to reflect a new set of priorities and gain the promised blessing? God switches the lights on, and the Christian begins to see the world through different eyes.

Opened: The maturing Christian develops a deeper understanding of obedience and discernment. This person begins to realize not only that the Bible has a lot to say about money, but also that it is central to the mission of Jesus' followers. He or she considers alternative options for earning and giving that would never have occurred to him or her before. It is only as the believer reaches this stage that he or she can begin to serve God.

Challenged: The mature believer faces the challenge to change and the accompanying demands. "What lifestyle is right for me?" "Where are my treasures and my heart?" "How do I allocate the money I earn?" "Whose money is it?" These are urgent questions. The Christian can only reach this point by knowing the word of God and being willing to be led by his Spirit.

> ☑ **ACTION:** Prayerfully reflect on this process of "changing your mind" – thanking God that he has transformed you by his grace, as no one else is able to do. Where would you identify yourself in this process? If you cannot yet say that you are "challenged", what do you need to do to move to the next level of maturity?

Rejecting God's design: The effects of materialism and consumerism

God's designs are flawless. But in matters of money and possessions we often reject God's perfect design, leaving it on the cutting room floor in favor of some flawed and selfish design of our own. Satan is anxious to distract us, to disrupt and even reverse the process outlined in Figure 3.1. Above all, Satan does not want us to call upon God's countervailing power. What is it about money that makes us want to put it beyond God's reach? There are two issues in particular that often tempt Christians to choose their own designs and ignore God's design.

1. Materialism: I have never met a Christian who wants to acknowledge that he is a materialist – it's just too nasty, violent and soiled a concept. Many western Christian communities have constructed a culture of denial about materialism. Yet Jesus gives us several very sharp warnings about it. "Watch out! Be on your guard against all kinds of greed; a man's life does not consist in the abundance of his possessions."[3] Moreover, it's a theme that recurs throughout the Bible and is invariably described in severe language. Paul observes, for example, "For the love of money is a root of all kinds of evil. Some people, eager for money, have wandered from the faith and pierced themselves with many griefs."[4] We cannot say that we have not been warned. But most of us are under the illusion that we have our money and possessions under control. While we see others doing it, we ourselves would never visit mammon's altar. As we have seen, not having money does not exempt one from being a materialist – it's a question of what occupies the heart and mind. Whether we have money or not, if our lives are centered around its accumulation we are materialistic. "What's the problem? Everyone else is. And don't we need to be working for economic growth and wealth creation for the good of humankind?" Yes – but not at the expense of Christ being the Lord of our lives.

"Materialism, open or disguised, is the logical result of thinking that above and beyond this world there is nothing else" – Stephen Alford

Materialism fosters amnesia concerning God's provision, eroding our ability to think straight and fostering a spirit of disobedience.

"When I fed them, they were satisfied; when they were satisfied, they became proud; then they forgot me"[5]

While we may trifle with materialism, God warns that it brings many dangers. The Bible stresses three of these dangers in particular. First, materialism destroys spiritual life. The Old Testament portrays Israel as a bride who has become a prostitute because of her love for material things. "'But you have lived as a prostitute with many lovers – would you now return to me?' declares the LORD."[6] Although we might shrink from the starkness of this metaphor, it reflects God's unequivocal stance. In a totally different time and culture, the Spirit told a church, "You say, 'I am rich; I have acquired wealth and do not need a thing.' But you do not realize that you are wretched, pitiful, poor, blind and naked. I counsel you to buy from me gold refined in the fire, so that you can become rich."[7] These words contain a grim diagnosis – but also a proven cure.[8]

Second, the Bible emphasizes the close association between materialism and pride. "Here now is the man who did not make God his stronghold but trusted in his great wealth and grew strong by destroying others!"[9] "For who makes you different from anyone else? What do you have that you did not receive? And if you did receive it, why do you boast as though you did not?"[10] The central issue here is this: if you have faith in yourself, who needs faith in the Lord? This is a particular challenge in an age that values individualism, independence and self-development. These are not evil in and of themselves, but if they divert our minds from faith in God they become both evil and destructive. John Blanchard once observed, "In the world in which we live today it takes a miracle for a man not to be a materialist". That miracle is the miracle of grace.

Third, the Bible shows us that materialism always distracts the Christian from his or her core purpose. Jesus explains the parable of the sower in this way: "The one who received the seed that fell among the thorns is the man who hears the word, but the worries of this life and the deceitfulness of wealth choke it, making it unfruitful."[11] When our concerns are materialistic, our lives are unfruitful. It is easy to see this in the lives of others. Can we see it in ourselves?

2. Consumerism: For our purposes here we define consumerism as the advocacy of a high rate of consumption and spending as the basis of a sound economy. Western culture implicitly tags on to that definition "... and as the basis for a sound life", and many people buy into that belief. We revel in stories of economic and financial success, which in turn become the basis for setting (often unrealistic) benchmarks for our own lives and those of our contemporaries. But I have a confession to make here. As an economist and businessman, I know that it is necessary for large numbers of individuals to strive to succeed and to be imaginative, entrepreneurial and innovative. This success is at the root of economic progress, generating finance for education, health and welfare. As a Christian, however, I also recognize the moral hazards inherent in this economic system. But I cannot be a hypocrite and argue that I do not think this striving is both important and necessary. The challenge is to manage these goals without being managed by them. I have long concluded that the solution to this conundrum begins and finishes with the motivation of the heart.

"Consumerism is an idol that Christians are in danger of being seduced by. It competes to become the story within which we live our lives" — Craig Bartholomew [12]

It is probably fair to say that, in our diverse and shrinking world, consumerism is *the* religion of the twenty-first century. It's the part of the globalization process that reaches into most corners of the world.

Although this phenomenon is not new, it has many new dimensions, including the incredible breadth of consumer choice as to what, when and how to purchase; products and services, with the marketing campaigns to match, tailored to the needs of individuals and households; the shortened life of products that generates a "use it and discard it" mentality that extends from possessions into relationships, including marriage; and the priority of customer satisfaction. All of these factors have further implications in terms of longer working hours and demands, higher standards of living, and so on. For many people, buying is living, shopping is religion, debt is nothing, pleasure is consuming.

Such an environment presents many difficult challenges for the Christian. Firstly, the imperatives of consumption can both define and distort our value systems. The list of "must have" items extends to all areas of our lives – what we wear and own can determine how we are perceived, how we conduct our relationships and so on. Secondly, our buying habits and choices sustain the assumption that freedom of choice is the inherent right of every consumer – whether or not the available choices accord with our principles. Consumerism becomes a perceived source of liberty – in everything. Thirdly, the spirit of consumerism is the mortal enemy of contentment. By definition, having everything is not having enough – since in the pursuit we constantly extend both our needs and wants. How should our Christianity shape our consumption? Consumerism, taken to extremes, destroys contentment and blinds us to a kingdom perspective.[13] We need to be alert to all of these issues as we pursue the answer to the question "Whose money is it anyway?"

Taking stock

Describe how materialism and consumerism affect your life.

Imagine yourself explaining to God how much of your mental energies you devote to money and possessions. Do you feel comfortable with what you would say? Why or why not?

Try writing a short profile of how your attitudes to money have changed since you became a Christian.

Think and pray about this statement by Franz Werfel: "Materialism is organised emptiness of the spirit."

Further reading

Blamires, Harry, *Recovering the Christian Mind* (Downers Grove, IL: IVP, 1989).
Rowe, Dorothy, *The Real Meaning of Money* (London: HarperCollins, 1998).
Sire, James W., *Discipleship of the Mind* (Downers Grove, IL: IVP, 1990).
Swinson, Antonia, *Root of All Evil?* (Edinburgh: Saint Andrews Press, 2003).

Endnotes

1 Rom. 8:5.
2 Phil. 4:7.
3 Lk. 12:15.
4 1 Tim. 6:10.
5 Hos. 13:6.
6 Jer. 3:1.
7 Rev. 3:17-18.
8 We will return to this passage in Chapter 5.
9 Ps. 52:7.
10 1 Cor. 4:7.
11 Mt. 13:22.
12 C. Bartholomew and T. Moritz, *Christ and Consumerism: A Critical Analysis of the Spirit of the Age* (Carlisle: Paternoster, 2000), p. 81. This series of essays provides thought-provoking insights into consumerism.
13 For a disturbing assessment of some of these dangers see David Wells, *God in the Wasteland: The Reality of Truth in a World of Fading Dreams* (Leicester: IVP, 1994).

4
Facing up to the Attack

"Command those who are rich in this present world not to be arrogant nor to put their hope in wealth, which is so uncertain, but to put their hope in God, who richly provides us with everything for our enjoyment." (1 Tim. 6:17)

Outline What role does spiritual warfare play in how we think about money? We need to clearly understand the battle in order to avoid and overcome further hazards.

Warfare? What warfare?
We don't stand a chance in the battles surrounding money unless we see the conflict for what it really is.

Case Study No. 1: David and Goliath
This familiar incident in David's life teaches us four lessons that we can carry into our spiritual battles with money.

Understanding the battleground
We are particularly vulnerable to attacks concerning money in five different areas: idolatry, trust, contentment, greed and slavery.

Case Study No. 2: Foundations
This section applies a familiar parable to the role that money plays in the foundations of our lives. We examine the project, the builders, the foundations, the lessons and the outcomes.

Warfare? What warfare?

While spiritual warfare is not often specifically associated with money and possessions, it should be. The battle metaphor also brings the issues into sharp relief. Materialism and consumerism consistently clamor for our minds and attention, but few Christians seem to want to fight against this. The battle is almost subliminal – the enemy can deploy all his resources, at times largely unopposed; resistance is often very weak; and surrender is almost inevitable. The habits of consumerism are so ingrained that none of us think we are addicts. This is a bleak picture with grave consequences. What do we lose, and what does the victor gain? The spoil includes captured Christian hearts; lots of kingdom money never meeting a kingdom cause; minds more preoccupied with earning than giving; and many Christians abdicating their role in allocating God's wealth on earth. It is agonizing to think that those who belong to Christ are serving money and Satan's cause rather than the God who created them and died to redeem them. Because forewarned is forearmed, however, we will examine the weapons that the enemy uses.

The Bible regularly reminds us that we are in the presence of hostile forces as we try to live for Christ. "For our struggle is not against flesh and blood, but against the rulers, against the authorities, against the powers of this dark world and against the spiritual forces of evil in the heavenly realms."[1] The power of money is a key component of that struggle. In his commentary on this verse, John Stott reminds us that the forces of darkness are powerful, wicked and evil.[2] In matters of money, these forces can easily convert what has such capacity for good into an all-consuming evil. It's not surprising, therefore, that this verse follows advice to "put on the full armor of God so that you can take your stand against the devil's schemes".[3] None of our enemies can overcome this divine offense and defense, as we will see in the story of David and Goliath.

"Keeping our heads despite the pull of pleasure is as hard a task as any for the affluent believer" – J.I. Packer

---

☑ **ACTION:** Read 1 Samuel 16 and 17.

Case Study No. 1: David and Goliath Our purpose in revisiting this familiar scene from Old Testament history is to extract the lessons that we can learn from David's victory over Goliath. Several of these lessons give us insights into our daily mental battles in a world besotted with money and possessions. The Philistine army was literally on David's doorstep, and a contest of champions was a common way to solve disputes between nations. David's battle with Goliath was physical, and the victory decisive – while our battles against the power and lure of money are often less visible, and their outcomes less evident. But there are still many similarities between these struggles, and the following are among the many lessons we can learn from this incident.

Go with God's blessing: God's affirmation, "All right, go ahead, and may the LORD be with you",[4] (NLT) enables David to approach this awesome task with a quiet confidence and assurance. David did not have the blessing of his brothers or his peers, but he did have God's. Do we look for God's blessing in our daily financial transactions? If we understood that it is a battle that is beyond our strength to win, we might seek God's blessing more urgently.

"There is no winning without warfare; there is no opportunity without opposition; there is no victory without vigilance"
— Alan Redpath

Know the enemy: Not all of life's enemies appear as large, visible, loud or assured as Goliath did. Many of our enemies are much subtler, but their threat to dishonor God's name is the same. Our reaction to these enemies should match David's sense of outrage towards Goliath. "Who is this uncircumcised Philistine that he should defy the armies of the living God?"[5] Goliath's destructive capacity was obvious, and everyone saw what was coming in the battle on the valley floor. Most of us fighting against materialism or consumerism do not see our battles ahead of us – not, of course, unless we ask God to alert us. We may not seek God's guidance and wisdom very often because we don't recognize our enemies as potential aggressors. Will it take losing the battle before we're even aware it's being fought for reality to dawn on us?

Be willing to fight: For David, motivation was everything. His confidence in God was foremost in his mind. "Let no one lose heart on account of this

"We are not here to commune with darkness but to conquer it" – Vance Havner

Philistine; your servant will go and fight him."[6] In preparation, David reviewed his spiritual bio and recalled the grace of God in his life on many previous occasions. Perhaps we simply give up fighting against the temptations posed by money sometimes because we have no memory of victory. We may find it all too difficult, too counter-cultural, too demanding. Sometimes the hardest victory is victory over self, and that can be true with regard to possessions.

Take the correct equipment: It's not surprising that King Saul wanted to equip David with his finest fighting gear – after all, he was his champion for the battle. But David knew that these were the wrong weapons – the trappings of the king would achieve nothing. So, guided by the Lord of the battle, he chose his own weapons. A shepherd's staff, a sling and five stones were enough to make the enemy laugh – long and hard. David, however, affirms his equipping with a powerful statement. "All those gathered here will know that it is not by sword or spear that the LORD saves; for the battle is the LORD's, and he will give all of you into our hands."[7] And he did! So, too, our battles with money and materialism can only be won when we acknowledge that "the weapons we fight with are not the weapons of the world. On the contrary, they have divine power to demolish strongholds."[8] With David, we need to praise God for this power and victory.

☑ **ACTION:** Do you seek God's blessing daily? What exactly are the battles you need to fight with regard to money and possessions? (Consider where your money goes and where your treasure is. Analyze the daily choices you make regarding your lifestyle – are you confusing desires with needs?) If you have ever recognized, fought and won a spiritual battle over money, thank God for that outcome and list the things you learned from that experience that you can use in the future. If not, equip yourself with the correct equipment and prepare for battle.

Understanding the battleground

Howard Dayton tells an interesting story about the Crusades in the twelfth century. The crusaders often employed mercenaries to fight on their behalf, but because they were in a "religious" war, they insisted that the mercenaries were baptized before fighting. As they were being baptized, they held their swords out of the water to identify the one thing in their lives that Jesus Christ did not control. In effect, they were saying that they had the freedom to use their swords in any way they wished.[10] That is exactly what many Christians do with money – setting it apart as something to be used solely at their own discretion, beyond the influence of the Spirit. So we might individually ask, "Am I holding my purse out of the reach of God's influence?" "Is it my intention to keep it there?" As we look at some of the ways in which we do this, we can identify the areas in our lives and aspects of our personality where God needs to transform us. The business term "change control" describes the important and continuous process whereby, in fulfilling a large contract, both parties have to formally agree to make changes in a project – and usually accept the cost consequences. So it is with the Christian life. The Spirit will teach us about what needs to be changed. The question is whether we will agree, obey and implement the change. It is a two-sided matter. Following are five of the areas in which we are most vulnerable to disobeying God in money matters.[11] One way or another, most of us need to change in all of these areas.

"Be self-controlled and alert. Your enemy the devil prowls around like a roaring lion looking for someone to devour" [9]

Idolatry: The Bible declares that there is a close link between avarice and vesting money with a divine status. Most Christians are appalled by this suggestion, knowing how serious a charge making a god out of money is. Yet God speaks some very sharp words on this subject. Before we quibble about that, remember that he knows us from the inside out. He has *all* the empirical evidence available. We know, therefore, that we need this advice – however unwelcome it sounds. Here are two of the many examples. "The images of their gods you are to burn in the fire. Do not covet the silver and gold on them, and do not take it for yourselves, or you will be ensnared by it, for it is detestable to the LORD your God."[12] Few things have the power to ensnare us as money does. And it usually traps us by stealth. "For of this you can be sure: No immoral, impure or greedy person – such a man is an idolater – has any inheritance in the kingdom of Christ and of God."[13] Most worshipers readily acknowledge their idols. But money is a special kind of god, because nobody seems willing to admit to being a worshiper. As we have seen, the worship of money is associated with many spending rituals and sacred symbols – including logos, brands and designer labels. And, if no one else did, God clearly saw wealth as a rival when it came to the call to worship. And, of course, he was right. Making an idol out of money can lead us to steal from God. "Will a man rob God? Yet you rob me. But you ask, 'How do we rob you?' In tithes and offerings."[14]

Trust: The text from 1 Timothy with which we started this chapter makes a strong connection between wealth and uncertainty. How is it, then, that many Christians associate money primarily with guaranteeing security – both their own and that of their families? At one level this seems quite normal and unremarkable. You might even argue that this is part of the obligation of the wage earners in any family, and I would agree. The many different ways in which wealth is subject to erosion today – economic and stock market crises, unemployment, technological change, taxation, social and political disruption and so on might make us more aware of that uncertainty. Yet we still cling to money as if it were durable and worthy of our trust. But is it? The problem is that we are tempted to place our confidence in money instead of trusting God. When we do that, we call into question our basic relationship of faith in God. Our trust is badly misplaced, wrongly directed and fundamentally flawed. Jesus clearly associated storing earthly wealth with decay, destruction and robbery.[15] We need to expect to lose it – or be disappointed with a life dedicated to achieving wealth. How many of us pray: "Give me neither poverty nor riches, but give me only my daily bread. Otherwise, I may have too much and disown you and say, 'Who is the LORD?'"[16] This idea does not sit well with our culture – nor was it meant to. It's the language of the citizens of heaven who know where to put their trust and who know how vital it is never to forget who is Lord.

"If we have not quiet in our minds, outward comfort will do no more for us than a golden slipper on a gouty foot" – John Bunyan

Contentment: Sometimes described as "an inexhaustible treasure", contentment is a rare commodity – not least among Christians, where God expects it to flourish.

Money fosters restlessness and discontent in so many people, both rich or poor. "Keep your lives free from the love of money and be content with what you have, because God has said, 'Never will I leave you; never will I forsake you.'"[17] This challenging verse contains a *promise* that underpins a disciple's contentment – *not* his or her income, savings, wealth or financial aspirations. This is particularly hazardous territory in the spiritual battleground. "How can anyone be content in a consumer driven society?" "I am on my way up the ladder of life – this is not the time to be content with anything" "I'm a businessman. If I'm content, society suffers because of my lack of drive and ambition – so what do you say to that?" "You have to understand that the important thing in life is to make money." We have all heard, spoken or thought these sorts of comments. They identify all the problems but ignore the promise. They focus on the external and deny the internal. It's like trying to live the Christian life without the Spirit. Contentment will not come from our wealth or our society, but only from the goodness of God. Paul observed that "godliness with contentment is great gain".[18] By this standard, many of us are poor in the midst of our affluence. Indeed, some of us may have become impoverished by our wealth.

"Some people are so poor they only have money" – Ivor Powell

Greed: In anyone's vocabulary, this is a nasty word. John Chrysostom called greed "an illness of the soul". Greed is another sin that few of us would ever confess, and one that we rarely notice in our own behavior. In telling the parable of the rich fool, Jesus warned, "Watch out! Be on your guard against all kinds of greed; a man's life does not consist in the abundance of his possessions."[19] In order to guard our lives from greed, we need to be aware of the different guises and characteristics of Christian greed. It can take the form of conspicuous consumption while discounting or ignoring the financial needs of others; of refusing divine interference regarding the allocation of "our" money; of upgrading our spending with no thought about the spiritual implications of being on a financial treadmill, and so on. Greed commonly surfaces in certain circumstances. For example, greed has destroyed many a family through a contested will and has unfairly enhanced the wealth of employers who exploit vulnerable employees. In the New Testament, the greedy were those who refused to share their possessions – God had touched their lives, but not their pockets.

"Most men pray more for full purses than for pure hearts." – Thomas Watson

Are we "greedy" in God's eyes? A famous philanthropist once observed that "to distribute my money is a harder and more anxious task than making it". Regardless of our financial position, many of us can identify with that sentiment. But distributing our money is so much easier when we look at it from God's perspective. The absence of any trace of greed is one of the marks of true discipleship.

Slavery: One of the unintended consequences of focusing on owning and accumulating money is slavery, or addiction. A commodity that was designed to be in our service gradually, almost imperceptibly, becomes our master. The central challenge for some people is that their spending either equals or exceeds what they earn. The image of the hamster on the wheel comes to mind – and the human exercise of becoming a slave of money is just as futile.

"Few people have the spiritual resources to be both wealthy and godly" – Erwin Lutzer

Many Christians are slaves to money – sometimes because they were prisoners of their careers and ambitions before they experienced Christ's freedom. Such people have many common characteristics. They are fiercely independent and individualistic – a slave to no one. They struggle in vain to find contentment. They are constantly readjusting their lifestyle to make sure that they remain at the same level as their peers. The short-term indicators for this include homes, cars, jewelry, clothing, vacations, prestigious schools for their children and much more. In this form of bondage, one set of invisible chains leads to the next. Paul's remark about lifestyle is incredibly relevant today: "we drifted along the stream of this world's ideas of living ...".[20] Many do drift, but some Christians have knowingly steered their lives in that direction. Is your present position due to drifting or steering? Regardless of the route, the result is serving mammon instead of God. Mammon is a demanding master, leading Christians to acquire money by whatever means, to sin to keep money (through cheating on tax returns, for example) and to hold on to money even when clearly prompted by the Spirit to give it away.

> ☑ **ACTION:** The paragraphs above portray some ugly conditions with some very negative consequences for both our personal lives and Christian witness. Identify the area in which you struggle most: idolatry, trust, contentment, greed or slavery. Decide upon one action you can take in this area to institute "change control". Based on what we learned from David's battle with Goliath, how will God equip you to make this change?

Some have much, and some have more,
Some are rich and some are poor,
Some have little, some have less,
Some have not a cent to bless;
Their empty pockets, yet possess
True riches in true happiness.
– John Oxenham

Case Study No. 2: Foundations

We have seen that an excessive preoccupation with money can lead Christians to build their lives on a very unstable foundation. Since all of the difficulties discussed above are by-products of that instability, we will turn now to consider what role money plays in the foundation of your life.

"Do not wear yourself out to get rich; have the wisdom to show restraint. Cast but a glance at riches, and they are gone"[21]

Since it has been so long since some of us last visited our foundation, this exercise may be more like going on an archaeological dig than visiting

"The sermon on the mount is not to be commended, it is to be carried out" — Martyn Lloyd-Jones

an active construction site. The story of the two builders who chose different foundations, and paid the consequences in a storm, comes at the end of Jesus' Sermon on the Mount. The teacher is edging his audience towards decision time. Having heard the words, his audience needs to respond by making some difficult choices.

✔ ACTION: Read Matthew 7:24-29.

The project: The Christian life is a project – with aims and objectives, a set of resources and tasks, a beginning and an end. Each of us, therefore, has to ask what we are trying to achieve and whose advice we are taking. This parable is founded on these assumptions. Twice Jesus refers to the advice that the two builders received "... these words of mine ..."[22] Now that our attention has been directed to what God has to say about money, our challenge is to build these principles into our project – or reinforce them, if they are already there. Both of the builders in the parable had been taught the theory of good building. But only one designed his project in the light of it.

The builders: People choose widely different project designs for their lives. But, in God's eyes, there are only two types of builders – the obedient and the disobedient. The two builders in this parable may have been working to a common house design, but they labored under quite different assumptions. Similarly, you and I might share the desire to live to God's design. (While our 'projects' as Christians take many different shapes, they have the same designer.) But one of us thinks that God has no interest in money, and lives accordingly. That one of us is disobedient.

The foundations: Every life is built upon some sort of foundation. Many people lay down several foundations before they get the right one. And some never seem to be able to find a foundation that they can build upon. All of us, therefore, need to ask "What is my foundation?" This is not an easy question, because the foundation is one of the least visible parts of a building. Few of us ask such questions about our lives. Among the many likely answers are family, business, sports, fitness, friends, church and so on. Some may even confess that, implicitly or explicitly, money is foundational to them. We continually build upon our foundation, assuming that it is in good shape. It might be good to reexamine yours, checking whether it has substance and verifying if it will survive God's scrutiny.

The lessons: Perhaps the most important lesson that this parable teaches is that we need to take time to think. Because one of these builders was in too much of a hurry when he built his house, he didn't pay enough attention to the foundation. All of us need to ask how busy we can afford to be.[23] For example, is money part of your foundation more by default than by intention? Busyness can be a product of career progression, peer pressure, the business or professional environment in which you work, or the neighborhood in which you live. While this parable implies that both builders were interested in the kingdom, only one believed the king. And ultimately that was revealed. The moral? Do not wait for the storms of life before checking your foundation.

The outcomes: The teaching of this parable is stark, uncompromising and unmistakable. The houses faced a single test, but there were two distinct results. One house stood, and one fell. The Bible emphasizes the accountability of Jesus' disciples. Our lives will be subject to test and evaluation. There are no grounds for thinking that our custodianship of money will be excluded from that evaluation. It is difficult to see how money alone – with all of its potential for good – could ever be seen as a "foundation on the rock".[24] On the contrary, money is like sand in that it shifts quickly and significantly in the storms of life. It holds no guarantees. No one should plan to approach the judgement seat of Christ with a life founded on money.

☑ **ACTION:** Do you have more in common with the wise builder or the foolish builder? Just how "foundational" is money in the project of your life? What might make a better foundation for your life?

Taking stock

Were you conscious of money being part of your spiritual warfare? Having read this chapter, how has your perspective changed?

Have you ever been conscious of greed affecting your willingness to give money away? If not greed, are there other words you would use?

Are you content with your attitude to money and possessions? Why or why not?

"Slavery to the power of money is always best seen in others." Do you agree? What can you see in yourself in relationship to such slavery?

What does an inspection of the foundation of your life reveal?

Further reading

Campolo, Tony, *Carpe Diem* (Dallas: Word, 1994).

Dunn, Jim, *God's Wisdom for your Money* (Eastbourne: Kingsway, 2002).

Stott, John, *The Cross of Christ* (London: IVP, 1986).

Warren, Rick, *The Purpose Driven Life: What on Earth Am I Here For?* (Grand Rapids, MI: Zondervan, 2002).

Endnotes

1 Eph. 6:12.

2 John Stott, *God's New Society: The Message of Ephesians* (Leicester: IVP, 1979), p. 265.

3 Eph. 6:11.

4 1 Sam. 17:37.

5 1 Sam. 17:26.

6 1 Sam. 17:32.

7 1 Sam. 17:47.

8 2 Cor. 10:4.

9 1 Pet. 5:8.

10 Howard Dayton, *Your Money Counts* (Wheaton, IL: Tyndale, 1997), p. 11.

11 For an excellent and penetrating treatment of these issues see Brian Rosner, *How to Get Really Rich: A Sharp Look at the Religion of Greed* (Leicester: IVP, 1999).

12 Deut. 7:25.

13 Eph. 5:5.

14 Mal. 3:8. We will explore the nature and consequences of that theft in Chapter 7.

15 Mt. 6:19-21.

16 Prov. 30:8-9.

17 Heb. 13:5.

18 1 Tim. 6:6.

19 Lk. 12:15.

20 Eph. 2:2 (J.B. Phillips).

21 Prov. 23:4-5.

22 Mt. 7:24, 26.

23 The question of busyness and service is developed in much greater detail in Neil Hood, *Whose Life is it Anyway?* (Carlisle: Authentic Lifestyle, 2002).

24 Mt. 7:25.

5
Placing Confidence in Prosperity

"'For I know the plans I have for you' declares the LORD, 'plans to prosper you and not to harm you, plans to give you hope and a future.'" (Jer. 29:11)

Outline What the Christian's expectations for prosperity should be, and how much confidence we should place in prosperity, is a controversial topic. This chapter focuses primarily on material prosperity – its significance, meaning and limitations.

A personal view
In this section I share some of my perspectives about economic prosperity in the hope that it will help you to consider your own views.

What is prosperity?
We explore the basic features of prosperity and consider biblical teaching about its meaning and our own expectations.

Why have confidence in material prosperity?
Biblical material helps us to test and apply a number of the more common reasons for our confidence in prosperity.

The mirage of prosperity
An unusual incident and a foolish church reveal this mirage – namely Jesus' cleansing of the temple and the affluent church at Laodicea.

From mirage to reality
What is true spiritual prosperity in which we can have confidence?

A personal view   The overall economic prosperity of countries is of great interest to me. I have a particular perspective on this topic that leaves me with occasional dilemmas. I both trust and distrust prosperity. I regard it as necessary, but never sufficient. I have long had both an academic interest and extensive practical involvement in economic development – particularly, but not exclusively, in my own country. My interest stems from technical and intellectual concerns, as well as Christian ones. I find the widespread under-use and misuse of human resources disturbing, and the chasm that exists in so many places between the rich and the poor is shameful. Many Christians agree with this diagnosis but struggle to know how to respond. God's design for humankind includes work, including paid employment, and the full realization of individual potential. Because people need appropriate skills, attitudes and behavior to achieve these aims, they are more easily achieved in places that are rich in opportunity. Above all, the realization of these goals requires some measure of economic prosperity. Christians should work to help achieve that prosperity wherever they can. I confess that I have spent a lot of time and mental energy pursuing that aim – and not always without criticism. I have been involved in inward investment, private equity, business and corporate development, designing and implementing economic development strategies and so on. The more an economy prospers, the better able it is to deal with the employment and social inclusion of its people – a goal consistent with so much of Jesus' teaching. Luke's Gospel in particular is full of people who were excluded by others but were included by Christ. Economic prosperity in and of itself, at either a national or a personal level, is not the solution to all of society's ills. It can solve none of its spiritual ills and only some of its social ones. Nonetheless, properly used and directed, prosperity is invaluable.

"Prosperity is only an instrument to be used, not a deity to be worshipped" — Calvin Coolidge

The text from Jeremiah with which this chapter began is critical. The Bible contains many promises that God will prosper Christians – but not necessarily with material wealth. In God's eyes, protection, security of soul and confidence in his purposes are much more important ingredients of "prosperity" than money. God's view of prosperity goes much deeper than that.

☑ **ACTION:** How would you explain to an interested inquirer the fact that many Christians in developed countries appear to be relatively prosperous? Your answer will reflect your own perspective on prosperity. It will be helpful for you to clarify your views on this before you read further.

What is prosperity?

What do we mean by prosperity in the life of a Christian? Standard dictionary definitions of the word "prosperity" include ideas about thriving, experiencing favorable circumstances, flourishing, being successful, having good fortune and so on. All of these concepts are part of the world's view of prosperity – a view shared by many Christians. In the New Testament, however, the word used for "prosper" refers to getting help on a journey. So when Paul is anxious to visit Rome he writes, "I pray that now at last by God's will the way may be opened for me to come to you."[1] This idea occurs in a different context when Paul encourages the Corinthian church members to set aside a weekly sum for giving "as God has prospered him".[2] They were to respond to God's goodness through giving. The Old Testament, while warning about the dangers of prosperity, emphasizes a different angle. Francis Bacon summarized the differences as follows: "Prosperity is the blessing of the Old Testament, adversity is the blessing of the New which carries the greater benediction and the clearer revelation of God's favour." In the Old Testament there is a clear link between God's blessing and material prosperity in the lives of the patriarchs. So, for example, for Abraham, Isaac and Jacob, blessing and prosperity were almost synonymous.[3] Some Christians see these texts and others as authenticating a gospel of material prosperity[4] – a concept that seems alien to so much of Jesus' teaching.

"The figure of the Crucified invalidates all thought that takes success for its standards" – Dietrich Bonhoeffer

While all Christians hold in common the core beliefs of forgiveness for our sins, the indwelling of the Spirit and the hope of eternal life, there are many different perspectives on what this new life in Christ looks like. There are many different opinions, therefore, on what the Christian's expectation of prosperity should be and what form it should take. The following examples highlight a number of these differences and may help you to clarify your own views on this subject.

Financial: "God has promised to bless me in every dimension of my life, and I see no reason why that should not include money. Indeed, that's what I expect. I've seen God bless others in that way."

Spiritual: "Jesus has liberated me from my sins and delivered me from a life of addiction. This fills me with joy every day. Each new day is a bonus. Of course I want to receive his blessings, but prosperity for me is to be able to grow in my knowledge of him. Frankly I'm content with that."

Mental: "I'm an anxious person and prone to depression. I can't handle stress anymore. I just pray that the peace of God would really reign in my heart. I want God to prosper me by ruling my mind, will and emotions all the time. I would be more than satisfied with that blessing."

Physical: "I have been sick for so long that I just want God to heal me. This is my daily prayer. I know that there is so much else to being a Christian, but at the moment I'm afraid this is the only prosperity that interests me."

☑ **ACTION:** What are your expectations of prosperity? Where have these expectations come from? If your particular expectations of prosperity are not financial in nature, what is your view of material prosperity?

Why have confidence in material prosperity? For many people today, this is not a question at all – achieving material prosperity is a central career and life goal. "Isn't this what life is about?" "Surely having enough money will bring the quality of life and sense of personal well-being that we all want." There are many Christians, too, who live as if prosperity is what life is all about. A few years ago, I met an old school friend at an international rugby

"Prosperity is good campaigning weather for the devil — C.S. Lewis

match. It had been thirty-five years since we had last met, and we were both amazed that we instantly recognized each other. We talked about how our careers had progressed. He had lived all over the world and was very successful in financial circles. He then asked if I was still a Christian. When I said that I was, his response surprised me. "That's really great to hear. And your life isn't all about money is it? My life always has been." While both of us had prospered in material terms, only one of us believed that it mattered. But I confess that his high expectation of Christians made me think. If only our lives always reflected his assumption – but they don't. Why do so many people, including some Christians, place their confidence in material prosperity?

TABLE 5.1 WHY HAVE CONFIDENCE IN MATERIAL PROSPERITY?	
It's achievable:	The input is work, the output is success, the scorecard is wealth.
It's tangible:	Prosperity can be earned, touched, counted, stored and retrieved.
It's demonstrable:	Prosperity allows us to buy what can be shown, measured, compared and even flaunted.
It's sustainable:	Prosperity is a result of achievement and success – and its loss is a distant prospect that only happens to others.
It's durable:	Prosperity can erode away, but not if those possessing it are prudent and well advised – and it can be passed on to future generations.
It's enjoyable:	We can gain pleasure from it in an untold number of ways – some good, some hedonistic.

As you read through Table 5.1, you will notice that there are not too many Christian words or ideas here. Yet many of these thoughts about prosperity feature in our own minds. Although there is much pleasure in prosperity that leads to selfless giving and deploying wealth to the glory of God, it is dangerous to place our confidence in material prosperity.

We can stand affliction better than we can stand prosperity, for in prosperity we forget God"
— Dwight Moody

Jesus met many people with supreme confidence in prosperity. The Pharisees, for example, apparently expected both health and wealth as a result of their thorough adherence to the law. For them, life's formula was prosperity through compliance. They despised those who failed to meet their standards. Hence their recorded disgust with Jesus: "This man welcomes sinners and eats with them."[5] Many of Jesus' contacts were total failures in their eyes. Jesus regularly made the connection between attitudes to prosperity and spiritual health. When Jesus confronted him, the wealthy and corrupt tax collector Zacchaeus immediately displayed radically new attitudes to his fortune. He set out to make retribution to those he had cheated. The repayment plan that he set up himself suggests that he had much to answer for in terms of his past behavior. Jesus explains this in simple but very direct terms: "Today salvation has come to this house".[6] No other explanation was needed. This new disciple did not have the same confidence in wealth today as he had yesterday. Does your attitude to material prosperity reflect the fact that salvation has "come to your house" (regardless of how recently or long ago that event occurred)? Although we may not be corrupt like Zacchaeus and may have much less to sort out, the effect of Jesus' touch on our lives should be exactly the same.

Because Paul, too, was a Pharisee, he probably saw the absence of "prosperity" in Jesus' life as an indication that he was not the Messiah. Among the many evidences of the transformation of Paul the believer, therefore, are his Christian views on adversity and prosperity. He writes, for example, "For it has been granted to you on behalf of Christ not only to believe on him, but also to suffer for him";[7] and he follows this by saying, "But whatever was to my profit I now consider loss for the sake of Christ."[8] You do not need a degree in theology to see where Paul placed his confidence. Nor was he slow to confront those whose confidence was misplaced. He sharply rebukes a self-satisfied and high-minded Christian group in Corinth, for example: "For who makes you different from anyone else? What do you have that you did not receive? And if you did receive it, why do you boast as though you did not?"[9] Paul clearly saw that the Christian route to prosperity was through humble service to God. It would have been an insult to ask Paul "Whose money is it anyway?" He probably would have pointed us to a church in Macedonia of whom he wrote, "Out of the most severe trial, their overflowing joy and extreme poverty welled up in rich generosity."[10] While Paul does not celebrate their poverty, he is overwhelmed by the confidence in God that led them to give generously even though they were very poor. They could not be confident in material prosperity, because they had none. The foundation of their confidence was much more solid.

☑ **ACTION:** What is your "confidence index"? On a scale of 1-10, how confident are you in material prosperity as you plan your everyday life? Use the same scale to rank your confidence in God's provision with reference to financial matters. Spend some time praying about what you have learned.

The mirage of prosperity

Material prosperity is, in many ways, a mirage. It can be "wondered at" from a distance and yet turn out to be wholly illusory at close quarters. It can reflect and distort images of happiness, self-fulfillment, contentment and security. The idea that more money guarantees happiness is a classic delusion – there is much evidence to the contrary and none to confirm its truth. An increase in wealth can make individuals happier for a short time, but invariably they get used to it and desire more. In the United States, for example, the average income has trebled since the Second World War – but the proportion of people claiming to be very happy has fallen. The pattern is similar in Japan and Europe. And some poor countries report levels of happiness well above those in affluent countries.[11]

"I can say that I never knew what joy was until I gave up pursuing happiness, or care to live until I chose to die. For these two discoveries I am beholden to Jesus" – Malcolm Muggeridge

Christians are not exempt from being misled by this "mirage". We will look at what we can learn from two different biblical examples.

1. The angry Jesus In John 2:12-22, we see that the followers of Jesus did not have to wait too long to discover the strength of his views on the inappropriate pursuit of material prosperity. They learned this lesson in an unexpected place. It was the Jewish Passover, in mid-April, and all of the Jewish males in the region were flocking to Jerusalem for the feast. Jesus was clearly appalled by the commercialism of the temple worship and the exploitation of the poor, so he scattered the coins of the money changers and overturned their tables. This rare picture of Jesus reveals his intense anger and aggression. He spoke sharply to those selling doves: "Get these out of here! How dare you turn my Father's house into a market!"[12] What was going on here?

Why was Jesus so angry? Money and the attitude of the principal actors were doubtless both to blame. The temple offered many opportunities for prosperity to those with shrewd business minds. People had to pay a temple tax to gain access. Because there were so many different currencies in use, the tax could only be paid in selected coinage. And – guess what – people could only change their money at the temple, where they were charged a high commission. Huge sums were amassed as a result – a fact confirmed in secular literature when, for example, Crassus captured Jerusalem in 54 BC. But there's more. Sacrifices had to be offered, and they had to be pure. People brought their finest sheep and goats, but if the inspectors did not deem the animal pure it was condemned. And – of course – they could buy another one at the temple for an inflated price. By such activity, both in spirit and in practice, the temple was desecrated and God's worship was diminished. That is what angered Jesus.

"To be angry against sin is a high and holy thing" – C.H. Spurgeon

What had happened to the house of prayer? In Mark's records of this event, Jesus said, "My house will be called a house of prayer for all nations. But you have made it 'a den of robbers.'"[13] The temple had been taken over by the pursuit of material prosperity. The temple staff had more enthusiasm for trade than they had for God, and the spiritual heart of the nation was polluted as a result. The people forgot their calling. There was too much noise and too many sideshows to either speak much to, or hear much from, God. Jesus saw that these leaders had almost forgotten the purpose for which the temple had been built. Is it true that Christians who place too much confidence in prosperity today are unlikely to spend much time in prayer?

Who gives you the right? The words and actions of
Jesus were not well received. But advice that
hits hard at either our income or its allocation
rarely is well received – whether or not it comes
from God. Those Jesus accused at the temple
wanted evidence of the credentials that justified
this outburst. He told them about the other
temple – his body – that would in due course be
destroyed and raised again. It is essential that
we give God the right to challenge our
relationship to material prosperity. When did you
last bring that before him for his evaluation? Notice how quickly Jesus saw
through the veneer of temple worship and was able to distinguish between
the form and the substance. He has not lost any of his ability to do so.

> *"Ultimately there is no better index of one's spiritual state and condition than one's prayers" –*
> *D. Martyn Lloyd-Jones*

Notice the mirage of temple worship here – the whole temple apparatus
was designed to please God, yet when his Son visited it he found the people
focused on material prosperity and its worship distorted beyond
recognition. This did not happen overnight. It took generations of focus on
the wrong things to get to this point. Our focus on God's purposes can wane
much more quickly – perhaps especially in the context of prosperity.

2. Laodicea Read Revelation 3:14-22, a graphic description of a church in an
affluent society. Laodicea was one of the most prosperous cities in Asia
Minor at the time. The historian Pliny described it as a "distinguished city",
famed throughout the Roman world for its banking, its linen and wool
industries, and its medical school. The latter was particularly noted for the
development of an eye ointment. Christ highlights all of these "fame
factors" as he condemns their spiritual poverty, nakedness and blindness.
"You say, 'I am rich; I have acquired wealth and do not need a thing.' But
you do not realize that you are wretched, pitiful, poor, blind and naked."[14]
God is able to make us look through different lenses to see ourselves as we
really are. This has to be one of the most challenging verses in the Bible
about placing confidence in prosperity. Externally, they were affluent;
internally, they were impoverished.

The myth: Arrogance, self-esteem and self-reliance ooze from the
Laodiceans. Theirs is the story of the self-made man who completely forgets

about God's contribution. His supreme confidence in prosperity is all very real and tangible to his peers, but it counts for nothing with his God. His prosperity is a myth of his own making.

The mind: Prosperity has achieved what his sin once did – it has dulled his mind to God's message. "But you do not realize ..." Prosperity has completely taken over his energies and thought processes. As Vance Havner says, "God wants no man to be more prosperous than his soul." Sadly that is what happened there – and can still happen today.

The message: God offers the Laodiceans the solution to their problem. "I counsel you to buy from me gold refined in the fire, so you can become rich; and white clothes to wear, so you can cover your shameful nakedness; and salve to put on your eyes, so you can see."[15] This solution did not merely entail reallocating their wealth – it required them to refocus their lives. The remedy for them, and for us, lies in rediscovering their relationship with the Lord.

The Master: The Laodiceans were invited to listen to the one at the door of their lives – the one whom affluence and self-sufficiency had excluded. He was knocking for permission to re-enter. "Here I am! I stand at the door and knock." If your view of prosperity has put Christ outside your door, will you invite him in again?

> "There is a burden of care in getting riches; fear in keeping them; temptation in using them; guilt in abusing them; and a burden of account at last to be given concerning them"
> — Matthew Henry
> (1662–1714)

The great encouragement of this account is that, in spite of his condemnation of the foolish members of this church, the Lord remains gracious. Indeed this grace extends to inviting them to sit in the place of highest honor at his throne. And he shows them the way. Everything about grace is amazing!

From mirage to reality

Although worldly prosperity is a mirage, the New Testament and the new covenant herald a radical shift in our understanding of true wealth. There *is* a prosperity in which Christians can have absolute confidence – spiritual prosperity. In Paul's prayer for the Ephesians, for example, he says, "I pray also that the eyes of your heart may be enlightened in order that you may know the hope to which he has called you, the riches of his glorious inheritance in the saints, and his incomparably great power for us who believe."[16] The same power that raised Christ is available to deliver us from the deceptions of false prosperity. To the Colossians Paul writes, "To them God has chosen to make known among the Gentiles the glorious riches of this mystery, which is Christ in you, the hope of glory."[17] This is a prosperity shared among all in the kingdom. Look again at Table 5.1 through spiritual eyes – the only item that does not apply to this prosperity is that it's not achievable. We cannot earn it; it's a gift from God. Spiritual prosperity thrives in the midst of both adversity and material prosperity.

"There is in every heart a spark of heavenly fire which lies dormant in the broad daylight of prosperity, but which kindles up and beams and blazes in the dark hour of adversity" — Washington Irving

"Give, and it will be given to you. A good measure, pressed down, shaken together and running over, will be poured into your lap. For with the measure you use, it will be measured to you."[18] This measure signals a different type of confidence and brings a whole new meaning to prosperity.

Taking stock

What have you noticed about the "mirage" qualities of material prosperity in your own circumstances? What do these observations teach you about the nature of prosperity?

How do you interpret the Bible's promise to bless you as one of Jesus' disciples?

How would Jesus react if he were to enter your "temple treasury"? Is there anything that might generate similar passions as those we saw in the incident from John 2?

How important is money to your sense of spiritual prosperity?

What is the nature of your confidence in spiritual prosperity?

Further reading

Barron, Bruce, *The Health and Wealth Gospel* (Downers Grove, IL: IVP, 1987).

Beisner, E. Calvin, *Prosperity and Poverty* (Westchester: Crossway, 1988).

Ellul, Jacques, *Money and Power* (Downers Grove, IL: IVP, 1984).

Harris, Richard, *Is there a Gospel for the Rich?* (London: Mowbray, 1992).

Endnotes

1   Rom. 1:10.

2   1 Cor. 16:2 (AV).

3   See, for example, Gen. 13:1-7; 26:12-14; 30:43.

4   Much has been written about this subject. For a recent and well-balanced critique of the word of faith movement, see A. Perriman (ed.), *Faith, Health and Prosperity* (Carlisle: Paternoster, 2003).

5   Lk. 15:2.

6   Lk. 19:9.

7   Phil. 1:29.

8   Phil. 3:7.

9   1 Cor. 4:7.

10 2 Cor. 8:2.

11 *The Times*, London, 26 June 2003, p. 7.

12 Jn. 2:16.

13 Mk. 11:17.

14 Rev. 3:17.

15 Rev. 3:18.

16 Eph. 1:18-19.

17 Col. 1:27.

18 Lk. 6:38.

6
Missing the Eternal Dimension

"He [God] has also set eternity in the hearts of men; yet they cannot fathom what God has done from beginning to end." (Eccl. 3:11)

Outline Christians often miss the bridge that connects money and earthly possessions with eternal values. The gap between accumulation and distribution, between the brevity of our time on earth and eternity, between holding on to what we know and letting go, can be both deep and wide. This chapter assesses the gap and offers some biblical wisdom for bridging that gap.

Living for the here and now
When we are obsessed with what we can see, we struggle with the implications of the unseen.

Money and eternal values
How can we reintroduce eternal values into our earning, saving, giving, spending, possessing and planning?

Eternity in the money parables
Jesus built the eternal dimension into six of his parables about monetary matters. Here we examine the links he made between the present and the future.

Giving an account to a holy God
God is holy and judges the way we live our lives – including how we handle our stewardship of his resources.

Living for the here and now While eternity is always a mystery, it is rarely a reality. Which of us is sufficiently conscious of eternity – its rewards, blessings and joys, its judgement and review? Because we are not thinking in this framework, eternity does not always inform our lives and influence our behavior as it should. Most religions and cultures have a concept of eternity. Christians associate eternity with the promise of salvation and with the reality of heaven and hell. Eternity has been described as a state wherein the horizon is not in view. Eternity is above and beyond time.

In sharp contrast, everything to do with money has an earthly horizon and is confined by time – and so it's not surprising that people rarely think about the connection between eternity and money. While Christians can and do invest money for eternal purposes through the extension of God's kingdom, in general money is about the here and now. But if its value is confined to earth, why amass it? Why hunger for it? Why live for it? And why cling on to possessions – none of which are going to accompany us into eternity? In order to assess accurately the implications of our core question, "Whose money is it anyway?" we need to carefully consider the concept of eternity. Paul helps to reorient us here. "So we fix our eyes not on what is seen, but on what is unseen. For what is seen is temporary, but what is unseen is eternal."[1] What would happen if you applied that verse to your preoccupation (however large or small) with money and possessions?

The following words from C.S. Lewis help us to focus on eternity. "I must keep alive in myself the desire for my true country, which I shall not find till after death; I must never let it get snowed under or turned aside; I must make it the main object of life to press on to that other country and to help others to do the same."[2] Every Christian (by definition) thirsts for the eternal – but so often we try to quench that thirst with the temporal, including money and possessions. As Ecclesiastes 3:11 implies, human beings were not designed to orient themselves according to their material possessions. Christians know that, but do we really want eternity to be in our hearts, minds and consciousness on a daily basis? Is it not more comfortable to file eternity in a "reassurance drawer" and bring it out when we need it – when we're faced with a life and death crisis beyond our control? Eternal life and eternal glory are the Christian's highest reward – and these promises rightly bring us great joy, peace and security, particularly in times of difficulty. For "in keeping with his promise we are looking forward to a new heaven and a new earth, the home of righteousness."[3] Meanwhile, however, life goes on – even for heavenly citizens – in this material world. Do you see anything of your own attitudes and perspectives towards money and eternity in Table 6.1?

TABLE 6.1 ETERNITY IN MY HEART? NO THANKS!
ON THE WAY UP: Graham was desperately ambitious. He had a first-class legal brain and a personality that easily connected with clients and judges alike. A specialist in corporate criminal law, his track record was outstanding – and he was highly respected. His boss regarded him as the brightest star in their firm for a generation. At the age of thirty-five, he was their top earner – he commanded fees beyond the wildest dreams of his colleagues. He described himself as a "passive" Christian – which meant that he participated at the margins of his church. While he did not deny having faith, his approach to Christianity was forensic and clinical. His faith was like a brief that he had read in a hurry before an urgently rearranged court appearance. He knew that he had all the main points in his mind, but he hoped that his assistants (whoever they were) had been working on the detail. For all his talents, he probably would have failed Theology 101. In a conversation with a Christian friend about wealth, stewardship and the future, he remarked, "I don't do eternity – because I can't get my mind around it. I really can't fathom what changes I would make in my life if I could. At any rate, I don't have time to think about it much. Maybe some time ..."
ON THE WAY DOWN: Mark had lapsed from Christian faith some years ago. The circumstances that crushed his faith were both unusual and sad. His wife died after a protracted illness, and the following week he lost his job. In the months that followed his son and daughter-in-law were a great support to him – but their marriage broke up within a year of his bereavement and both moved away from the area. He became depressed. His perception was that the center of his life had disappeared. Many of his Christian friends kept in touch and he appreciated their kindness – but most of the time he just wanted to be left alone with his thoughts. He was an avid reader and buried himself in his favorite historic novels and a wide range of

other books. It seemed important to him to think about time – its passing, how it was recorded and interpreted. The book stores were full of new age literature, and he developed a keen interest in that genre. He liked the idea of rediscovering himself and became fascinated by astral guidance for life and time, by the holistic nature of religious beliefs and so on. He also read *A Brief History of Time* by the incredibly perceptive Stephen Hawking – but he was not ready for some of the thoughts that book stirred in him about the link between time and eternity. Whatever eternity was about, he associated it with personal accountability – and he was not ready for that. So he decided to read a book about the Napoleonic wars next.

ON THE WAY BACK:
It was a great day for Harry. He had just completed the sale of his heating and ventilation company for more than twice the asking price. "What a deal!" he was musing to himself. "Now I have the rest of my life to think about ways to spend it – with no one else to answer to." He was on the way back home, having deposited the settlement money in the bank. He had told the manager, "This is the one deposit that only I could make – it's the product of the past twenty years of my life. And, believe me, this business got all my attention for all of that time". Harry thought that the celebratory glass of champagne in the bank manager's office was a small recompense for all the bank charges he had paid for years. Such was the brilliance of the sunshine on this special day that he decided to leave his BMW in the bank parking lot and walk home. He passed through the town center, where a group of young people was playing in a band. They were so talented and enthusiastic, he sat on an adjacent bench to listen. After all, he thought, the pressure has gone – it's all about enjoyment now. His relaxation was short-lived, however, as two of the young people started to pass out literature. He thought it would be a flyer for a college gig or a local charity event – but it wasn't. They were young Christians from a nearby summer camp. The flyer he received had Ecclesiastes 3:11 on the front. He had always thought that "eternity" was a new affinity card from one of those innovative retailers anxious to build long-term customer relations. "God doesn't have much of a sense of humor", he thought as he tore up the flyer. "To try to make me think about eternity today of all days – you must be joking! You'd think God would have a better sense of timing."

Why have many Christians lost a consciousness of eternity in their hearts? An immediate consequence, as Ecclesiastes 3:11 implies, is that our awareness of God's sovereignty and purposes also disappears. We lose this perspective by many different means – as we are absorbed by the immediate and tangible, as other worldviews subtly work their way into our minds, as we cultivate a spirit of independence, as we lose our sense of mystery about the afterlife, as we are busy and preoccupied with work, as we find satisfaction through materialism and consumerism.

☑ **ACTION:** Can you recall a sense of eternity ever making *any* difference to your attitude to money and possessions? Has your sense or awareness of eternity grown or diminished in recent years? And what has influenced that progression either way?

Money and eternal values Too many Christians regard earth as their heaven. They see their faith as a security pass for the future but hope that they won't need to use it for a long time. They own a precious gift called "eternal life" but resist the idea that this gift has any bearing on their earthly life, because it would lead to radical changes in their behavior. Eternal life is not some abstract concept for theologians and philosophers. All who have it gained it through acknowledging the only true God and his Son, Jesus Christ. Part of that acceptance was a pledge to adopt eternal values. As Jesus prayed to the Father, "Now this is eternal life: that they may know you, the only true God, and Jesus Christ, whom you have sent."[4] There are only four ways to know God and understand his eternal values. In the power of the Spirit of God, and through the Bible, we use our minds to think, our eyes to see, our hearts to love him and our ears to listen to him. We use all of our God-given faculties in this life to prepare ourselves for eternity.

"I thank thee, O Lord, that thou hast so set eternity in my heart that no earthly thing can ever satisfy me wholly" – John Baillie

The Bible is a window through which we may look into eternity. As such, the Bible also fleshes out the implications of eternal values with regard to money and possessions, as we see in the following three examples. A persecuted group of Hebrew Christians was commended, "You sympathized with those in prison and joyfully accepted the confiscation of your property, because you knew that you yourselves had better and lasting possessions."[5]

They had a good grasp of both their earthly and heavenly assets – but they understood that one set was infinitely more valuable than the other. The disciples learned this lesson first from Jesus, through his teaching on heavenly treasure. "But store up for yourselves treasures in heaven, where moth and rust do not destroy, and where thieves do not break in and steal."[6] In another passage, Peter highlights the moral imperatives that flow from believing in the second coming of Christ. He recognizes the certainty of the ultimate destruction of heaven and earth – "Since everything will be destroyed in this way, what kind of people ought you to be? You ought to live holy and godly lives as you look forward to the day of God and speed its coming."[7] What kind of people ought we to be? And how ought we to think about money and possessions? Most of us fit into one of two broad categories. Eternal values make a big impact on some people – eternal security, the certainty of salvation, the possession of eternal life and a sense of the brevity of time are central to the way they live their lives. For others, however, eternal values are less important and really make a minimal impact on how they determine their priorities, allocate their money and possessions, on the quality and consistency of their stewardship and on their commitment to Christian service.

> "This was the strength of the first Christians, that they lived not in one world only, but in two, and found in consequence not tension alone, but power, the vision of a world unshaken and unshakeable" –
> Harry Emerson Fosdick

Based on biblical principles, Table 6.2 sets out some of the many possible effects of truly understanding God's wealth and our relationship to it. As we investigate how God features in our accounts, we discover the contents of our spiritual balance sheet.

How many of us approach challenging teaching with the attitude that we will prove it wrong? Sometimes we decide instead who would *really* benefit from hearing this. Either way, we divert its application away from ourselves.

TABLE 6.2 BRINGING ETERNAL VALUES TO MONEY AND POSSESSIONS

If we understood that the money and possessions in our stewardship are God's wealth, what would we do about ...

EARNING? We would pay more attention to how we earn and at what cost to those around us. We would be more content to optimize rather than maximize what we earn – matching what we have to a revised list of needs and wants. We would seek specific guidance on how our earning capacity is connected to how much God expects us to give.

SAVING? We would seek God's perspective on how much we are or should be saving and what we are saving for. We would check whether we have ever really used God as our financial adviser and actually taken his advice.

GIVING? We would elevate giving to the top of our financial priorities and keep it there. We would look carefully and systematically at applying the principles of stewardship to all of the assets under our current ownership – not just income.

SPENDING? We would totally reappraise our spending patterns. We would ask how they line up with God's principles. We would consider how what we spend relates to our capacity to give according to God's call on these resources.

POSSESSING? We would compile a list of all the assets that we possess and try to prayerfully assess how effective our stewardship of them is. Based on the biblical evidence, we would ask if God approves of our asset register. We would consider what plans he might have for using our assets for his purposes.

PLANNING? We would consider what role we have assigned to God in our future planning of money and possessions. If we have not allowed God to participate in our planning, we would repent, ask for his guidance and be willing to make some radical changes according to kingdom values. We would realign our inheritance planning to kingdom objectives.

"If you want a religion to make you comfortable, I certainly don't recommend Christianity" —
C.S. Lewis

God is able to speak into every circumstance that underlies your personal response to the material in Table 6.2. There are, of course, many situations in which applying these principles would not be easy. For someone bearing the very high cost of living and accommodation in many capital cities, for example, a comprehensive spending review would be challenging. Such a review would also be difficult for many single-parent families with limited means and for retired couples living on low and declining pensions. But the material in Table 6.2 addresses an attitude of heart and mind rather than giving specific detailed guidance. That is where the Holy Spirit and biblical guidance take over – molding and shaping your responses in your particular situation.

✔ **ACTION:** It has been said that we should hold loosely everything that is not eternal – but that is a very exacting standard. Think and pray about how you answer the question in each of these six areas in Table 6.2. Which areas pose the greatest challenge for you personally? How will you respond to what you have learned here?

The following verse from Romans helps us to keep a godly perspective on money and possessions in a materialistic age. It assumes that we keep eternity in view. "Do not conform any longer to the pattern of this world, but be transformed by the renewing of your mind."[8] Applying the material in Table 6.2 requires that we conform to a new pattern and radically transform our thought processes. This verse calls for a Spirit-led reformation and, when we apply it specifically to money, we need to consider just how far we are from this spiritual goal. How much of this week's shopping wish list – or this year's holiday plan – has more to do with conforming than with being transformed? Have you considered God's plans when formulating your savings and investment plan? Is your asset register a product of conforming to your peers in this world or does it reflect the work of God in transforming your needs and wants?

Exercise:

1. Estimate what you have earned in the past ten years – even in broad terms, without going through a big accounting exercise.

2. Determine where you could, or should, invest money in God's kingdom for eternity.

3. Calculate the actual percentage of your income that you have allocated to these ministries in the past.

4. Add to this figure the percentage of net gain (or loss) of the value of your assets over the past ten years.

5. What percentage of that asset gain is presently earmarked for eternal purposes? Keep checking throughout that your perceptions of eternal values are the same as God's – they might differ when you get this specific.

Eternity in the money parables

The previous section presented some difficult but practical lessons which, as we will see, are deeply rooted in the parables of Jesus. We have seen how much of Jesus' teaching related to money, and we will see that he also linked money with eternity in much of that teaching. If Jesus makes these connections so explicit, so should we. The following six parables on money matters highlight some of the eternal dimensions of the lessons they teach. Jesus clearly wants eternity to be in the hearts of his disciples.

Rich young man:[9] He complied with the law, but he evidently had a blind spot when it came to his possessions. When Jesus instructed him to sell and give to the poor, he was consumed with sadness. Money meant more than obedience. The idea of treasure in heaven was lost on him, so he never invested in it. What might Jesus tell you is the "one thing you lack"?

The seed in the thorns: The farmer had done his work, but this particular seed landed in a bed of thorns. "But the worries of this life, the deceitfulness of wealth and the desires for other things come in and choke the word, making it unfruitful."[10] The consequence for such people is no joy, no fruit, no reward. They are victims of deceit and preoccupation as the tangible crowds out the eternal.

The treasure and the pearl:[11] Both of these treasures fall into the "must have" category of spiritual possessions. From the moment of discovery, we recalibrate all values according to them – as we should do from the moment we meet Christ. Knowing the relative values of earth and heaven, disciples are to be prepared to sell all they have. This is a parable about a new horizon and new values – both of which are eternal.

Rich fool: Here we meet a highly successful and rich farmer with great technique and a strategic sense second to none. His whole focus was on accumulation. Such is his skill in planning that he can now take life easy. Everything on earth has been taken care of. Eternity is not in his game plan, nor had he anticipated that the Lord would call for his life on his day of celebration. "This is how it will be with anyone who stores up things for himself but is not rich toward God."[12] How rich are you toward God?

Unmerciful servant: Two men are in debt. The one in greater debt is mercifully and generously forgiven. But the forgiven debtor is totally unforgiving to someone who owes him much less. The parable highlights how human beings separate their forgiveness from God's. There is no evidence of eternity in the heart of this servant, nor of the effect of the love of the heavenly Father in his life. Once again, we see here the fatal disconnection between earth and heaven.[13i]

Counting the cost:[14] There are two parables here – one about not having enough money to finish a tower, the other about not having a large enough army to defeat an enemy. Both are about imperfect calculations of the costs of completing a task. Jesus spells out the lesson. "In the same way, any of you who does not give up everything he has cannot be my disciple."[15] What do we need to give up to be his disciple? Recalculate the cost of discipleship and decide what the first step in obedience is.

✔ **ACTION:** Your response to the challenges presented in this book will reflect your response to the word of God. Which of these parables speaks most directly to your situation today? Why? Try writing a case study about how your attitudes to money and possessions have changed over the course of your life as a Christian. What would someone reading your case study learn?

Giving an account to a holy God As Christians we have many opportunities to shape our stewardship to eternal values. There are many reasons for our failure to take these opportunities, but two reasons stand out in particular. The first is our insufficient appreciation of God's holiness, and the second is our inadequate understanding of review and judgement. If we properly understood both, we would be unlikely to respond to biblical challenges regarding money and eternity with thoughts or remarks such as the following. "This is fine, but it's not realistic – I can't live my life in the shadow of something that I don't know." "I simply cannot change all my financial arrangements. There are a lot of things other than eternity to be considered – family, old age, unknown needs ..." "Yes, I know it's God's money, but I'm carefully looking after it for him. No, I haven't recently considered whether he might have further instructions for me. Do you think that I should?" "This kind of book makes me feel guilty and uncomfortable. That's not how God wants me to feel." "I've never really thought about eternity and money, but neither have lots of people I know. I might think about it if others started to, but this isn't a popular topic of conversation among my friends." Whether or not we echo some of these sentiments, we need to remember that rationalizing our behavior before our peers and friends is one thing. Formally explaining it to a sovereign God is an altogether different matter.

> *Life is a glorious opportunity, if it is used to condition us for eternity. If we fail in this, though we succeed in everything else, our life will be a failure" –*
> *Billy Graham*

1. God is holy Holy is the word that the Bible uses to communicate all that is distinctive and transcendent in God's nature and character. Holiness speaks of both difference and distance between God and us. Isaiah's is one of the classic biblical encounters with the holy God.[16] He is clearly struck by the profound contrast between God's purity and his own sinfulness. His observations help us grasp the realities of God's holy character. He is enthroned as Lord, great, high and exalted, yet he is near. He is pure, and Isaiah felt defiled before him. He displays mercy to his undeserving servant. Nothing would ever be the same for Isaiah after that vision. That day he learned a deeper set of lessons about his relationship with God. A fresh vision of God's holiness would help us all to apply the truths about eternity in our own lives. How can we see eternity clearly when our minds are soiled by philosophies that aim to "dumb down" God and bring him to our level so that we can negotiate with him about resources that are his to start with?

Jim Packer builds on these points by connecting God's holiness to our daily living.[xvii] This holiness needs to be in our hearts – the desire to please God at the center of our lives, not at the periphery. It affects our temperaments – God acting to shape our reactions and behavior. Holiness permeates our humanness – we aspire to the model of God as man, seen in Christ alone. It transforms our relationships – God has to stamp his pattern on all of our multi-dimensional relationships. As Packer observes, the central problem is a self that has not learned to die. "Ascribe to the LORD the glory due to his name. Bring an offering and come before him; worship the LORD in the splendor of his holiness. Tremble before him, all the earth!"[19] Does the offering we bring reflect our awareness of God's glory and holiness, our worship and trembling before him? One glimpse of God's holiness would transform us.

"But get one glimpse of the holiness of God, one tiny, brief glimpse, and any notion of personally created adequacy shrivels, withered and scorched by the absolute and uncompromising holiness that threatened to break out upon Israel at Sinai" — Dominic Smart[18]

2. God is judge Most of us are so familiar with annual appraisals, performance reviews and assessments that we take them in our stride. It is hard to imagine a world without accountability. Most of us would prefer, however, to be reviewed for secular rather than spiritual performance. But in this matter we have no option. "So then, each of us will give an account of himself to God."[20] Are you ready for a personal appraisal of your stewardship of money and possessions?

"We will stand before the judgement seat of Christ on the basis of our performance, not our profession. We will go past the judgement seat of Christ in single file" — John Blanchard

Judgement, which will involve an overall assessment of our lives, is one of the great moral incentives of the Christian life – whether we like it or not. The abiding concern of the apostles was with the quality of new Christian life in the light of accountability. They focused on living habits and behavior patterns. For example, "make every effort to be found spotless, blameless and at peace with him";[21] "And this is my prayer: that your love may abound more and more in knowledge and depth of insight, so that you may be able to discern what is best and may be pure and blameless until the day of Christ, filled with the fruit of righteousness that comes through Jesus Christ – to the glory and praise of God".[22]

"It ought to be the business of every day to prepare for our final day" – Matthew Henry

"I am not judged by the light I have, but by the light I have refused to accept" – Oswald Chambers

At the judgement seat God is not concerned with determining the Christian's destiny, but rather with assessing our works and character. But a sharpened awareness of the coming judgement helps us to follow without fear, to be dependent and not depressed, to be awake and not to slumber.

Taking stock

What can we learn from the response of the rich young man and others who first heard Jesus' parables about money and eternity?

Discuss the implications of the material in Table 6.2 with those closest to you, your study group, or a group of Christian colleagues in similar circumstances.

Complete this sentence prayerfully: "If I knew that I would be judged on my attitudes to money and possessions a month from today, I would …"

Further reading

Alcorn, Randy, *Money, Possessions and Eternity* (Wheaton, IL: Tyndale, 1989).

Schneider, John, *Godly Materialism: Rethinking Money and Possessions* (Downers Grove, IL: IVP, 1994).

Stowell, Joseph M., *Eternity* (Chicago: Moody Press, 1995).

Wuthnow, Robert, *God and Mammon in America* (New York: Free Press, 1994).

Endnotes

1 2 Cor. 4:18.

2 C.S. Lewis, *Mere Christianity* (New York: Macmillan, 1960), p. 120.

3 2 Pet. 3:13.

4 Jn. 17:3.

5 Heb. 10:34.

6 Mt. 6:20.

7 2 Pet. 3:11-12.

8 Rom. 12:2.

9 Mt. 19:16-30.

10 Mk. 4:19.

11 Mt. 13:44-46.

12 Lk. 12:16-21.

13 Mt. 18:23-35.

14 Lk. 14:28-33.

15 Lk. 14:33.

16 Isa. 6:1-8.

17 J.I. Packer, *A Passion for Holiness* (Cambridge: Crossway Books, 1992).

18 Dominic Smart, *Grace, Faith and Glory* (Carlisle: Authentic Lifestyle, 2003), p. 38. The passage he refers to is Exod. 19:23-25.

19 1 Chr. 16:29-30.

20 Rom. 14:12.

21 2 Pet. 3:14.

22 Phil. 1:9-11.

7
Failing the Tests of Stewardship

"Each man should give what he has decided in his heart to give, not reluctantly or under compulsion, for God loves a cheerful giver."
(2 Cor. 9:7)

Outline   What is Christian stewardship? Why should we practice it, how can we measure it and what are the pitfalls to avoid?

Thinking about stewardship
How do we learn about stewardship, and what is the test at the end?

The meaning of stewardship
Stewardship is about much more than money, and it is based on the master-servant relationship.

The motivation for stewardship
Why do we practice stewardship? For reward? For love? Or both?

Measuring stewardship
Guidelines and tests based on biblical practices help us to assess stewardship. What can we learn from tithing, jubilee and *koinonia*?

The enemies of stewardship: A review
What are the enemies we need to conquer in order to be effective stewards?

Thinking about stewardship People react to the demanding concept of stewardship in different ways. Some are in denial: "I practice good stewardship – but I see a lot of bad practice around me." Some prefer to avoid it: "I squirm whenever this subject is mentioned, it's far too confrontational and demanding." Others feel inadequate: "I feel like a complete failure whenever I think about stewardship – I just wish that I could honestly come to terms with it." While God has the power to transform all of us at any stage, we probably need to wrestle with the concept of stewardship enough to be able to voice this last thought before we can begin to make progress. Let's begin by asking the following two questions.

1. A personal decision? 2 Corinthians 9:7 beautifully captures the essence of Christian giving – one fundamental aspect of stewardship. But many poor stewards have cited this verse in defense of their own decisions about giving – decisions that bear little relationship to God's standards. With dulled consciences they give at an undemanding level that enables them to continuously enhance their standard of living. They feel neither reluctant nor compelled in matters of giving because they live well within their own "easy to comply" zone, where they are secure and satisfied. I have often heard Christian people say that they have completely clear consciences about their giving. This is fine provided they have recently and repeatedly examined their consciences at the only stewardship recalibration station recognized by God – the Bible. I have not always had a clear conscience about my giving, and so I have been back to that service station many times and tried to adjust my life accordingly. The key question is whether our giving is inspired and led by the Spirit. Is it "in tune" with God's teaching? Is it based on careful consideration and consultation? If so, the decision will meet the criteria in 2 Corinthians 9:7, be wholly cheerful and readily blessed. While our giving is a "personal" decision, it needs to be an advised and an informed decision made in the light of biblical teaching.

"God has given us two hands — one to receive with and the other to give with. We are not cisterns made for hoarding; we are channels made for sharing"
— Billy Graham

2. A personal test? Like any other discipline, stewardship requires a learning process.

The subject needs to be taught: The Bible contains lots of teaching about stewardship, but churches don't tend to teach a lot about it. Have you tried to learn all you can about it? Or have you designed your own strategies for avoiding it?

The teacher needs to be skilled: Some of those who "teach" us about stewardship by example are good role models – others are not. God alone is uniquely qualified to teach us about it.

Practice makes perfect: Few of us pick up and apply concepts the first time – we usually need to repeat and practice them over time. Examples and illustrations help – and in this area we have both in abundance.

Monitoring progress: We need to regularly ask for the insight of the Holy Spirit to review our progress. Our ultimate accountability is before God at a date to be determined. Few of us like the prospect of either of these reviews.

A lot of Christians are uncomfortable with the idea of a "test" being associated with stewardship, but it is inherent in all of God's teaching on the subject. We don't need to satisfy the expectations of anyone except God. "There is only one Lawgiver and Judge, the one who is able to save and destroy. But you – who are you to judge your neighbor?"[1] Yes, it is tempting – but always unprofitable.

☑ **ACTION:** How did you arrive at your present practice of stewardship? How, by your own practice, are you teaching others about it?

The meaning of stewardship   Christian stewardship is about managing God's resources to please him. As we examine this challenging (and invariably unpopular) subject, it is important to remember that "We are not trying to please men but God, who tests our hearts".[2] Pleasing other people – even Christians – by our stewardship can be relatively easy. We can present both our giving and Christian service to others with the goal of impressing them. But only God, the owner of all of these resources, knows what we have given and what we have held back. None of us, therefore, are in any position to judge each other's hearts. Nor should we try to do so – although it's a common preoccupation of Christians.

The New Testament word for "steward" refers to someone who administers the property of another. Stewardship involves much more than money, although money will be our prime concern here. The three components of what we hold in stewardship are as follows.[3] The Bible makes it clear that each of these belongs to God.

Natural talents from birth These are the distinct elements of our personality, skills and aptitudes that constitute the differences and similarities between us.

The truth of the gospel, his indwelling Spirit and the gifts received from God These things were passed on to us, and we have experienced their impact in our lives.

Possessions acquired during our lifetime Money and all our material possessions fall into this category, along with all that we have accumulated in terms of skills and experience.

Christians are to administer all of these resources faithfully. It is difficult to separate these three groups of resources and claim, for example, that we will specialize in one area. To do so would repeat the error of the single talent holder who buried his in the ground.[4] Moreover, being selective about our stewardship would imply that God had passed out a self-assessment form to let us decide what to manage for him. He hasn't, and he won't. A person is unlikely to be a good steward of God's money if he or she is not also a good steward of other things.

"However painful or difficult, or, on the other hand, however inconspicuous or humdrum life may be, the Christian finds his peace in accepting and playing his part in the master plan" —
J.B. Phillips

Recognizing the master-servant relationship between God and his disciples is central to good stewardship. We have to be prepared to live within that relationship and not seek to redefine it. To set our own parameters for our relationship with God can be very tempting at times. Stewardship is about God handing over control of the assets he owns for a period of time. But most of us prefer both owning and controlling – especially with money that we have earned, saved or invested. Many times, our failure in stewardship starts here.

"Christianity proposes not to extinguish our natural desires. It promises to bring the desires under just control and direct them to their true object"
— William Wilberforce

Christian stewardship can only flourish within the framework of the master-servant relationship and cannot survive outside it. It is more important to concentrate on getting the relationship right than it is to try out a series of curative spiritual recipes that address the symptoms of poor stewardship but miss the root cause. The foundation stone of stewardship is Lordship. Table 7.1 summarizes the major components of this relationship with principles from the parables on stewardship.

TABLE 7.1 THE MASTER AND THE STEWARD	
The Master ...	**The Steward ...**
Owns many resources	Manages but does not own resources
Is powerful	Recognizes the Master's authority
Places trust	Accepts that trust
Expects a good return	Acknowledges personal accountability
Goes away	Knows he will come back
Reviews performance	Submits to his judgement
Is both generous and severe	Waits with confidence and apprehension

☑ **ACTION:** How do you perceive your relationship with God in the context of stewardship? Identify any areas in Table 7.1 with which you struggle and pray about how you can adjust your attitudes and actions in order to be a good steward.

The motivation for stewardship Different forms of incentive are used to motivate all types of behavior – from making sure trains run on time, to getting hospital beds ready for patients, to passing examinations and so on. But Christians look at spiritual rewards differently. Although we regard them as desirable, somehow we feel that it is a bit hypocritical to obey Christ only for the reward. Indeed it is – and we should recall that we love (and obey) him because he first loved us. At the same time, seeking God's approval is a key part of our Christian journey. As Paul says, "Everyone who competes in the games goes into strict training. They do it to get a crown that will not last; but we do it to get a crown that will last forever."[5] Or, again, "I have fought the good fight, I have finished the race, I have kept the faith. Now there is in store for me the crown of righteousness, which the Lord, the righteous Judge, will award to me on that day – and not only to me, but also to all who have longed for his appearing."[6] Consider Jesus' own motivation for obedience and the reward he anticipated. "Let us fix our eyes on Jesus, the author and perfecter of our faith, who for the joy set before him endured the cross, scorning its shame, and sat down at the right hand of the throne of God."[7] We are on very solid ground when our heavenly reward motivates us to be good stewards. A good steward aims to please his master, welcomes the opportunity to manage his resources and looks forward to giving an account – because to do so he will need to be in his master's presence.

But reward is not the only factor that motivates the Christian to good stewardship. For the God who calls us is the sovereign Lord. It's his wealth – it doesn't belong to some demigod, benign uncle or friendly bank manager who has extended our credit limits. The resources in stewardship are all on his balance sheet. He allocated them to us and looks for a return. Who is this God we serve? "Know therefore that the LORD your God is God; he is the faithful God, keeping his covenant of love to a thousand generations of those who love him and keep his commands."[8] A disciple serves out of gratitude, love, reverence and hope.

> Tune me, O Lord, into one harmony
> With thee, one full responsive vibrant chord;
> Unto thy praise, all love and melody,
> Tune me, O Lord.
> – *Christina Rossetti*

> ☑ **ACTION:** Samuel Wilberforce once said that Christian discipleship could be stated in four words – admit, submit, commit, transmit. Do you admit that your resources belong to God? Do you submit to God's authority in the master-servant relationship? How much of your time and energy do you commit to being a good steward? What messages about God and his resources does your behavior transmit to others?

Measuring stewardship In many ways it is impossible to measure good Christian stewardship of money. But there is plenty of guidance available, as well as tests. We need to be serious about seeking and following that guidance and sensitive to the testing. I have advised many individuals and organizations and have often said, "You ask, and pay, for my advice; I give it to you in good faith and on the basis of some experience – but you can always ignore it if you don't want to take it." In the area of stewardship, too, many Christians wrestle with the biblical advice but end up discarding much of it. "Good to know, but impossible to follow – it's too intrusive, too prescriptive, too demanding." But let's stop to take a good look at some of the highlights of that advice as we seek to answer the question "What should I give?"

Beyond measurement Foundational to our understanding of the biblical model of giving are two promises that God gives us. Both of them point towards an open-ended model of liberal giving.

Promise 1: "Give, and it will be given to you. A good measure, pressed down, shaken together and running over, will be poured into your lap. For with the measure you use, it will be measured to you."[9]

Promise 2: "... remembering the words the Lord Jesus himself said: 'It is more blessed to give than to receive.'"[10]

These promises speak of an attitude of profound and boundless generosity, of a symbiotic relationship between giving and blessing, of trusting God and of confidence in his purposes. In short, they speak of a kingdom whose citizens know that they are managing God's money. We are these citizens; we are in that kingdom; these are our promises.

In a world of counting, financial planning, budgets and spreadsheets, these are foreign concepts. They might sound too idealistic. What relevance do these promises have in the context of my home loan, credit card debt and the soaring costs of living and education? With such enormous demands on my money, how can I think about giving money away? To say that God is not capable of enabling us to apply these principles in our generation, however, is to take a very narrow view of God and to imply that Christian discipleship is time- and culture-bound. This is not to deny the financial pressures of modern life, but to remind you of the Christian answer to "Whose life is it anyway?" Allocating resources has always been difficult, but it depends on our priorities. Most of us are bombarded daily by messages from those whose mission it is to constantly redefine our needs and reshape our financial priorities – without any thought of the lordship of Christ. We need the divine counterbalancing force of the Spirit of God to proclaim and act upon these biblical promises. Above all, the Christian's stewardship of money is a response to the one who gave everything for us on a cross. That is beyond measurement. Giving, therefore, is an act of worship, neither a chore nor an obligation.

> *"Giving is not God's way of raising money – it's God's way of raising people in the likeness of his Son"*

Applying biblical measures Now we consider more quantitative approaches to giving. In most spheres of life, as soon as something is quantified, there is debate – whether it is a golf enthusiast describing his best round on his favorite course, a traveler talking about the relative merits of different airlines or a doctor debating with colleagues about the efficacy of a new drug. Questions concerning the unit of measurement, the type of statistical data, its method of collection, its interpretation and so on are all parts of these conversations. We ask the same questions with regard to Christian giving – particularly if numbers are given, as is the case with tithing. But the Bible brings other relevant principles and practices to our attention.

> *"The world asks, 'How much does he give?' Christ asks, 'Why does he give?'"*
> *– John Raleigh Mott*

Tithing, which preceded the Mosaic law, was a test of obedience.[11] Abram gave a tenth of the booty from a battle to God, through his priest Melchizedek.[12] Some five hundred years later, as the law was given, the principle of tithing was established. "A tithe of everything from the land, whether grain from the soil or fruit from the trees, belongs to the LORD; it is holy to the LORD."[13] The Old Testament standards of tithing were very demanding, since they required far more than ten percent of income and assets. The law specified not only the quantity of giving, but its quality as well. "Honor the LORD with your wealth, with the firstfruits of all your crops."[14] Through both tithing and bringing "the first and the best" this nation produced a return on God's resources. Giving did not stop at tithing, since there were additional freewill offerings (for example, for rebuilding the temple) as God moved the hearts of the people. What was tithing designed to accomplish? "So that you may learn to revere the LORD your God always."[15] This systematic provision ensured that God came first, reminded the giver of his indebtedness and encouraged him to give thanks for all of God's blessings. The tithe set a minimum, not a maximum, for giving.

What did Jesus teach on the subject? Tithing was probably practiced in his home as he grew up, by his disciples and among his community. He did not teach against it, nor did he specifically advocate it for his disciples. He did, however, sharply criticize the way in which tithing had become a legalistic ritual among the Jewish hierarchy. He made it clear that his disciples were to be more sacrificial and generous in their giving than the Pharisees were. In short, a tithe would not have been enough of a demand for Jesus to place on his followers – then or now. Tithing is biblical, but is it Christian? One striking feature of the early church was the people's self-sacrificing attitude to giving and sharing (partly in response to special financial needs resulting from the social and economic disruption caused by people becoming Christians). It is likely that some members of the early church did give a tithe, based on their Jewish tradition. Paul, who has a lot to say about finance and giving, does not advocate tithing but encourages believers to set aside a sum of money according to their income.[16] Some might argue that this sounds a bit like tithing. The apostolic writings in general contain few references to tithing – perhaps to avoid mechanistic and legalistic approaches to giving and to emphasize the new spirit of love and generosity flowing from the grace of God in their lives. Tithing became a form of unwelcome taxation in subsequent centuries, with much of its original design being lost to the reluctant givers. Over the centuries the practice fell into disrepute, was used to exploit the poor and became a source of misery and conflict.

Christians differ in their opinions today regarding whether tithing should be the basis for determining their giving. Although I think that there is much to be said for rediscovering the principle of systematic giving by tithing as a point of departure, we have to recognize its dangers. These dangers include giving a tithe and nothing else to God and assuming that a correctly calculated donation will assuage God. Tithing can also be an unjust demand when resources are distributed so unevenly. It is more important to evaluate our whole attitude to God's wealth than to comply with a formula. It is more challenging, and more crucial, to repudiate the worship of money and possessions, to institute lifestyle changes that enable a radical reappraisal of giving and to come to terms with the many issues touched on in Chapters 3–6. Having said all that, there could be great benefit to the kingdom if an average of ten percent of the income and assets under the stewardship of Christians were actually pledged to God.

☑ **ACTION:** What measure do you use for giving? Are you satisfied with it? Do you think God is? What, if anything, needs to change in your practice of giving?

Learning from other practices There are two other sets of principles and practices that could guide our stewardship of money. Both are open-ended in their demands and remind us of the close connections between stewardship and discipleship.

Jubilee: The Old Testament introduces the remarkable concept of the year of Jubilee.[17] Every fifty years the Israelites were to free slaves, cancel debts, return land to its owners and allow a period of rest for the countryside. These radical actions were a costly reminder that they really owned nothing and that all they had was in trust from God. The year of Jubilee avoided extremes of wealth and poverty and was both a searching spiritual and profound social event. It offered the poorer members of the community a new beginning – but it gained little popularity with the rich. While there is not much evidence to suggest that it was commonly practiced in Israel, the ideal of jubilee is found throughout the prophets as part of their teaching on release and restoration.[18] The parables of Jesus also contain jubilee concepts, not least the parables referring to release from debt and redistribution of goods to the poor.[19] And, of course, Christ came to proclaim the ultimate year of jubilee – sins forgiven and salvation through faith through his death. The early church also espoused jubilee ideals, as when the Christians in Jerusalem sold assets so that "There were no needy persons among them."[20] What, then, can we learn from this concept? Firstly, most of us need to radically reappraise what we give in the light of God's grace. That is the ultimate test. In so doing, we will probably find that it leads to "jubilee" effects on all other parts of our stewardship. Be careful how you do this ... it could change your life, and you won't be able to wait another fifty years before doing it again. Secondly, the gospel was designed to be "good news to the poor". The way we live our lives as Christians might explain in part why the gospel is not always in high demand from the poor – so too might the way we respond, or not, to God's challenges on giving.

Koinonia: This word describes a unique quality of fellowship that should characterize Christian life. The word has many dimensions including partnership, joint participation, communion and community. Its root meaning is "commonness". In the communion meal, for example, it refers to the joint participation in the body and blood of Christ.[21] But *koinonia* was also an economic term. Paul, for example, uses the word to describe "practical sharing" in connection with the collection for the poor Christians in Jerusalem.[22] This perspective helps us to see that we give with other members of the Christian church as partners in an enterprise. This idea lies at the heart of the early church and was one of its defining characteristics. "They devoted themselves to the apostles' teaching and to the fellowship, to the breaking of bread and to prayer."[23] Part of this was an ongoing and voluntary process of wealth redistribution. What, then, do we learn from this? Firstly, it is striking to see the joy, willingness and enthusiasm that surrounded this form of financial fellowship. It is spontaneous – much closer to a jubilee than to the mechanics of tithing. There was nothing niggardly or calculated about what they gave. Do we have that joy in our giving? Secondly, there was evident generosity and sacrifice in its application. This brand of fellowship could not possibly be viewed as an easy option – because there were no limits to what they gave. Thirdly, there was an element of equality in this fellowship – both in the Christian community and beyond. Sharing resources was not a unique event, but a way of life.

☑ **ACTION:** Can you trace any evidence of the concepts of jubilee and *koinonia* influencing your giving? If they are absent, what could you do to foster them?

The enemies of stewardship: A review

Having acknowledged the spiritual warfare that surrounds the deployment of money in Christian hands, we identify here some of the most aggressive enemies of good stewardship. Their effectiveness lies in their capacity to attack the relationship with God that underpins all stewardship.

Personal greed: Ever present, greed is fueled daily by the materialism that surrounds us.

Worship of money: We often worship at a private and secret altar, rarely admitting it to ourselves – but this worship determines our priorities and shapes our lives.

Lack of contentment: This is a widespread problem – but there is a cure. We should find contentment if we know God, take his view of the world and cultivate thankfulness.

Trust in wealth: As we have seen, this is a misplaced confidence that is common. It can often grow from early adult life as relative levels of prosperity are experienced.

Resistant spirit: Sometimes our response to God is determined much more by earth than by heaven, more by peer pressure than by the persistence of the Spirit.

There are many defenses against these enemies – perhaps chief among them is grace. Of the early church, Luke records, "With great power the apostles continued to testify to the resurrection of the Lord Jesus, and much grace was upon them all."[24] That grace influenced everything they did. It was the meaning, motivation and the measurement of their stewardship. We could do no better than follow their example.

Taking stock

Which of the five enemies above do you have the greatest problem resisting? Why? Where does grace come into your calculation of giving?

Our relationship with Christ, rather than money, is the true measure of wealth. How has your relationship with him changed in a way that will affect your stewardship?

Money is an important consideration when choosing where we work, and consequently where we live. This in turn becomes the basis of our family finances. Sometimes living in a high cost environment can trouble Christians who feel "locked in" to a financial straitjacket. Has this affected your stewardship of money? If so, can you see any short- or long-term solutions?

"Money, designed as a tool, has become a drug to many." Is this true of your relationship with money? If so, how can you free yourself from the addiction?

For the Christian, money is also a way of communicating the grace of God. How do you, or could you, transmit God's grace to others through your stewardship?

Further reading

Dayton, Howard, *Your Money Counts* (Wheaton, IL: Tyndale, 1996).

Maiden, Peter, *Take my Plastic* (Carlisle: OM Publishing, 1997).

Murray, Stuart, *Beyond Tithing* (Carlisle: Paternoster, 2000).

Rusbuldt, Richard, *A Workbook on Biblical Stewardship* (Grand Rapids, MI: Eerdmans, 1994).

Endnotes

1 Jas. 4:12.

2 1 Thess. 2:4.

3 See also Neil Hood, *Whose Life is it Anyway?* (Carlisle: Authentic Lifestyle, 2002), p. 41.

4 Mt. 25:14-30.

5 1 Cor. 9:25.

6 2 Tim. 4:7-8.

7 Heb. 12:2.

8 Deut. 7:9.

9 Lk. 6:38.

10 Acts 20:35.

11 For a comprehensive and thought-provoking treatment of this topic, see Stuart Murray, *Beyond Tithing* (Carlisle: Paternoster, 2000).

12 Gen. 14:18-20.

13 Lev. 27:30.

14 Prov. 3:9.

15 Deut. 14:23.

16 1 Cor. 16:2.

17 Lev. 25:10-41.

18 See, e.g., Isa. 61:1-11; Amos 9:11-15.

19 See, e.g., Lk. 16:1-12; 18:22.

20 Acts 4:34.

21 1 Cor. 10:16.

22 As, e.g., in Rom. 15:26 and 2 Cor. 8:4.

23 Acts 2:42.

24 Acts 4:33.

8
Neglecting to Put Jesus First

"I am the Alpha and the Omega, the First and the Last, the Beginning and the End." (Rev. 22:13)

Outline   By far the greatest hazard of all those we have looked at throughout this section is neglecting to put Jesus first. Each of us needs to ask whether Jesus is first or last in our lives.

Jesus, first or last?
What does it mean to call Jesus the "alpha and omega"? And what are the practical implications of this confession of faith for our discipleship generally and in the area of money and possessions in particular?

How far have we come?
What could happen if we really saw Jesus as first and last? How do we apply this truth to each of the themes from Chapters 3, 4, 5, 6 and 7?

A call to worship
The call to worship in Psalm 95 requires a response of rejoicing and reverence. How do we worship God with our money and possessions?

Learning from others
What can we learn from the biblical examples of Achan, Ananias, and Sapphira and Daniel, as well as three contemporary case studies about the challenges of putting Jesus first?

Jesus, first or last? This final hazard is the most dangerous one because many people, causes and imperatives aspire to be first in our lives. If we don't give Jesus the place that he deserves in our hearts, priorities and devotion, we will keep "our" money and possessions beyond his reach. We may be content to take everything else that he offers us – and even give thanks for these blessings, including material prosperity. When we make other things more important, Jesus slides down our scale of priorities toward the bottom. You may think that this is improbable or impossible, but look within yourself and then look around the Christian community. And Jesus' relative position in our lives has a lot to do with how we handle money.

For many years I have struggled to fully understand and apply the verse above from Revelation 22. As Augustine of Hippo wrote in the fourth century, "What I want is not more certainty about you ... but to be more certain in you." Within this verse lies the key to all Christian life and service. If the Lord is both alpha and omega, he is also everything in between – the whole spiritual alphabet. There is not one word, idea or concept in our Christian vocabulary that is not composed of him. If we do not regard him as alpha – built into the beginning of our lives – he cannot govern the rest, nor will he be omega – the goal toward which we strive.

Christ as the alphabet: Everything written in the English language – regardless of the subject, author, style or country of origin – uses only twenty-six letters. We need every one of them, from A to Z. There are no more – but those twenty-six letters enable us to express ourselves in an almost infinite number of ways, both written and spoken. Jesus is alpha and omega in every alphabet, from every culture, from every language, both past and present. He is the beginning and end of all things. Christianity can neither exist nor be explained without Christ. He is sovereign Lord and our savior. But if he is everything and everywhere, why do we pay him so little heed in our acquisition, consumption and allocation of money? And in how many of our words and sentences about money does Jesus feature?

Alpha and omega is characteristically a title for God. In the words of Isaiah, "I, the LORD – with the first of them and with the last – I am he."[1] "This is what the LORD says – Israel's King and Redeemer, the LORD Almighty: I am the first and the last; apart from me there is no God."[2] Ancient Greek commentators saw God as the beginning, the creative cause of all things; the end, the goal of all things; and the middle, equally present in all things. Revelation 22:13 specifically refers to Jesus Christ the Lord and ascribes to him these distinctive qualities of God.

What does this title mean? There are several great Christian principles associated with this title. The first is that the Lord is total and complete. He has all power, wisdom, knowledge, goodness and so on. In contrast, at our best we are partial and incomplete in all such qualities – and we can only find completeness in him. The second is the idea of continuity throughout history and eternity – he is the same yesterday, today and forever. As the first and the last, all time is in his hands. We rejoice in his continuous and instant availability to all who call on him at every stage of life. And we have committed our eternal future to him. The third principle is that, as the beginning and the end, the Lord is not just the source of all things but the goal of all things – including our lives.

What are the implications for me? In terms of our overall discipleship, if the Lord is first in all things by God's reckoning, how dare I (by intention or default) make him second? Or third? Or anything but first? If he is complete, how can my Christian service be effective if I exclude him from important areas of my life? Many who are Christians lead lives that are fragmented and mixed up because of this exclusion. We grant God a form of "restricted access" or a quota of "visiting hours" and thereby diminish our effectiveness as servants. Strange as it may seem, we may recognize that he has all knowledge and wisdom but choose not to listen to him. Why? We have a better answer – ourselves! On the matter of continuity, his canvas is not only cosmic and eternal. It is also human and personal. He wants to shape each aspect of our lives at all ages and stages. Some Christians open and shut doors to God at various stages of their lives but never quite get to the point of ongoing personal surrender. We need to surrender to God in order for him to be the goal of our lives.

> "Everyone wants the kingdom of God, but few want it first. Everyone wants high achievement, but few want to pay the price. Everyone wants God, but few want him first" –
> Charles Venable

What impact does this title have on money and possessions? These three principles all affect the way we handle money and possessions. If God is complete, then his sovereignty should be evident in the way we handle money. "Evident to whom?" you might ask. It would certainly be evident to God, and most probably to all who know us as well. Is there any other way to have a clear conscience before God concerning money? In terms of continuity, we need to continuously ask God to oversee how we handle money and possessions – throughout our lives. Few of us do. This process would entail, for example, implementing many of the self-checks found throughout this book. If God has the first and last word in matters of personal finance, the standard will be a demanding one. Finally, how does God being the source and the goal affect our finances? "For from him and through him and to him are all things. To him be the glory forever! Amen." [3] For from him and through him and to him are our money and possessions. Once we have acknowledged God as the source, we need to involve him as we think about the goals to which such resources are to be directed, and when and how. Involving God in every aspect of our everyday affairs is part of bringing God glory.

☑ ACTION: If you were to seriously confess God as "alpha and omega" over your money and possessions, what aspects of your behavior and practice would have to change? How you would achieve this and over what time period?

How far have we come? How might taking God seriously as "alpha and omega" deepen our understanding of what we have learned in Chapters 3 to 7? If Jesus were truly the alpha and omega of our money and possessions, what would that look like in our lives? Table 8.1 summarizes a series of responses to this challenge.

Truly acknowledging the Lord as both alpha and omega is an act of worship. Who or what we worship determines what we become. The challenge is to translate our worship into behavior that honors him. What, then, does a true worshiper do with God's money? In answer, we turn to one of the classic Old Testament calls to worship.

**TABLE 8.1 ACKNOWLEDGING JESUS AS THE FIRST AND THE LAST …
WHAT MIGHT THAT LOOK LIKE?**

Money on our minds: Being freed from a preoccupation with money, we would be tuned instead into God's grace. We would be victorious over the temptations of materialism and consumerism.

Facing up to the attack: We would be acutely aware of the reality of the battle and the perils of money worship. We would find contentment, have a passionate aversion to greed and resist the bondage of money's invisible chains.

Placing confidence in prosperity: Knowing the architect, we would build our lives according to his perfect plans. We would place no confidence in temporary material prosperity. We would have an insatiable appetite to know him better. Knowing Christ to be the algorithm of life, we would not look to money for answers but assign it to its proper place in our lives.

Missing the eternal dimension: There would be no danger of missing the significance of eternity, because the alpha and omega enables us to realize that "the reality … is found in Christ".[4] We would apply eternal values to everything, including money, and our lives would reflect a transformed holistic view of giving and stewardship. We would have no fear of giving an account to a holy God.

Failing the tests of stewardship: We would devote much greater care on a continuing basis to ensuring that we were good stewards – simply because our motivation would be totally revitalized. Good stewardship would become *the* topic of conversation among Christians regarding money, and it would become an important part of our prayer lives.

☑ **ACTION:** Read Psalm 95.

A call to worship   The psalmist here invites the reader to join in praising God. C.H. Spurgeon compares this summons to the pealing of church bells. The first peals are lively, reflecting the mood of rejoicing. The final peals, however, are slow and sad, as for a funeral, as those who were disobedient and consequently perished in the desert are remembered. This psalm may have been used at the dedication of the second temple – one of those occasions when the nation needed to be reminded of the fundamentals of their worship. Psalm 95 highlights three important attitudes we need to have in coming before God.

Rejoicing: The psalm issues a summons to which the people respond. We, too, respond to that summons. Their rejoicing in verses 1-5 had three dimensions. Firstly, they were to sing – probably because it was the best way to express their collective love for God. "Come, let us sing for joy to the LORD; let us shout aloud to the Rock of our salvation."[5] Secondly, they were to come with thanksgiving. We find this emphasis on thanksgiving and confession throughout the psalms. Thirdly, they had to come knowing. "For the LORD is the great God, the great King above all gods."[6] This was a type of creed, an affirmation of what they believed. Do we come before the Lord rejoicing (singing, thanking and knowing) when we want to talk with him about money? Are God's instructions regarding money and the allocation of his resources a source of pleasure to us, or a nuisance? Does our worship match our behavior in these practical dimensions of life?

Reverence: "Come, let us bow down in worship, let us kneel before the LORD our Maker; for he is our God and we are the people of his pasture, the flock under his care."[7] The tone here is deeply reverential. The worshipers lower themselves by bowing down and kneeling as they approach God's presence – the God who is Creator and shepherd. The covenant between God and humankind is vital in this verse: "he is ... we are". It is so fitting to bow our heads, bend our knees and prostrate ourselves before him. How often are our hearts filled with reverence when we think about money?

Response: The worshipers are to respond to hearing his voice – but it is conditional and followed by a dire warning. "Today, if you hear his voice, do not harden your hearts as you did at Meribah, as you did that day at Massah in the desert, where your fathers tested and tried me, though they had seen what I did."[8] Hearing his voice is one of the central acts of worship. The two place names for quarreling and testing sum up the skeptical and disobedient spirit of Israel. They often heard, but they rarely obeyed. The psalm ends abruptly, recalling the forty years during which God was angry and disgusted with his people. The heart of worship is not wonderful music or a lofty building – it is, rather, bending our wills to the will of the Lord.

> ☑ **ACTION:** Worship is the submission of all our nature to God, it is the quickening of conscience by his holiness, the nourishment of the mind with his truth, the purifying of the imagination by his beauty, the opening of the heart to his love, the surrender of the will to his purpose. – William Temple
>
> How do you worship God with your money? Do you submit yourself, including all of your resources, to God? Does his holiness quicken your conscience regarding money matters? Do you nourish your mind with his truth, found in the Bible's teaching, regarding money and possessions? Does God's beauty purify your imagination regarding how you could allocate his resources? Does your stewardship reflect the opening of your heart to his love? Do you surrender your own will in money matters to his eternal purpose?

Breathe, O breathe Thy loving Spirit
Into every troubled breast;
Let us all in Thee inherit,
Let us find Thy promised rest.
Take away the love of sinning
Alpha and Omega be;
End of faith, as its beginning
Set our hearts at liberty.
– *Charles Wesley*

Learning from others
1. Biblical examples

The Bible is refreshingly honest about people and their imperfections and gives us many illustrations of both good and bad practice when it comes to making God first or last in money and possessions. Do you identify with any traits or tendencies in the following four examples?

Achan: This is a sad story.[9] Achan had been greatly blessed by God, had seen God's power and knew that he was not to be treated lightly. When God displayed this power again here, by opening up the city of Jericho in a miraculous way, God also gave his people a clear warning. "But keep away from the devoted things, so that you will not bring about your own destruction by taking any of them."[10] The people were to bring all the spoils to the Lord in recognition of his victory and their unswerving obedience.

But Achan just couldn't resist taking some of the booty for himself and hiding it – thereby putting his personal desire above the glory of God and the welfare of God's people. Achan had been specifically told that these riches belonged to God, but he chose to ignore and disobey these instructions. The calamitous story ends with his death and the deaths of many others. The crime? He robbed God of what was his by right.

Rich ruler: This distinguished man had some very good instincts. He was interested in eternal life and went to the correct source, Jesus himself.[11] Millions of people today never make that connection. On the other hand, he appeared content to keep Jesus in the "good teacher" category, rather than follow him as Lord. He thought that he could achieve eternal life through his good works and was happy to do more of them. "What good thing must I do to get eternal life?"[12] But the one thing he would not do was give up his personal idol – his money and possessions. In this man's mind, Jesus was up there with the best, a unique and gifted teacher, a man of standing and integrity – but he was not first. Jesus' call to renounce his wealth falls on deaf ears. There are many Christians who, sadly, will listen to God about anything – except their relationship with money.

Ananias and Sapphira: In many ways this story is similar to Achan's.[13] Ananias and Sapphira were a privileged couple in the early church, and their story reminds us that even in that special Spirit-filled environment Satan's intrusions were evident. They sold a piece of property that was rightfully their own and which they were not obliged to sell. We have to assume that, before the sale, they had committed to give all of the proceeds to the church – and therefore to the Lord. Instead, they kept some for themselves – thereby being both dishonest and deceitful. Peter focuses on their hypocrisy, "What made you think of doing such a thing? You have not lied to men but to God." [14] The punishment, their subsequent sudden deaths, seems severe – but the sin was grave and the impact of the incident profound. The Lord was not alpha and omega to this couple. Have we fulfilled the promises we have made to God in the disposition and deployment of our resources? Few of us have, but by his grace all of us can.

Daniel: The story of Daniel is less about money than it is about values.[15] But our values determine how we handle God's money. Daniel's Babylonian captors probably assumed that Daniel and his compatriots would eventually adopt their values about food. After all, it was only a matter of reeducation. But they misunderstood his knowledge of God, his resolve and the strength of his obedience. Daniel experienced plenty of peer pressure to comply, but he resisted it all. The ten-day period without the king's food was a real test, but he passed the test and was rewarded. "At the end of the ten days they looked healthier and better nourished than any of the young men who ate the royal food." [16] Many of us experience enormous peer pressure not about food or religious practice, but in the area of money and possessions. We are surrounded by the equivalent of "Babylonian" values. Our only antidote is the same as Daniel's – know and obey your God.

2. Contemporary case studies We face opposition to God's values and priorities daily. The following three case studies remind us that these challenges, in their complexity and variety, have not changed that much since biblical times.

Wilson and Margaret: Drifting. Life had been kind to this pair of fifty-year-olds. They had succeeded in their respective professions, had a fine family and many friends and were both well respected in their community. They were also very involved in the work of their local church and were a great encouragement to many people. For years, they had made God and his work their priority. And then they began to drift, for reasons that even they did not fully understand. Their friends were baffled. Yes, there were disagreements in the church and some big disappointments from people they respected which caused bitterness and some disillusionment. But the larger issue was affluence – its consequences and enjoyment. They had to free up weekends to take advantage of the many holiday options that were open to them. Then they bought a vacation home and radically reappraised their lives to make more free time. "We have done our bit for others – now it's our time to enjoy ourselves. Besides, we're not sure how we fit in any more." Their affluence led to a very determined pursuit of self-interest, and God did not feature much in their resource allocation decisions. In fact, he had never featured less. During a vacation in Spain, they listened to the local Christian radio station one morning while relaxing at the pool. The topic was money and Jesus being the beginning and the end of all things. Margaret was pensive. "I suppose we once lived as if that were true, but not now," she thought. "I can't remember when we last prayed about what we do with our money". More focused and aggressive by nature, Wilson quipped,

"Actually we're rearranging the alphabet a little to suit ourselves at the moment. I'm not sure where we will end up, and I haven't lost my faith – but always making Jesus first is a bit of a bind sometimes – especially when it comes to money." Somehow giving had taken second place to living. That was the way they wanted it to be.

Rachel: The benefits of a pattern. Rachel had had a modest income for most of her career as a primary school teacher. For her, money was always secondary. Twenty years later, she still felt a deep sense of vocation about her job. Her friends admired this greatly, as did the parents of her students. "Isn't it great to find no trace of cynicism about teaching in her attitude – after all these years?" one grateful parent remarked. Rachel was a Christian who had made an early commitment to tithing. She still remembered the calculation she made the first day she was paid. The memory was almost a sacred one, based on the realization that she had the capacity both to earn and do a job she loved. She saw the tithe as her way of keeping God at the top of her priorities every month. When she was in her early forties, her financial circumstances changed dramatically and unexpectedly. Within a year, she inherited substantial sums of money and property assets. She had no idea that her ninety-year-old aunt was so wealthy, until her lawyer called three weeks after the funeral. Nor did she have any idea that she would inherit from a childless uncle nine months later. It turned out that he had invested well in several major companies. Rachel found all of this overwhelming. She had never needed financial advisers, but now they hovered like vultures over her fortune. She prayed that she would be obedient to God in all of this and struggled to find out what she was really worth. "Tithing used to be easy," she told her bemused church treasurer. "But it's going to take me months to sort this all out, meet my inherited tax liabilities, and know how to be faithful to the Lord in what I do with it." Her pastor wisely assured her with the words of Matthew 6:21 about the treasure and the heart. Because she knew where her treasure was, she knew she would eventually be able to reestablish the pattern of a lifetime and use this unexpected wealth for God's glory. She set up a trust with Christian objectives and good advisers and, although Rachel died in 1965, the product of her stewardship lives on to the great benefit of many Christian ministries. The kingdom still benefits from Rachel putting Jesus first.

Robert: The past lives on. Robert had lived a complicated and godless life. He had spent twenty years in the military. His work had taken him to a dozen different countries, and he often spent extended periods in dangerous environments. While he thrived on this and enjoyed the risks, the teamwork and the challenges, his long absences made life at home difficult. Jenny, his childhood sweetheart and wife of twelve years, did not enjoy military life and they steadily drifted apart. Both admitted to extramarital affairs. There were many tense and difficult months on the way to divorce, even when both parties had pledged to ensure the proper upbringing of their two children. Their daughter, Maria, was severely disabled and would always require extra care. Their son, Jonathan, was exceptionally able and, for quite different reasons, would also require special attention. Robert fully recognized his obligations to his family as part of the divorce settlement. The financial burdens were great and would extend over many years. A year after the divorce, while on duty in the Middle East, he became a Christian as a result of the persistent witness of a colleague. The impact on his lifestyle was very clear and immediate. He was convicted that God had to come first in every area of his life – but he wasn't sure how he could fully achieve that. He tried reconciliation with Jenny, but this proved futile. She simply did not understand his new motivation and to pursue it further could have destroyed even the poor relationship he did have with her. To make things worse, they were having arguments about money and the costs of caring for the children. Jenny suspected that Robert was not being honest in his income declarations. Robert was confused. "I want to move God to the top of my priorities, but I have so much baggage from my past. And as a Christian I know that I can't ignore these obligations. In the area of finance, I have to regard my obligations to my family as part of my giving to God." As a young Christian, Robert wasn't sure whether that was right or whether it was an excuse – but it was a reality. "I'm a new creation in Christ," Robert prayed daily, "but I'm not free from my past – show me the way to please you in this situation, Lord."

☑ ACTION: Assuming that they would listen, how would you try to help Wilson and Margaret make Jesus first again? What can you learn from Rachel's example about putting God first and last? How would you advise Robert in his complex circumstances?

Taking stock

The theme text for this chapter, Revelation 22:13, is set in the context of Christ's return. How should you prepare to give an account of your stewardship of God's money?

Is Christ your "alphabet", or frame of reference, in all things? How does God feature in your language and thought processes regarding money?

Do your attitudes and behavior in the area of money and possessions reflect the fact that God is complete, continuous and our ultimate goal? If not, why not?

Which areas in Table 8.1 require the greatest attention in your situation? What actions will you take toward achieving the goals presented here?

Further reading

Barclay, William, *Jesus as they Saw Him* (London: SCM Press, 1962).

MacArthur, John, *Whose Money is it Anyway?* (Nashville: Word, 2000).

Packer, J.I., *Knowing God* (London: Hodder and Stoughton, 1973).

Yancey, Philip, *Reaching for the Invisible God* (Grand Rapids, MI: Zondervan, 2000).

Endnotes

1 Isa. 41:4.

2 Isa. 44:6.

3 Rom. 11:36.

4 Col. 2:17.

5 Ps. 95:1.

6 Ps. 95:3.

7 Ps. 95:6-7b.

8 Ps. 95:7c-9.

9 Josh. 6:18-19; 7:1-26.

10 Josh. 6:18.

11 Lk. 18:18-23.

12 Mt. 19:16.

13 Acts 5:1-11.

14 Acts 5:4.

15 Dan. 1.

16 Dan. 1:15.

PART THREE
THE OUTCOMES

9
Taking God's Advice about Money

"... remembering the words the Lord Jesus himself said: 'It is more blessed to give than to receive.'" (Acts 20:35)

Outline In this final section we consider the outcomes of really believing that all we possess belongs to God. We first pause to chart our progress with this topic, and ask how open we are to the Lord's advice on this subject. This leads to a review of the comprehensive scope of that advice; before taking a specific and more in depth look at the spirit and nature of our giving – the area of money and possessions that the Bible spends most time on.

The search for advice
Are you prepared to appoint the Lord of your life as your financial adviser? How do you choose advisers and assess the nature and source of the advice about money that guides your behavior?

The scope of God's advice
Here we consider some questions that God could legitimately ask about each and every aspect of our handling of money and possessions – our "money cycle".

Focus on giving
Why, when, how, what and to whom do we give?

Case study: The Jerusalem collection
What can we learn from Paul's classic appeal to the Corinthian church to help their Christian brothers and sisters in Jerusalem?

The search for advice   As we have sought God's advice about money and possessions, we have seen that this advice is extensive and direct, challenging and immediate, relevant and contemporary – regardless of how little or how much money we have. We have also noted that God's advice on money is only part of the overall instruction given to us on Christian discipleship. We acknowledge that we have free will to either take or reject this advice.

"God does not force his presence on us. When lesser gods attract, God withdraws, honoring our fatal freedom to ignore him"[1] – Philip Yancey

If we do not plan to ignore God's advice, we need to consider the outcomes and ask the question: "Am I ready to appoint God as my financial adviser?" If God is already well established in that position in your life, praise God that this is so.

Businesses and individuals commonly follow the three-stage process below when appointing a financial adviser. Although few of us would take such a structured approach to identifying the sources of advice that influence our behavior, this is an important tool for self-analysis. This process may help not only to clarify the range of possible outcomes, but also our response, to the question "Whose money is it anyway?"

Identify the range of potential advisers: Our peers, the media, the market place and our own inclinations bombard us daily with gratuitous advice about money. Who do you listen to? And which sources have you acknowledged as capable of changing your behavior? If you listen to God's advice about money, do you listen to him alone? Or is he one among many advisers, depending on your feelings, mood or circumstances? As we have seen, money breeds independence – and independence is the enemy of advice. It's also the enemy of trust and faith.

Check their credentials: In business affairs it is relatively easy to check credentials, since the advisers bidding for our attention are very willing to give us evidence of their experience and performance. But how many of us have ever seriously reviewed the spiritual credentials behind financial institutions or major retail groups that advise us to maximize our spending or credit card indebtedness? Although we may not think in these terms or look for "advice" from such sources we get it anyway – because the spirit of our age explicitly fosters the worship of the God-substitute that is money. Offering us more and more money on extended credit terms is one subtle way of stimulating greed and shifting our focus. The advice to borrow may claim to be neutral and value-free – but its effects on the Christian are neither. Are we convinced that even our Christian peers are honoring God as they pursue a lifestyle that pays homage to mammon? Of course not. Our obligation is to be informed from a higher source, and therefore to make quite different decisions.

> "Knowledge is horizontal. Wisdom is vertical – it comes down from above" – Billy Graham

Make a choice: Most Christians probably make one of two errors regarding their choice of financial adviser. Some think that they don't have to make a choice about whose advice to seek regarding God's money. Others think that they have made a valid choice in listening to different voices at different times. The biblical assumption is that we continuously need to make wise decisions about how to allocate God's money. If we acknowledge this, we acknowledge that he is the only legitimate source of advice. It's both his money and his choice, but he leaves us to implement these decisions. The trouble is that, in matters regarding money and possessions, we often think that we know better than God.

> "God always gives his very best to those who leave the choice with him" – James Hudson Taylor

---

☑ **ACTION:** Apply each of these three stages – search, check and choose – to your own stewardship. How much (or how little) attention have you paid to God's advice over the years? Are you ready to appoint God as your financial adviser? Or is he still on your "to do" list?

The scope of God's advice

Whenever we choose an adviser, we need to determine the nature of his brief and set the scope of his remit. What exactly do we want that adviser to do, and under what terms? When we proclaim Jesus as Lord, we concede that his brief is wide and his scope limitless. Anything less would be a denial of our faith.

"You cannot have the gifts of Christ apart from the government of Christ" —
A. Lindsay Glegg

We have glimpsed the comprehensive nature of God's interest in these dimensions of our lives in Chapter 2 on treasure and in Chapter 7 on stewardship. In Chapter 6, we identified six areas of our financial stewardship in which God wants to make a difference – earning, saving, giving, spending, possessing and planning. These six areas, covering most of the things we do that concern money, constitute our "money cycle". All of these elements fall under the scope of God's advice – but are we prepared to place all of them under his scrutiny?

We will focus on one of these elements, namely giving, in this chapter. But this "money cycle" is an integrated whole, and Table 9.1 poses some of the questions that emerge from the biblical teaching in these six different areas. These are questions that the Lord might reasonably ask each of us. In his earthly ministry, Jesus often began with a question before giving advice. He began his conversation with the rich young man, for example, with "Why do you ask me about what is good?"[2] Jesus made his point to the rich fool with the question: "Then who will get what you have prepared for yourself?"[3] He introduced the parable of the wise and foolish builders by asking, "Why do you call me 'Lord, Lord,' and do not do what I say?"[4] For the purposes of brevity and clarity, I have confined myself to a few questions under each heading. The Lord might validly ask us any one of them. They all call for answers – although there are several that most of us would prefer to avoid.

☑ **ACTION:** Answer the questions in Table 9.1 as if God were specifically addressing them to you – he might actually do that some day. It is one thing to answer the questions, and quite another to evaluate the consequences of your answers. Take some time to reflect and pray about these consequences.

TABLE 9.1 AN INTERVIEW WITH JESUS
Earning: Do you earn your money in a way that is consistent with God's values? What do you want to achieve by earning more money? Have you established the limits to which you would go to earn more? If so, what criteria have you used?
Saving: Who has advised you in this so far? Are you saving for yourself or for me? What is the ultimate purpose of your accumulation of wealth?
Giving: Are you content with how much you give and your pattern of giving? Why or why not? Can you explain to me the principles on which you base your giving? If I called for greater resources from you, how would you respond?
Spending: Did you ever ask my advice about your spending habits? Can you explain to me how I fit in to them? How could you change these habits if I asked you to do that?
Possessing: Are you content with what you possess? Why or why not? What motivates you to accumulate possessions? Can you show me how my teaching on stewardship relates to what you own?
Planning: How have I featured in your financial planning in the past? What would you say is the connection between your plans for my money and my plans? Will you invite me to play a different role now?

Focus on giving

Of all the elements in the money cycle, we will focus here on giving. There are several reasons for this. The first reason is found in the verse above, Acts 20:35, in which Paul quotes an otherwise unknown axiom of Jesus. This principle of love and self-sacrifice clearly exerted a powerful influence over the early church. The radical attitude to giving and sharing that the early Christians exhibited was one of the first evidences of the impact of the lordship of Christ on their lives. It also had a huge impact on the community around them. Where has that spirit gone? And what have we lost in terms of Christian testimony? Another reason for focusing on giving

"Men give advice; God gives guidance" — Leonard Ravenhill

here is to reflect the biblical emphasis – the biblical passages on money and possessions talk more about giving than about anything else. Christian giving is the thermometer of love. As you read, check your personal temperature in this area.

We can only determine our approach to giving in the light of what we have learned so far – about the treasure and the heart, eternity, stewardship, putting Jesus first and last and so on. Apart from this, giving is an intrusion and an imposition. If we are seeking to please God in all of these different areas, our giving will please the Lord. What is this attitude that pleases God and which must therefore characterize Christian giving?

> "There is no portion of our time that is our time, and the rest is God's; there is no portion of money that is our money, and the rest God's money. It is all his; he made it all, gives it all, and he has simply trusted it to us for his service. A servant has two purses, the master's and his own, but we have only one." – *Adolphe Monod*

Access denied? In order to reinforce the truth of our custodianship of God's money, imagine a bank account owned by God but held in your name. Although there is normally no distinction between ownership and control, in this case the bank records clearly show not only the balance, but also God's ownership of this account. Only you, as the named signatory, can access the money for withdrawal. The only way the owner can get the money is if you transfer it to him. Suppose the owner asks for money to meet a particular need. You respond not as someone *giving to*, but as someone *giving back*, releasing resources at the request of the owner. Because the account is only under your stewardship and not your ownership, you always knew this would happen some day. And what if, for any reason, you refuse the owner's request to make his money available? You can only expect to have poor and deteriorating relationships with him. Many Christians find themselves in this situation. Pray that you do not join their ranks and make sure that you are not denying the owner access to his resources.

The following five questions will help us to examine our attitudes to giving.

1. Why do we give? The Christian gives because God gave the greatest gift of all. Loving and giving are inextricably linked. "For God so loved the world that he gave his one and only Son, that whoever believes in him shall not perish but have eternal life."[5] "If I give all I possess to the poor and surrender my body to the flames, but have not love, I gain nothing."[6] As God loved and gave, so we respond in love and give. "Not that I am looking for a gift, but I am looking for what may be credited to your account."[7] Our giving is an essential act of worship as we make investments for eternity.

"If giving is merely to a church, a ministry or a needy person, it is only charity. But if it is to the Lord, it becomes an act of worship" — Howard Dayton[8]

2. When do we give? We give when God asks us to give. We expect such requests to come continuously so that we can give systematically. We have seen how Paul encouraged the Corinthian church: "On the first day of every week, each one of you should set aside a sum of money in keeping with his income, saving it up, so that when I come no collections will have to be made."[9] As we establish this pattern, we do so with joy. "Each man should give what he has decided in his heart to give, not reluctantly or under compulsion, for God loves a cheerful giver."[10] These passages assume that giving is a personal, considered and premeditated decision. While we can also be spontaneous in our giving, such gifts are offered above and beyond what is planned. In fundraising for Christian causes I have witnessed the massive contribution that is made by regular, planned giving – often of small donations. All of us need to be alert to discern when and what God asks from his accounts.

3. How should we give? There is so much biblical guidance here, we have no excuse for not following it. Following are four of the attitudes that should characterize Christian giving.

(a) With generosity: The woman who broke the alabaster jar of perfume and poured it on Jesus' head gives us a beautiful example of this attitude – although the disciples did not understand her gift. "Why this waste of perfume?" they muttered indignantly.[11] It seemed to them to be far too generous. What is generosity? It has as much to do with the spirit in which we give as it does the quantity. Having said that, C.S. Lewis made the following thought-provoking observation about quantity. "The only safe rule is to give more than we can spare. If we live at the same level of affluence as other people who have our level of income, we are probably giving too little away." What might the consequences be of applying that principle to your own circumstances?

(b) With modesty: God is quite specific here. "But when you give to the needy, do not let your left hand know what your right hand is doing, so that your giving may be in secret."[12] This instruction was given in the context of giving that was grossly and publicly flaunted. Not all of our giving today can be done in secret, because the accounts of Christian charities and other financial structures are open to public scrutiny. Some Christian fundraising methods also identify donors for specific reasons. Even so, we do not announce our own generosity, and we do well to apply this wisdom for all kinds of practical reasons as well. It avoids the false adoration of the generous, it reminds us that we give as to the Lord who already knows all about it, and it protects the dignity of the recipient.

(c) With joy: The theme of joy is repeatedly connected with giving in the Bible. As Joash restored the temple, for example, it was recorded that, "All the officials and all the people brought their contributions gladly, dropping them into the chest until it was full."[13] On such occasions there was a profound sense of national purpose, and the people expressed their joy at being part of a great project dedicated to the worship of the Lord. We also see this idea in the verse from Acts 20:35 at the beginning of this chapter. Elsewhere we are told, "God loves a cheerful giver."[14] We saw in our discussion of tithing in Chapter 7 that giving reluctantly, under pressure and according to a formula can be joyless. But reflect on the joy of giving a gift that was reported by the recipient as being "just in time", or one that was given as a result of guidance well beyond ourselves. Moreover, part of our joy in giving flows out of our gratitude for what God has given us.

"Grace and gratitude belong together"
— Karl Barth

(d) With sacrifice: Many of us, particularly in Western Christian communities, find this characteristic of giving most difficult. Many of us give much less than we are able to give. Does this reflect a love deficit? Probably. Too much comfort? Certainly. Are we insensitive to the needs of others? Assuredly. One of the most moving examples of giving in the New Testament is that of the Macedonian church. "Out of the most severe trial, their overflowing joy and their extreme poverty welled up in rich generosity."[15] What did they know about giving that we don't know? They certainly knew the joy of radical obedience and profound trust in God. David, anxious to build an altar and offer sacrifices, vowed, "I will not sacrifice to the LORD my God burnt offerings that cost me nothing".[16] How would you apply David's principle to your giving? Far too much of our giving costs us little or nothing – because we have so much left over.

4. What do we give? Too many Christians decide what they give based on their chosen lifestyle. Maintaining that lifestyle is the priority that determines the amount of their discretionary income – from which their giving is (wrongly) derived. Much giving, unfortunately, is out of the residual – the dregs at the bottom of the cup of blessing. Think carefully about your lifestyle. Is it compatible with biblical principles regarding God's money? It is possible to spend so much of God's money on what we perceive to be our needs that God has access to very little of what belongs to him. Having said that, the New Testament portrays a wide variety of lifestyles – from the itinerant and rootless lives of the disciples and the apostles to the more settled patterns of Christians in the market towns and cities. Within a number of the Christian communities to whom some of the apostolic letters were addressed there was wealth as well as poverty. While we can conclude that variety did exist, the biblical teaching on money and possessions strongly encourages us to reappraise our lifestyles to determine what is appropriate for the Christian disciple. The personal discipline of financial re-evaluation (for spiritual rather than material reasons) is largely missing in the Christian church in the West today. The norm, instead, is the preservation and enhancement of lifestyles regardless of the cost to the kingdom. Each of us needs to respond to the radical behavior found in Acts 2 and Acts 4. "There were no needy persons among them. For from time to time those who owned lands or houses sold them, brought the money from the sales and put it at the apostles' feet, and it was distributed to anyone as he had need."[17] Are passages like this merely of historic interest? Does this behavior merely reflect the social and economic disorder that faced many families who had turned to Christ at the time? Or is there an enduring principle embedded here? All that we have learned regarding our stewardship of God's money would suggest the latter. When he asks, we hardly want to offer excuses in response.

5. To whom should we give? Christians often say that they are bewildered and confused by the number of causes to which they could give. Having decided what to give, the next decision is to whom? Prayer and the guidance of the Spirit are essential here. Scripture gives us much practical guidance concerning the relative demands of family, mission and poverty. For example, we are advised (in the context of widowhood and poverty) to meet financial needs within our family. "If anyone does not provide for his relatives, and especially for his immediate family, he has denied the faith and is worse than an unbeliever."[18] We need to consider this verse in context, however. It is not a defense for increasing a family's material wealth or an excuse for giving lesser priority to Christian mission.

> "Obedience to the Great Commission has more consistently been poisoned by affluence than by anything else" – Ralph Winter

Funding mission work through church and para-church activities should be a central part of Christian giving. Yet, according to surveys, it is an area in which churches and individuals often fail spectacularly. Many Christian workers are very poorly financed, and this situation is often justified by people who should know better (and who could not survive on the level of income that they deem adequate for others) making unrealistic assumptions about the economics of their lives. The under-funding of leading Christian workers is not new. Paul commended the church in Philippi (and implicitly criticized others), "... when I set out from Macedonia, not one church shared with me in the matter of giving and receiving, except you only."[19] Surely no one would fail to support someone like Paul, we might think – but apparently plenty of Christians did fail to do just that.

> "The measure of our success will be the measure of our ability to help others" – F.B. Meyer

How should Christians respond to poverty? The Old Testament fosters a proactive attitude to poverty. For example, "He who is kind to the poor lends to the LORD, and he will reward him for what he has done."[20] Jesus, too, shows profound compassion and concern for the poor. "The Spirit of the Lord is on me, because he has anointed me to preach good news to the poor."[21] Throughout his ministry, the poor feature more than most other groups. We are to feed them, treat them with justice, invite them to the banquet, show them kindness and so on. In allocating our giving, we have to remember that Jesus' mission is our mission. If we neglect the poor, we are unlikely to please him.

What kind of giver are you?

There are three kinds of giving: grudge giving, duty giving, and thanksgiving. Grudge giving says, "I hate to", duty giving says, "I ought to", thanksgiving says, "I want to". The first comes from constraint, the second from a sense of obligation, the third from a full heart. Nothing much is conveyed in grudge giving since "the gift without the giver is bare". Something more happens in duty giving, but there is no song in it. Thanksgiving is an open gate to the love of God. – Robert N. Rodenmayer

What kind of giver are you? And with what results? If you do not give with thanksgiving, what would transform your approach to giving?

☑ **ACTION:** Ask yourself the five questions above. Which of your answers are you least comfortable with and why? What is your basic motivation for giving? Are you sensitive to God's timing in your giving? Are your attitudes consistent with the biblical ideal? Are there different lifestyle choices that you are willing to make to enhance your giving? Do you seek God's wisdom and guidance in the way you allocate your giving?

Case study:
The Jerusalem collection

One of the classic New Testament cases on Christian giving involves Paul's extended efforts to mobilize financial support for the poor in the church in Jerusalem in 2 Corinthians 8 and 9. Can you relate to the givers? To the recipients? What do you learn from the context, challenges and consequences for your own ministry of giving?

Context: Paul had a special burden for the Christians in Jerusalem. Many of them had suffered both socially and economically on account of their Christian faith. It is not hard to imagine how they were regarded within the rigid social structures and ingrained traditions of their families and community. Famine and penal taxation imposed by the occupying powers further contributed to their poverty. Paul had been on the case for up to five years by the time he wrote to the church in Corinth. It's possible that some had questioned his motives for this fundraising effort, but that did not stop him from making every effort to meet this need. Indeed, he records this mission as dating from the time of his acceptance by the other apostles when Peter, John and James welcomed and briefed him. "All they asked was that we should continue to remember the poor, the very thing I was eager to do."[22]

Challenges: The response had been mixed. The example of the Macedonians was stellar, and there were hopeful signs elsewhere – but there was still work to do. So Paul held up the example of the Macedonians as he appealed to the Corinthians and challenged their thinking on several grounds.

i) *Capacity* – The Macedonians gave "as much as they were able, and even beyond their ability".

ii) *Privilege* – The Macedonians "pleaded with us for the privilege of sharing in this service to the saints".

iii) *Lordship* – "They gave themselves first to the Lord and then to us".

iv) *Grace* – As the Corinthians excelled in other areas, Paul exhorted them to "see that you also excel in this grace of giving".

v) *Testing* – Paul did not issue a command but wanted "to test the sincerity of your love".

vi) *Reality* – If they are willing, Paul says, "the gift is acceptable according to what one has, not according to what he does not have".

Consequences: It is almost as if Paul worries that the Corinthians will not quite grasp the significance of their giving for the bigger Christian picture in the whole region. He spells it out for them.

i) *Seed sowing* – generous giving leads to generous reaping

ii) *Joy* – in the heart of both God and the giver

iii) *Thanksgiving* – directed to the Lord because of their generosity

iv) *Immeasurable* – our giving stems from God's giving and is benchmarked by it. "Thanks be to God for his indescribable gift!"[23]

Taking stock

By default, many different people and groups can become our advisers on our stewardship of God's wealth. Which advisers currently exercise the most influence on you and detract your focus from God's advice?

Can you recall any occasions when God gave you clear advice about money and you ignored it? If so, think through the consequences of your response. How might you respond differently now to the same situation?

Jesus' teaching on money emphasizes that we need to break free from its power. Can you honestly say that you experience that freedom?

> Two mites, two drops (yet all her house and land),
> Falls from a steady heart, through trembling hand;
> The other's wanton wealth foams high, and brave,
> The other cast away, she only gave.
> – *Richard Crashaw (1613-49), "The Widow's Mite"*

Further reading

Anders, Max, *The Good Life*: *Living with Meaning in a 'Never Enough' World* (Milton Keynes: Word, 1993).

Catherwood, Fred, *God's Time, God's Money* (London: Hodder & Stoughton, 1987).

Mann, Adrian, *No Small Change: Money, Christians and the Church* (Norwich: The Canterbury Press, 1992).

Meadows, Peter, *Rich Thinking about the World's Poor* (Carlisle: Authentic Lifestyle, 2003).

Endnotes

1 Philip Yancey, *Rumors of Another World: What on Earth Are we Missing?* (Grand Rapids, MI: Zondervan, 2003), p. 51.

2 Mt. 19:17.

3 Lk. 12:20.

4 Lk. 6:46.

5 Jn. 3:16.

6 1 Cor. 13:3.

7 Phil. 4:17.

8 Howard Dayton, *Your Money Counts* (Wheaton, IL: Tyndale, 1997), p. 74.

9 1 Cor. 16.2.

10 2 Cor. 9:7.

11 Mk. 14:4.

12 Mt. 6:3-4.

13 2 Chr. 24:10.

14 2 Cor. 9:7.

15 2 Cor. 8:2.

16 2 Sam. 24:24.

17 Acts 4:34-35.

18 1 Tim. 5:8.

19 Phil. 4:15.

20 Prov. 19:17.

21 Lk. 4:18.

22 Gal. 2:10.

23 2 Cor. 9:15.

10
Measuring the Impact

"But whatever was to my profit I now consider loss for the sake of Christ." (Phil. 3:7)

Outline This final chapter asks what is the appropriate response to our core question, "Whose money is it anyway?" and invites us to test our response to the biblical principles set. We then pursue the very basic question of pleasing ourselves or pleasing God in money matters.

God's wealth: What's the answer?
With our five biblical principles in mind, we check the basics, confirm our love and challenge our lifestyle.

The stark discipleship question
James helps us to examine the ultimate discipleship question about obedience and apply it to money and possessions.

Time, work and money: The trilogy completed
How are these three topics inextricably linked, what are the challenges they present, and how can we be encouraged to persevere?

God's wealth: What's the answer? This book is about recalibrating our lives. Without consistent biblical teaching, our thinking about money will be shaped by various misleading and potentially damaging views. The verse above, from Philippians 3, is one example of how Paul recalibrated his life to Christ. He was, of course, referring to his whole life – not just his attitude to money and possessions. We must do the same so that we can truly understand God's money in the context of a life lived for Christ.

I chose to write about this subject out of a deep conviction that most of the financial and material resources in the possession of Christians were unlikely ever to be released to God. I came to this stark conclusion primarily by witnessing the marks of materialism in the lives of so many Christians. The demands of maintaining a certain lifestyle had (to their minds) progressively reduced their financial flexibility and (by definition) reduced what they had left over to give. I saw, too, the attitudes of many Christians towards this subject – ranging from indifference to hostility. I noted the consistently low level of funding that Christians as a whole donate to mission activities. I observed widespread resistance to changing personal behavior in response to the truth of "God's wealth". I also have ample evidence of these tendencies in my own heart – perhaps you do, too. My own relationship with money is far from perfect, my responsiveness to the Lord's calling is at times sluggish and my mind is too often absorbed with the subject in the wrong ways. The weight of all of this evidence might suggest that the challenges are too big, the consequences too far reaching, for the situation to change. I also know, however, of many excellent contemporary and historic role models who have managed God's money to good effect. Above all, I believe in the power of the Spirit and of God's word to convict, convince and transform.

We know that all we have belongs to the Lord – *it literally is God's wealth*. But can he have more of the money and possessions that we manage for him – as and when he asks? We cannot answer that question by adhering to a rule book or applying a formula. The biblical answer lies primarily in the quality of a relationship. We need to understand the nature of discipleship before we can see God's perspective on money and possessions. This is one of the central causal relationships in the Bible – as we believe, so we behave. Acknowledging that it is indeed God's money, we begin to respond by doing three things.

Check the basics: Test your behavior and practice against the five overarching biblical principles that we identified in Chapter 1. These principles set the framework within which we handle God's wealth. We are unlikely to please him if we operate outside them. Answering the questions below is a practical, if demanding, way of inspecting your foundations.

A design for good: Do you think of the money and possessions that you have as a gift from the Lord? Or do you explain them in some other way? And do you regard your circumstances as equipping you to do good deeds in his name?

An inherent capacity to distract: Just how much have you been absorbed by money and possessions? And would an honest appraisal lead you to confess that you have directed forms of worship and misplaced love towards them?

A transformation in stewardship: Have you ever experienced such a transformation? How does your present stewardship measure up against biblical principles?

A redistribution challenge: Are you conscious that God may be asking you to further mobilize and redistribute his resources? If so, what is your response? If not, pray for discernment and wisdom in this area.

An essential spiritual link: Would you say that the material and spiritual dimensions of your life are integrated or separated? How does eternity feature in your behavior regarding money?

Confirm the love: For the Christian, the motivation to respond to God's instruction is always love. This love often needs to be rekindled, yet we look to other explanations for our practices and to other remedies for our faults.

> "Every love has its own force; and it cannot lie idle in the soul of the lover. Love must draw the soul on. Do you, then, wish to know the character of a love? See where it leads" —
> Augustine of Hippo

Where has our love for the Lord actually led us in the realm of money and possessions? Few of us like applying "the love test" to this subject, but there is no other test for disciples. We prefer to measure our behavior by less exacting standards such as those of our peers, our community, our own past and so on. When it comes to money, are you only a clanging cymbal? "If I speak in the tongues of men and of angels, but have not love, I am only a resounding gong or a clanging cymbal."[1] What would it look like if true Christian love shone through in all of our dealings with money?

> Love ever gives,
> Forgives, outlives,
> And ever stands
> With open hands.
> And while it lives,
> It gives.
> For this is love's prerogative –
> O give, and give, and give.
> – *John Oxenham*

Challenge the lifestyle: As we have seen, the lifestyles that we have adopted or aspire to are a major factor in determining our giving. It is tempting to accept our lifestyles and associated financial commitments as "given". There are many reasons for resisting radical change. After all, we have worked hard to attain our lifestyle and many of us can remember when we were less affluent – a state to which we are reluctant to return. Our lifestyle may be the product of success rather than the goal of success, and we may therefore regard it as a form of blessing. Our lifestyle may also grant us many social and professional connections and privileges that we want to maintain. Changing our lifestyle might affect so many other people in our families that we wonder if it is reasonable to ask them to bear such burdens. Finally, we struggle to know exactly what the new standards might be. We would have to carefully examine these reasons against the biblical principles we have seen, however, before deciding against any change in our lifestyle to free up more of God's resources. Some of these reasons would be more persuasive if we were using a society magazine as our textbook instead of the Bible.

"Those Christians who succumb to the lure of materialism may understand Christianity, but they don't accept it in their soul" – Alexander Solzhenitsyn

We can do none of this in our own strength. But God is waiting for us to ask him: Please guide me to the lifestyle that is appropriate to my standing as a custodian of your money.

> ☑ **ACTION:** Carefully and prayerfully check the basics, confirm your love and challenge your lifestyle. Based on this assessment, formulate a plan of action. You may need to come back to these exercises periodically if you plan to take "God's money" seriously from now on.

The stark discipleship question The question that constantly confronts all Christian disciples, who were called "to the obedience that comes from faith",[2] is this: "Do I want to please myself or God?" Our answer to this question will determine how we handle God's money. It is primarily a matter of will.

Our obligation is obedience. For it is obedience that brought us to Christ and sustains us in good fellowship with Christ.

"One act of obedience is better than one hundred sermons" – Dietrich Bonhoeffer

James 4:1-12 is not explicitly concerned with money and possessions, although it has some financial undertones. It is more about relationships between quarreling Christians and between them and the Lord. What can we learn here about correct relationships that will underpin correct behavior? Who do we want to please? This passage divides into two sections: pleasing self and pleasing God.

Pleasing self **Desires that battle:** Internal warfare within the Christian heart is the explanation for the dissension that characterizes the relationships between these believers. These desires (sinful pleasures) are firmly rooted in the world and are quite distinct from the eternal blessings of discipleship. They reflect the priorities that dominated their lives before coming to Christ.[3] This preoccupying internal struggle makes it difficult to hear God's voice about anything – not least about money and its allocation.

Requests that are resisted: "You do not have, because you do not ask God. When you ask, you do not receive, because you ask with the wrong motives, that you may spend what you get on your pleasures."[4] James paints a picture of people who pray, but with impure hearts, and who ask by formula.

Their relationships with each other and with God are broken, and this brokenness is reflected in their dialogue with him, which is unreal and unfulfilling. Such phenomena result from a master-servant relationship gone wrong.

Friendships that are foreign: God sees these consequences clearly. These sharp words address their disloyalty and unfaithfulness. "You adulterous people, don't you know that friendship with the world is hatred towards God? Anyone who chooses to be a friend of the world becomes an enemy of God."[5] James does not pull his punches. Friendship with the world in these terms places us squarely in the realm where everything is assessed by human standards. In the realm of money and possessions the choices are daily, small, but cumulative. We may need to reassess some "foreign friendships" in our lives.

Pleasing God

Greater grace: Ever practical, James confronts the challenge that what he advocates is impossible. Who can ever give this level of devotion to God? He reminds us that God's grace – imparted inner power – far exceeds the rigorous demands of discipleship. So he quotes the proverb, "God opposes the proud but gives grace to the humble."[6] We need an abundance of that inner power in order to handle God's money properly.

Firmer resistance: "Submit yourselves, then, to God. Resist the devil, and he will flee from you."[7] The basic biblical cure for pollution from the world is submission to God. James launches into a series of commands here, demanding immediate response. But do we respond immediately? Or at all? There were apparently plenty of estranged drifters among the audience that James was addressing. How much resisting of the devil have we done in matters relating to money?

Closer devotion: "Come near to God and he will come near to you. Wash your hands, you sinners, and purify your hearts, you double-minded."[8] James was very conscious of the defiling effects of the world around him. Many of us need to have a heightened awareness of this issue – of its subtle and invasive nature. We will never resist the devil if we are distant from God.

Renewed spirit: James saw a need for true penitence after the disloyalty that these people had shown to God. Penitence could mark the beginning of a new relationship with money. It's not a rejection of joy, but a way to new joy. "Let there be tears for the wrong things you have done. Let there be sorrow and deep grief. Let there be sadness instead of laughter, and gloom instead of joy."[9]

Better perspective: James illuminates the route to pleasing God in his injunction: "Humble yourselves before the Lord, and he will lift you up."[10] As we have seen, the Christian community would never have mislaid the answer to "Whose money is it anyway?" if we had kept the power, majesty and eternity of God in closer view.

"Nothing influences a man so much as that which he calls his own" — C.H. Spurgeon

There is a particular historic context that we need to address here. In Western countries, a major transfer of wealth has been underway for a generation and more as economic growth and affluence have generated unprecedented assets within the Christian community. This will continue over the next twenty to thirty years at least. What will happen to these assets? Will they support ever better lifestyles for the few? Or will they be invested in eternity as we recover a biblical perspective on stewardship?

✔ **ACTION:** Spend some time soul searching to determine the extent to which your management of God's wealth is a product of pleasing self or pleasing God.

Time, work and money: The trilogy completed The idea for this trilogy emerged from a simple question. The question follows a statement of faith that most of us will have used on many occasions. "I have given my life to Christ." Christians recognize that this decision is a step of faith, an acknowledgement of love, a response to grace and so on. But the question that inevitably follows, and which reverberates over the subsequent years as life unfolds is, "What does that mean?" At one level it can mean quite a lot; at another level it can mean very little. It always means that much has been received; but it does not always mean that much has been given. That perceived imbalance was my starting point. I was aware that many Christians preferred to keep God at a distance from some critical areas of life. Sometimes this was short-term – the product of pressures of the moment; in other cases it was more long-term – the product of a life that had been redesigned since that first enthusiastic commitment was made to the Lord. Both conditions were reversible – but there seemed to be relatively few Christians who were able or willing to revisit the rhythm of their lives in order to remedy these situations.

People have separated themselves from God, thereby denying his lordship, in three key areas. The first area is time. It is possible for Christians to be so busy and preoccupied that they have little or no time to offer service to the Lord. So many of us have confused God's time with our time – and so we proceed to live according to our own agenda. The second area is work, and in particular the practice of keeping work and faith apart – making two worlds out of one, thus robbing the Lord of so many opportunities for effective witness in the market place. The third is money. We have seen the serious consequences of separating the earthly and heavenly dimensions of money.

The books in this trilogy are designed to help busy people – by being direct, accessible, rooted in Scripture and experience, with short sections and items for thought, prayer and application. Above all, I hope that you find them honest – I have not conquered all the issues, but I have thought deeply about them for many years. I have long hoped that more people struggling with these issues in their professional lives would write Christian material – but I know why they rarely do.[11] Writing these books has been personally challenging at every level, and I pray that God will use these pages to transform your life, too.

The one thing I want to avoid is engendering a sense of failure in my readers. Although few of us are in the shape that God wants, he is working on it – if we are willing. And there is always a way back. As C.S. Lewis encourages us, "No amount of falls will really undo us if we keep picking ourselves up each time. We shall of course be very muddy and tattered children by the time we reach home ... It is when we notice the dirt that

God is most present in us; it is the very sign of his presence." In many ways these books have been about "noticing the dirt", pointing the way to cleansing and pointing toward the great kingdom benefits. Recognizing that we need God's instruction, the Bible shows us the life that God approves. We make constant choices as to whose instruction to listen to in every aspect of Christian discipleship. As the psalmist says, "Blessed is the man who does not walk in the counsel of the wicked or stand in the way of sinners or sit in the seat of mockers. But his delight is in the law of the LORD, and on his law he meditates day and night."[12]

Taking stock

It has been suggested that it is only when we understand ourselves and our attitudes to money that we can understand our relationship with God. How has your understanding (on both counts) changed as you have engaged with the material in this book?

Campbell Morgan once observed that the issue for the Christian is not to catch the spirit of the age but to correct it. How much correcting have you done?

How would you apply Paul's testimony in the verse with which we began this chapter, Philippians 3:7, to money and possessions? Is there anything that you once counted as profit that you now consider loss for the cause of Christ?

Look back at Table 1.2 in Chapter 1 of this book. How has your position changed, if it has, since you first encountered these different categories?

Further reading

Bartholomew, Craig, and West, Andrew, (eds.), *Praying by the Book: Reading the Psalms* (Carlisle: Paternoster, 2001).

Cymbala, Jim, *Fresh Faith* (Grand Rapids, MI: Zondervan, 1999).

Stott, John, *The Incomparable Christ* (Leicester: IVP, 2001).

Tozer, A.W., *The Pursuit of God* (Milton Keynes: Authentic Media, 2004).

Endnotes

1   1 Cor. 13:1.

2   Rom. 1:5.

3   As in this passage in Titus that uses the same words: "At one time we too were foolish, disobedient, deceived and enslaved by all kinds of passions and pleasures" (Tit. 3:3).

4   Jas. 4:2-3.

5   Jas. 4:4.

6   Jas. 4:6, quoting from Prov. 3:34.

7   Jas. 4:7.

8   Jas. 4:8.

9   Jas. 4:9 (NLT).

10   Jas. 4:10.

11   A testimony to this lies in the fact that the books were all designed while on the move – *Whose Life Is It Anyway?* in Portland, Oregon; *God's Payroll* in London, England; and *God's Wealth* in Venice, Italy.

12   Ps. 1:1-2.